MARILYN
MONROE
DAY BY DAY

MARILYN MONROE DAY BY DAY

A Timeline of People, Places, and Events

Carl Rollyson

ROWMAN & LITTLEFIELD
Lanham • Boulder • New York • London

Published by Rowman & Littlefield
A wholly owned subsidiary of The Rowman & Littlefield Publishing Group, Inc.
4501 Forbes Boulevard, Suite 200, Lanham, Maryland 20706
www.rowman.com

16 Carlisle Street, London W1D 3 BT, United Kingdom

British Library Cataloguing in Publication Information Available

Library of Congress Cataloging-in-Publication Data

Rollyson, Carl E. (Carl Edmund)
  Marilyn Monroe day by day : a timeline of people, places, and events / Carl
Rollyson.
      pages cm
  Includes bibliographical references and index.
  Includes filmography.
  ISBN 978-1-4422-3079-8 (hardback : alk. paper) — ISBN 978-1-4422-3080-4
(ebook) 1. Monroe, Marilyn, 1926-1962—Chronology. 2. Motion picture
actors and actresses—United States—Biography. I. Title.
  PN2287.M69R79 2014
  791.4302"8092—dc23

                                                                2014014494

♾™ The paper used in this publication meets the minimum requirements of
American National Standard for Information Sciences—Permanence of Paper
for Printed Library Materials, ANSI/NISO Z39.48-1992.

Printed in the United States of America

To Lisa

Contents

Acknowledgments

I'M GRATEFUL TO DOROTHY PARKER biographer Marion Meade for pointing out Parker's interest in Marilyn Monroe. As always, I have had the excellent assistance of my wife, Lisa Paddock, in preparing this book for publication. Thanks to Jeff Mandor at the Larry Edmunds Bookshop for locating the photographs that appear in this book, and to David Wills for sharing with me his formidable understanding of Marilyn Monroe iconography. Stephen Ryan, my editor at Rowman & Littlefield, was an early believer in this book, and I appreciate his acumen in bringing my work to publication. Thanks also to Tara Hanks and Laura Grieve for proofreading and spotting errors and to Rosemary Clark for giving this book her scruting before publication.

Introduction

SHORTLY AFTER COMPLETING *Marilyn Monroe: A Life of the Actress* (1986), I began to conceive of another book about her, one that could include material left out of a narrative that had to be selective in order to tell a persuasive and succinct story. Since a biography—no matter how authoritative—cannot contain all of the facts and events of an individual's life, I wanted to do a sort of documentary detailing the days of Marilyn Monroe. In this way, I could partially restore what is left out in a narration of her life. Such a book would also illuminate the gaps—and the discrepancies—that still exist in our knowledge of her biography. I have done my best to get the dates and days right, but several of my sources conflict, requiring me to work out what seems like the most reliable account. Different sources give different release dates for Marilyn's films, for example, so I have decided to follow Richard Buskin's practice of using the dates established by the Margaret Herrick Library of the Academy of Motion Picture Arts and Sciences.

I had a model for the kind of book I contemplated: Jay Leyda's *The Melville Log*. Leyda spent decades attempting to discover where Melville was and what he was doing on any given day. While such an effort may seem like drudgery to some, establishment of chronology and documentation has an intrinsic fascination and importance for the researcher and, I hope, for the reader—and especially anyone who delights in discovering all aspects of becoming and being a self, any self.

Although I originally thought I would include a chapter about the aftermath of Monroe's life, in the end what fascinated me most was how her life unfolded. The literature about what she became after her death is so voluminous that it requires another book. I wanted the calendar of this book to be the one that she composed and that was composed in response to her living presence.

I began by recording Marilyn's activities without commentary. But gradually I saw that excerpts from her diaries, journals, and letters—and the reports of others—were a part of her day-to-day world. And so certain of her days are vividly brought to life in her own words, and even by the checks she wrote and the receipts she kept. I have usually written the entries in the present tense to keep alive the sense of life as it happens.

My annotated bibliography specifies my indebtedness to books and websites about Marilyn, and I have also used that space to describe the photographs published in those books. In the chronology I have, wherever possible, documented Marilyn's life using the photographs taken of her. I have also included a source list for photographs mentioned in calendar entries.

With the exception of Colin Clark's two books about the making of *The Prince and the Showgirl*, I have shied away from references to dubious sources such as Robert Slatzer, Ted Jordan, Hans Jorgen Lembourn, and Lena Pepitone. Reputable biographers like Lois Banner and Donald Spoto have exposed the unreliability of such books. Taking Clark's measure is a more difficult task, since he was present during the making of *The Prince and the Showgirl*, when he apparently kept a diary. None of the other principal personages involved with the production mention Clark, but as third assistant director he was on the periphery—although still occupying a position from which he could record his impressions. I give him the benefit of the doubt mainly because his work does seem to reflect the tension that characterized the production, and because he seemed to understand Marilyn's need to find allies. When a given event may be doubtful, I sometimes identify the biographer from whom I have drawn information. Otherwise, I do not cite sources for entries that seem part of the established record of her life.

For my descriptions of Marilyn's appearances on magazine covers, I am indebted to the reproductions in Clark Kidder's invaluable *Marilyn Cover to Cover*. His book provides a comprehensive, although not exhaustive, look at how Marilyn's career developed in this country and abroad. Following the sequence of her cover photographs reveals fascinating aspects of her evolving public persona. At times—in the mid-1950s and even later, for example—shots of early Marilyn dating from before 1950 appeared, so that, in a sense, her image was out of sync with the maturing woman and actress. These magazine covers suggest that she appealed to several different audiences. Some wanted a wholesome Marilyn, even a rusticated down-home Marilyn, while others were attracted to her appearances as a seductress, an alluring mature woman, a comedian, a sexual object, an intelligent woman with a teasing intelligence. In short, over time a variety of Marilyns emerged to suit a variety of audiences around the world.

One of the chief virtues of this book is that it does not force Marilyn to conform to any one biographical narrative. Reading about her activities day by day and year by year may well yield many different Marilyns and, I hope, a sense that she had choices to make, that her life was not foredoomed, and that circumstances and cultural forces had roles to play in the outcome of her life. This book, in other words, may just be a starting point for readers and writers still attempting to take Monroe's measure and to see her from a new set of angles and perspectives.

A Brief History of Marilyn Monroe

Family History and Early Years (1876–1944)

Marilyn Monroe did not know a great deal about her family history, and what she did know seemed grim. Donald Spoto makes a compelling case for disputing her belief that mental illness in her family was a congenital condition, but of course the facts in Marilyn's case mattered less than her worry that she had inherited some kind of family disposition that would deprive her of her sanity. Counteracting this belief, however, was her early exposure to Christian Science, which compelled her to believe in her own salvation.

Evil and pain could be overcome, her "Aunt" Ana Lower counseled her. Marilyn may have exaggerated the traumas of her childhood in service of creating a good story her studio could exploit. But there is no doubt about the disruptive nature of her early years, when she could not count on her mother and did not know who her father was, and when she had to choose among conflicting role models afforded by the religious and secular families that cared for her. Early on, she was obliged to perform in a number of different roles and in circumstances over which she had little control. The possibility that she was sexually molested—and then disbelieved when she tried to tell what had happened—could only have added to her uncertainty about her place in the world.

1

By the time Norma Jeane—as she was called then—married, she had a troubled awareness of the world that was quite remarkable for a young woman, as can be seen in the note she wrote to herself shortly after her marriage (see the entry for late 1943). She tried to make the marriage work; she also tried to make contact with family members living apart from her, such as her half-sister, Berniece Miracle. While marriage might have meant a settled world to her first husband, the events of Norma Jeane's early years led her to question what could be truly permanent and enduring in her own life. It is not surprising, then, that she should so readily and completely adopt the prospect of a modeling and movie career when it seemed within her grasp. She had so little to relinquish in order to become the next Jean Harlow, a future her guardian, Grace Goddard, had said was in store for her beautiful charge. In retrospect, the marriage to Jim Dougherty seems doomed, but at the time of her wedding Norma Jeane appears to have believed she was in love, and the truth about her own ambitions only became clear to her when the opportunity to model for a wartime photographer arose.

EARLY CAREER (1945–1952)

Norma Jeane did not give up on her marriage all at once. She expected that her husband would take an interest in her work as a model, and was deeply disappointed when he could see no outlet for her other than as a conventional stay-at-home wife. But it is doubtful her marriage could have been sustained, because she pursued her opportunities in such a relentless way, developing an ambition that simply had no place in her husband's world.

By August 14, 1945, Norma Jeane—soon to be renamed Marilyn Monroe—was given a screen test and seemed on her way to fulfilling her dreams. But this initial success was not followed by much actual work at the studio, and Marilyn took her place among a legion of starlets hoping to win the favor of studio heads. These young actresses were used mainly as extras and bit players. Despite her rapport with photographers, Marilyn found it daunting to deal with an industry hierarchy over which she had no control and which regarded her as just another blonde.

Although studio personnel and producers did not yet see Marilyn as a valuable property, it is remarkable how many powerful and talented men she attracted—not only because of her beauty, but also because of her yearning to achieve her own kind of greatness. This cast of male supporters includes: Johnny Hyde, a powerful William Morris agent; Joe Schenck, one of the founding producers of Hollywood; Elia Kazan, a celebrated New York director already well established in Hollywood; and Arthur Miller, who sensed Marilyn's potential long before she acquired a starring role. Hard-working professionals like Fred Karger and Natasha Lytess helped her hone her singing and acting skills.

Equally important to her confidence in herself were the many sessions she spent with photographers, trying out poses, scrutinizing different layouts, and consulting with publicity professionals about the best way to project herself in the media. Indeed, she became better known from her photographs than from the minor roles the studios assigned her.

Marilyn's apprenticeship period ended in 1949, just as the story about her posing for a nude calendar shot broke. The event, three years earlier, could now be dismissed as just a job that a struggling actress and model—chaperoned by the photographer's wife, of course—felt obliged to take in order to support herself. Marilyn, without seeming defensive, won the public to her side. She did so again when it was revealed that her mother was not dead, but, as Marilyn explained, carefully shielded from the public so as to protect her. Although she had killed off her mother to elicit sympathy and make her story more dramatic, Marilyn turned her mother's revival into yet another kind of drama that the public seemed to enjoy just as much—if not more—than her bogus biography.

Middle Years (1953–1959)

Although Marilyn still had not starred in a major motion picture, by 1953 she was receiving volumes of fan mail—the kind of adulation that only the biggest stars enjoyed. Her particular niche as a screen sex symbol had yet to be established, but in news stories and photographs, she had already forged an identity in the public mind. And with the release of *Niagara* in January, her face and figure became a wonder, presented in CinemaScope and full color. It was as if film noir director Henry Hathaway had left behind the closed-in world of 1940s films, opening now to a blonde femme fatale who seemed intriguing to some viewers and outrageous to others. Sexuality was no longer confined to the dark corners of popular film but became, in itself—and in Marilyn—the centerpiece of 1950s cinema.

So shocking was Marilyn's appearance in *Niagara* that the studio felt compelled to dress her in far more demure gowns in *Gentlemen Prefer Blondes*. These new gowns still flattered her figure, but they covered her cleavage and made her more of a child-woman than a seductress. This infantilizing does not, however, diminish Marilyn's sexual appeal; instead the transformation makes it more of a joke. Director Howard Hawks persuaded Fox head Darryl Zanuck that Marilyn's gift was for comedy, and that despite her good work on *Don't Bother to Knock* and *Niagara*, it was a mistake to cast her in dramas. Hathaway argued that she could do serious roles—and indeed, he wanted to cast her as Grushenka in *The Brothers Karamazov*. But the overwhelming success of *Gentlemen Prefer Blondes*, and the studio's concern that Marilyn's sexuality not seem threatening or scandalous, meant that she would be typecast as a dumb blonde who was also a sex symbol. Marilyn's challenge was to create a persona that had more resonance than her roles actually called for. It was this disjunction between her desire to create art and the studio's mission to create commercial vehicles that caused an inevitable collision between the actress and her employers.

Beginning in 1953, Marilyn began to grapple with how to get what she wanted out of studio contracts that gave her almost no say over her creative life. She turned to DiMaggio, Charles Feldman, Milton Greene, and others for assistance. In effect, she had to figure out how to cope with and, ultimately, defeat the corporate interests aligned against her. Biographer Barbara Leaming has covered the business side of this struggle, showing how Marilyn was by turns hesitant and then adept in dealing with studio executives. This battle continued to rage until the very end of her life.

Marilyn's low point during this period was her work on *There's No Business Like Show Business*. DiMaggio objected to the vulgar display of her body in this picture, and Marilyn was disappointed that her role and musical routines were so derivative of other films and musical stars. But DiMaggio had no solution except to urge her to quit Hollywood, and even agents like Charles Feldman seemed powerless to change her working conditions. This is why an outsider like Milton Greene, who had shown his prowess with a camera, seemed so vital to her future. Because of Greene, the prospect of a life in New York City, where she began to see Arthur Miller and attend Actors Studio classes, became a kind of yearlong sabbatical from Hollywood. And when Marilyn stood her ground, the studio finally capitulated, giving her much of what she wanted: a list of approved directors and the right to make films independent of Fox.

Even so, it was a trying time for Marilyn. The studio warned her that her marriage to Arthur Miller was risky since the House Committee on Un-American Activities had, in effect, identified him as a subversive. And then, when Miller seemed unable to intervene in her head-to-head confrontations with Laurence Olivier, her co-star and director on *The Prince and the Showgirl*, Marilyn began once again to feel she was on her own. Even the triumph of *Some Like It Hot* failed to satisfy her, since however great her performance, she was still playing the ingénue—if more chastened now and with a subtlety no other actress could have brought to the role. As Billy Wilder would say after her death, a whole category of films vanished with her departure from the screen.

LAST YEARS (1960–1962)

Let's Make Love was a terrible comedown after *Some Like It Hot*. The former is a very poorly written and directed film, and Marilyn knew it, delivering a rare lackluster performance. Arthur Miller tried to help by improving the script, but he did not have a gift for light comedy, and his services only diminished him in Marilyn's eyes, since the playwright she respected had no business working as a hack motion picture doctor. Miller also had his mind on *The Misfits*, about which Marilyn had grave doubts. These were shared by Elia Kazan and John Huston, although Huston, like Miller, was determined to make the picture. When Miller left Marilyn's side to consult with Huston in Ireland about the script, she felt betrayed and turned to her sympathetic co-star Yves Montand. He found her irresistible, even though he had a high regard for Miller, who had recommended Montand for his role in *Let's Make Love*.

To cope with her anxieties Marilyn began consulting Ralph Greenson, a Los Angeles psychiatrist with many Hollywood patients. He eventually became involved in Marilyn's career, not only advising her but also meeting with studio executives. But Greenson found it difficult to stabilize Marilyn, especially in view of her deepening involvement with Frank Sinatra and his friends, and with Peter Lawford and the Kennedys. In both cases, she seemed distracted by a social life that impeded her effort to overcome her anxieties in her therapy sessions with Greenson.

Director George Cukor found it difficult indeed to deal with Marilyn's lateness, her absences, and her reliance on Paula Strasberg. Arthur Miller tried to help Cukor and was grateful for the director's kindness to Marilyn, but neither man was able to assuage her anger about her participation in such a mediocre film after the high hopes she had entertained for Marilyn Monroe Productions. Her affair with Yves Montand during the making of *Let's Make Love* seemed only a momentary diversion during her estrangement from Miller, an estrangement that culminated during work on *The Misfits*. Miller remained committed to his script, which idealized Roslyn Taber, the character based on Marilyn, but Marilyn was upset that she had to play a character who was a lie because she did not express Marilyn's dark side.

The divorce from Miller devastated Marilyn. She was hospitalized and seemed to be coming apart, although she was not like the mentally ill people she encountered at the Payne Whitney Clinic. Her letters and notes reveal a woman who still had inner resources and a sense of self-worth and dignity. In the last eighteen months of her life she struggled to re-establish herself, buying a home in Los Angeles, but also maintaining her contacts with the Strasbergs and with New York City, which she saw as a personal and cultural antidote to Hollywood superficiality. Yet she could not escape that Hollywood world, which is perhaps why, in the end, she chose to end her life—disappointed in herself, disappointed in the life she had created, but perhaps also believing she had achieved as much as possible, given her psyche and her circumstances. As with many suicides, her ultimate intentions are not clear and are susceptible to many different interpretations, including, perhaps, an expression of the desire to be saved.

Principal Personages

(In alphabetical order)

Rupert Allan (1913–1991): Allan first met Marilyn while doing a story about her in *Look*. He was impressed with her intelligence, ambition, and talent and went to work for her as a publicist. She relied on him both as a professional advisor and as a friend.

George (1877–1968) **and Maude Atkinson** (?): These British actors become Norma Jeane's foster parents during an especially hard period for her mother, Gladys. They were easygoing and presented quite an alternative to Norma Jeane's earlier foster family, the religious Bolenders. George Atkinson was a stand-in for actor George Arliss, and it is likely he and his wife shared Hollywood stories and gossip with Norma Jeane. One account has her praying for them.

Gladys Pearl Monroe Baker (1902–1984): Like her daughter Norma Jeane, Gladys married young. In fact, she was not quite sixteen when she married John Newton Baker, the first of three husbands. The erratic Gladys showed both a fun-loving secular side and a religious, indeed almost fanatical side. Norma Jeane never knew which person she would encounter, and by the time she reached her teens, having lived with foster families and in an orphanage, she was unable to make genuine contact with her mother.

From time to time Gladys seemed to rise out of her demented state, but she never could support, let alone understand, her daughter's desires. Indeed, Gladys addressed one of her later notes to her eldest daughter to Mrs. Norma Jeane Miller. Institutionalized for most of Norma Jeane's early career, Gladys made brief and usually disturbing appearances in her daughter's life.

Bruno Bernard (1912–1987): One of the greatest portrait photographers in the history of Hollywood, Bernard formed a friendship with Norma Jeane. He liked her freshness and ease in front of a camera, and he showed her photographs to Ben Lyon at Twentieth Century Fox. But Marilyn would always remain Norma Jeane to him, his daughter Susan suggested.

José Bolaños (1935–1994): A Mexican playwright and actor, Bolaños acted as Marilyn's escort in Mexico and in Los Angeles. If they were involved in an affair, it was brief and inconsequential. He appeared in public as her congenial date—and perhaps a bit more.

Ida (1887–1972) **and Wayne Bolender** (1883–1974): The Bolenders were Norma Jeane's evangelical Christian foster parents. Wayne was a gentle, caring foster father. Ida was strict and disapproved of the worldly pleasures Gladys and her friends indulged in. At the same time, Ida and her family provided a source of stability for Norma Jeane. Gladys relied on the Bolenders to take care of her child, even though Gladys did not share all their beliefs.

John Carroll (1906–1979): An actor who bore a slight resemblance to Clark Gable, Carroll encouraged Marilyn's ambitions. Accounts differ as to whether or not she had an affair with Carroll.

Michael Chekhov (1891–1955): Chekhov was one of Marilyn's acting teachers. He played character roles in Hollywood films and wrote a well-regarded text, *To The Actor*, which elaborates on Stanislavsky's method. Marilyn relied on Chekhov not just for acting lessons, but also for learning a way to approach the world as an artist.

Colin Clark (1932–2002): As third assistant director on *The Prince and the Showgirl*, Clark kept a diary of the fraught production.

Montgomery Clift (1920–1966): Marilyn's co-star in *The Misfits*, Clift would also have starred with her in *Freud* if Marilyn had not turned down a role in the film after she learned that Anna Freud opposed John Huston's production. Of all of Marilyn's male co-stars, Clift felt closest to her and shared a reciprocity of feeling that was unique in her experience. They both had a tender regard for their fragile psyches.

Harry Cohn (1891–1958): The owner of Columbia Pictures, Cohn was considered the crudest and most vulgar producer in Hollywood. At Joseph Schenck's urging, Cohn signed Marilyn to a six-month contract at Columbia, where she starred in a B picture, *Ladies of the Chorus*. Marilyn spurned Cohn's sexual advances, and he canceled her contract.

Jack Cole (1911–1974): Cole became Marilyn's favorite choreographer when she first worked with him on *Gentlemen Prefer Blondes*.

David Conover (1919–1983): Conover was a photographer who visited Radioplane and took the first professional pictures of Norma Jeane. With his encouragement, she began to believe that a modeling and acting career might be within her reach. She said that he treated her with respect and admiration.

George Cukor (1899–1983): Renowned for his excellent work with actresses, Cukor was on the list of Marilyn's approved directors. He agreed to film *Let's Make Love*, but he found fault with the script and asked Arthur Miller to do rewrites. In spite of his reputation for working well with women, Cukor established little rapport with Marilyn on her last two films. Just before she was fired from *Something's Got to Give*, the director indicated that Marilyn was no longer capable of doing a good job.

Andre de Dienes (1913–1985): One of Norma Jeane's first important photographers, de Dienes discovered that she excelled at location shooting. Initially, she resisted his advances, but according to de Dienes the couple did have a brief romance. Although this photographer is associated mainly with the discovery of Norma Jeane, he continued to work with her through 1953, capturing key moments in her transition from starlet to star. His earliest photographs of her also kept circulating, especially in European magazines.

Joe DiMaggio (1914–1999): This baseball legend played a crucial role not only in Marilyn's life but also in the pivotal period 1952–1953, when she was figuring out how to deal with Hollywood and her desire to find better roles and be recognized for her achievements. DiMaggio's business sense served her well, although he never understood what acting—or art—meant to her. Jealous and possessive, DiMaggio criticized her flamboyant performances, pressuring her to retire and spend the rest of her life as his wife. And yet after they divorced, Marilyn and DiMaggio continued to see one another frequently and became good friends. Indeed, until her marriage to Arthur Miller, DiMaggio remained the most important male figure in Marilyn's life. He became increasingly important after she divorced Arthur Miller. DiMaggio got Marilyn released from the horrors of Payne Whitney, and he dined with her frequently, occasionally spending a night with her. He took care of all the funeral arrangements for Marilyn, making sure to exclude all but her very closest friends and family.

James Dougherty (1921–2005): Dougherty was a star athlete and an amateur actor in high school. His mother and Grace McKee Goddard encouraged him to take Norma Jeane out on dates. He married her just after she turned sixteen. His own accounts depict their marriage as happy until Norma Jeane began working as a model and aspiring actress. But Norma Jeane's own feelings about this early marriage seem to have been mixed, and in retrospect Marilyn Monroe saw it as a mistake. Although Dougherty made it clear he did not want his wife to work as a model or actress, in the early phases of her career Norma Jeane continued to expect that he would come around to her point of view and even signal his approval.

Charles Feldman (1904–1968): This Hollywood agent and producer took an active interest in Marilyn's career after Johnny Hyde died. Feldman introduced her to several important people in the industry and tried to obtain for her a measure of independence from her restrictive Hollywood contract. One reason Marilyn turned to this high-powered individual is that he had shown he could deal with the large Hollywood studios. She expected a great deal from Feldman—a renegotiated contract that would give her some say over scripts and directors, for example. Not even the biggest stars could make such demands unless, like Cary Grant, they were truly independent contractors, negotiating with more than one studio.

Clark Gable (1901–1960): Often called the king of Hollywood, Gable treated Marilyn with unfailing courtesy and respect on the set of *The Misfits*. He was the star she idolized and the man she fantasized was her father.

Stanley Gifford (1898–1965): Gifford was a salesman for Consolidated Film Industries, where Gladys worked. He was apparently what used to be called a ladies' man. Norma Jeane was later given to believe that Gifford was her father. She made a few efforts to contact Gifford, but he rebuffed her.

Ervin "Doc" Goddard (1904–1972): Goddard was a handsome aspiring actor who married Grace McKee. He had children from a previous marriage, and Grace, anxious to accommodate her younger husband, placed her ward, Norma Jeane, in an orphanage—promising that this was only a temporary measure. Goddard later made some sort of pass at Norma Jeane.

Grace Atchinson McKee Goddard (1895–1953): Gladys's friend who became Norma Jeane's guardian. Like Gladys, Grace worked in the movie industry and was star-struck. She projected her desire to be an actress into stories she told Norma Jeane, going so far as to encourage the young girl to believe she could be the next Jean Harlow. Although she tried to do her best by Norma Jeane, Grace's romantic notions and her desire to have a good time made her far from reliable as far as Norma Jeane was concerned. On the one hand, Grace told Norma Jeane to pursue her dreams of movie stardom; on the other hand, Grace complicated and perhaps confused Norma Jeane by arranging for the girl's marriage to James Dougherty. Although at that time Grace was no longer involved in the day-to-day doings of Norma Jeane's life, she and Norma Jeane continued to communicate in notes and letters. Norma Jeane felt obligated to tell Grace that the marriage to Dougherty was a success—and even (contrary to all available evidence) that Dougherty approved of Norma Jeane's new career. Grace continued to make sure Marilyn's mother, Gladys, was well cared for, but Marilyn no longer saw much of Grace after the divorce from Dougherty and no longer felt quite the same sense of obligation to her former guardian.

Lotte Goslar (1907–1997): Goslar was a famous mime who often helped Marilyn with the physical business required by her roles.

Sheilah Graham (1904–1988): Graham is most famous for her affair with F. Scott Fitzgerald, which Graham wrote about in *Beloved Infidel*. She was a Hollywood gossip columnist of some influence, although not as important as Louella Parsons or Hedda Hopper. Still, Graham was the kind of Hollywood figure Marilyn cultivated by—among other things—showing up at important events such as Graham's wedding.

Milton Greene (1922–1985): This photographer and eventual Marilyn Monroe business partner first met her at a party in September 1953. At the earliest stage of their relationship, Marilyn knew Milton Greene as a photographer and social acquaintance. They became friends, and she confided in him her concerns about the limitations of her roles. He worked to make her head of her own production company so that she could secure better acting parts and have a say in how her films were made. It is said they may have had a brief affair. It was not until late 1953 or 1954 that he entered her life as an advisor, dealing with her desire to break out of her Hollywood contract and roles that confined her to impersonating sex symbols. But Greene's inexperience as a producer and inability to deal with the tensions produced by Marilyn's work with Olivier, and Arthur Miller's increasing involvement in Monroe's business affairs, eventually forced Greene out of his role as vice-president of Marilyn Monroe Productions and ruined Greene's friendship with the star.

Ralph Greenson (1911–1979): Marilyn consulted the psychiatrist for the first time in Hollywood on the recommendation of Dr. Marianne Kris, who was treating Marilyn in New York. Greenson gradually supplanted Dr. Kris as Marilyn's psychiatrist. Greenson explored unorthodox therapies, which included bringing Marilyn to his house and encouraging her friendships with his children. Eventually, Marilyn called on him for assistance almost daily.

Howard Hawks (1896–1977): One of the great directors of Hollywood's Golden Age, Hawks early on determined that Marilyn's gift was for light comedy verging on farce. This is how he employed her in *Monkey Business* and *Gentlemen Prefer Blondes*, two important pictures that made it virtually impossible for her to do dramatic roles, since her studio profited so much from her comedies.

Ben Hecht (1894–1964): Because he worked on so many important films, Hecht was often called the Shakespeare of Hollywood. He was one of the writers on *Monkey Business*, and after he took an interest in Marilyn, the two worked on a plan to publish a series of autobiographical articles. The project ended when DiMaggio disapproved of it and when Hecht's agent unscrupulously published part of Marilyn's autobiography in a British tabloid, *Empire News*. Later Marilyn gave a manuscript of her collaboration with Hecht to Milton Greene, who published it in 1974 as *My Story*—without mentioning Hecht's role in creating the book.

Margaret Hohenberg (1898–1992): Marilyn began seeing this psychoanalyst when she moved to New York City in late 1953.

During some periods, Hohenberg treated Marilyn on an almost a daily basis. Hohenberg became increasingly involved in her patient's life and career, until Marilyn's estrangement from Milton Greene in 1956.

Hedda Hopper (1885–1966): Like her rival gossip columnist Louella Parsons, Hedda Hopper, through her column and radio program, wielded powerful influence in Hollywood. She could deliver devastating rebukes to misbehaving stars and elaborate compliments to her favorites. Like other stars, Marilyn catered to Hopper's requests for interviews and exclusives.

John Huston (1906–1987): One of Hollywood's great directors, Huston first employed Marilyn in a small role in *The Asphalt Jungle*. He agreed to work with Miller and Monroe on *The Misfits*. Although he expressed admiration for Miller's script, in fact Huston demanded extensive revisions. Marilyn became increasingly resentful about the Huston-Miller collaboration, which seemed to leave her out of discussions of a script closely based on her own story. As the tensions between Marilyn and her husband mounted on the set of *The Misfits*, Huston seemed to withdraw, gambling all night and falling asleep during the filming of certain scenes. When Marilyn's health worsened, he shut down production—in part to give himself time to secure funding to cover his gambling debts and enable filming to continue.

Johnny Hyde (1895–1950): A powerful William Morris agent, Hyde worked indefatigably on Marilyn's behalf and fell in love with her. She rejected his plea that they marry, but she felt deeply indebted to him. He secured her first important role in *The Asphalt Jungle*, directed by John Huston. Hyde died shortly after obtaining a new seven-year contract with Fox for Marilyn.

Joseph Jasgur (1919–2009): Jasgur, one of Marilyn's early photographers, realized early on that if Norma Jeane was to be successful, she would need to work on her physical appearance, eliminating as many flaws as possible and enhancing her look by becoming a blonde. Even though he saw her potential, he was surprised by how far she exceeded his expectations.

Fred Karger (1916–1979): Karger was a vocal coach at Columbia Pictures. Marilyn worked with him diligently, and he prepared her well for her starring role in *Ladies of the Chorus*. Although the two became romantically involved, he did not think she was suitable for marriage or to be the mother of his children. Marilyn did not name Karger in *My Story*, but she obviously had him in mind when she described her sorrow over this failed affair with one of her mentors.

Elia Kazan (1909–2003): One of the founding members of the Group Theatre in the 1930s, and a prominent New York and Hollywood director, Kazan became Marilyn's lover and also her advisor. After their affair ended, Marilyn continued to see Kazan but was disappointed that he never cast her in a film. He seemed wary of using her because she had become such a huge star. The Monroe persona was liable to overwhelm any character she played. Miller counted on Kazan's advice, although the playwright was unable to quell the director's qualms about *The Misfits*.

Tom Kelley (1914–1984): Kelley was the photographer who persuaded Marilyn to pose for her famous nude calendar shots, for which he paid her fifty dollars. In most poses her face is obscured, but in one upright shot, she is recognizable. The pictures were taken at a time when she was largely unknown, and Marilyn was willing to risk showing more of her body than was permissible during an era governed by the censorship of the Hollywood production code.

John F. Kennedy (1917–1963): Although Marilyn met the president on a few occasions and allegedly had sex with him once (according to Ralph Roberts, her confidant), the exact nature of her connection to Kennedy remains unclear. It seems unlikely that their relationship was either as close or as portentous as the many books about Marilyn and the Kennedys suggest.

Robert Kennedy (1925–1968): In the last months of Marilyn's life—as her interest in politics peaked—Robert Kennedy supplanted his brother John as a focus of the star's attention. She was concerned about civil rights and quizzed Kennedy about the subject. He seemed to welcome her attention, and though much has been said about an affair between them, not much can be proven. It is true that Marilyn called the Justice Department several times, and that Kennedy was known to be fascinated with Hollywood figures, including Judy Garland. But it is likely that what Marilyn sought was his help getting her reinstated at the studio after she was fired from *Something's Got to Give*. Conflicting testimony has been given about whether Robert Kennedy visited Marilyn on the last day of her life.

Marianne Kris (1900–1980): Marilyn's New York psychiatrist, Dr. Kris made the mistake of putting Marilyn in the Payne Whitney Clinic, which treated psychiatric patients. Marilyn was frightened and angered, since she did not believe her mental distress warranted this kind of institutionalization. Although her tie to Kris was severely tried by this incident, Marilyn remained grateful for the help the psychiatrist extended to her over several years.

Peter Lawford (1923–1984): Lawford is mentioned as a casual acquaintance of Marilyn's during her early years in Hollywood. Their friendship did not develop until early 1960 during JFK's campaign for the presidency, a period when Lawford was married to Kennedy's sister Patricia and lived near Marilyn's Hollywood home. Lawford received a call from Marilyn on the last night of her life that made him worry she might be in trouble.

Joshua Logan (1908–1988): One of Marilyn's most sensitive directors, Logan worked closely with her to develop the role of Cherie in *Bus Stop*. Even so, she brought to the set her usual distrust of directors as company men who rarely viewed scenes from her point of view. Yet Logan never seemed to resent her suspicion, and he continued to work with her, filled with admiration for her sensitivity and intelligence.

Ana Lower (1880–1948): Norma Jeane lived for a time with this devout Christian Scientist, who had a powerful influence on the maturing girl, who tried to follow the principles of this church. Lower was sensitive to Norma Jeane's needs, and Norma Jeane relied on her both for advice and for encouraging words that bolstered the young woman's self-esteem. Continuing her role as Norma Jeane's confidant, Lower remained supportive when her charge embarked on a modeling career and signed a movie contract.

Ben Lyon (1901–1979): This actor, later Fox studio executive, was impressed with Norma Jeane and arranged for her first screen test. He wanted to capture her visual appeal, so he had the test shot in color but without sound.

Natasha Lytess (1913–1964): An acting coach at Columbia Pictures, Lytess was assigned to Marilyn Monroe. Although Lytess did not think much of the struggling actress, the coach agreed to work with Marilyn on her diction and on acting exercises. Gradually, Lytess became an essential part of Marilyn's program to improve herself, and although Lytess remained so during preparation for filming and on studio sets, her demands for a higher salary and desire to dominate troubled Marilyn, who resented the burdens Lytess placed upon her. By 1956, Marilyn had replaced Lytess with Paula Strasberg.

Arthur Miller (1915–2005): On a movie set, Elia Kazan introduced Marilyn to a smitten Arthur Miller. The playwright, suffering in a troubled marriage, listened sensitively to Marilyn's concerns, but then flew back to New York. Marilyn seemed already to be considering a life with Miller, even though there was no immediate prospect of acting on her desires. The playwright began seeing Marilyn almost as soon as she moved to New York, announcing her break with Fox. He was circumspect and met her alone or at social engagements with a few trusted friends like Norman and Hedda Rosten and Sam Shaw. He seemed besotted with Marilyn but also cautious, never quite revealing his commitment to her until he testified before the House Committee on Un-American Activities

(HUAC). Their wedding was broadcast in the press as the union
of the egghead and the hourglass. She stood by him during his
HUAC testimony, even when the studio advised her to keep her
distance from Miller. When she refused to do so, studio executives
expressed the hope that Miller would be a "cooperative witness,"
meaning that he would "name names"—that is, identify friends and
associates he knew or suspected were Communists. Miller refused
to assist HUAC and was cited for contempt of Congress and convicted in a court of law. Eventually, an appeals court overturned his
conviction. But Miller's role as admired hero disintegrated as Marilyn relied more and more on him to deal with her career—which
Miller could not fix. As he lost Marilyn's confidence, he withdrew
into himself, making Marilyn feel, once again, that she had been
abandoned and was alone in her fight for integrity and a serious
career. Miller worked on rewrites for *Let's Make Love*, although
he was not credited with the work because of a writers' strike in
Hollywood. He did not want to be perceived as a strikebreaker or
as a hack writer who doctored movie scripts. He wanted to help
Marilyn, but his efforts only seemed to diminish him in her estima-
tion. When he left her to consult with John Huston on the script of
The Misfits, she regarded this departure as a sign of abandonment
and began an affair with Montand. Miller's efforts to pay tribute to
Monroe in *The Misfits* only worsened matters, because she detested
his idealization of her and his unwillingness to deal with the darker
sides of her character. The marriage dissolved as soon as *The Misfits*
concluded filming.

Isidore Miller (1886–1966): Marilyn maintained a close relation-
ship with Arthur Miller's father even after she and his son divorced.
She visited Isidore in Florida and also took him as her guest to the
Madison Square Garden celebration of JFK's birthday.

Berniece Miracle (1919–): Berniece was Norma Jeane's half-sister.
Although the sisters saw one another sporadically, their blood tie was
important, providing first Norma Jeane, then Marilyn, with some
sense of continuity and family history. Marilyn kept in contact with
Berniece through notes, reporting her progress and prospects.

Della Hogan Monroe (1876–1927): Marilyn's maternal grandmother was a restless woman who married several times and who was a fitful presence in her daughter Gladys's life. Marilyn claimed that her grandmother tried to smother her with a pillow, although Marilyn was not much more than a year old when Della, who had become insane, died of a heart attack.

Yves Montand (1921–1991): Marilyn was not discreet about Montand, and their affair became public knowledge. Her studio seemed not to mind and perhaps even abetted stories about the couple as part of the publicity for *Let's Make Love*.

Martin Edward Mortensen (1897–1981): Mortensen is listed on Norma Jeane's birth certificate as her father. But he is almost surely not, even though he married Gladys. Gladys never treated him as her child's father, and he apparently never asserted his paternity. Described as a meter reader, he is one of the more shadowy figures in Monroe's biography.

Eunice Murray (1902–1994): At Dr. Greenson's urging, Marilyn hired Murray as a housekeeper. In fact, Murray was something more than a housekeeper and something less than a psychiatric nurse. She worked closely with Greenson and accompanied Marilyn on her trip to Mexico. Some biographers suggest Marilyn became dissatisfied with Murray and intended to fire her. Murray has come under some suspicion because her accounts of Marilyn's last hours have been contradictory.

Jean Negulesco (1900–1993): Marilyn's director on *How to Marry a Millionaire*, Negulesco worked hard to earn Marilyn's confidence and to share his aesthetic sensibility with her. His main problem was Natasha Lytess, who interfered with his direction, interrupting production with her constant conferences with Marilyn.

Pat Newcomb (1930–): This publicist became Marilyn's friend and took over the role Rupert Allan played during Marilyn's formative years. Because Newcomb went to work for the Kennedys, she often figures in conspiracy theories about Marilyn's death. New-comb has said very little about Marilyn's final days.

Laurence Olivier (1907–1989): When he was turning fifty, this distinguished actor regarded a film with Marilyn Monroe as a way to revive his leading-man image. She, in turn, believed that acting with him would enhance respect for her as an actress. Neither of them understood the other very well. Olivier seemed condescending to Marilyn, and she seemed undisciplined and unprepared to him. Monroe could not act on command, and Olivier had no patience with the Method's emphasis on relating the role to the actor. Like nearly all of her directors, he resented the presence of Marilyn's coach—in this case Paula Strasberg, who seemed to Olivier simply an interfering sycophant. Marilyn, on the other hand, relied on Strasberg, since she found herself shut out of the company Olivier kept with the crew, individuals who had worked with him for years.

Louella Parsons (1881–1972): Parsons was the first important Hollywood gossip columnist. She took an early interest in Marilyn's career and usually defended Marilyn when the actress was criticized. Marilyn knew the value of cultivating Parsons's good will and would often feed her stories that were exclusives.

Ralph Roberts (1918–1999): Marilyn's masseur and confidant, Roberts became increasingly important to her in her final days, and before that during her divorce from Arthur Miller, her stay at Payne Whitney, and her troubled work on *Something's Got to Give*. Dr. Greenson, however, was concerned that figures like Roberts were making it more difficult for Marilyn to confront her anxieties, and for a time, Roberts was excluded from her inner circle. But toward the end of her life, she often confided in Roberts, both in person and on the phone.

Jane Russell (1921–2011): Russell co-starred with Marilyn in *Gentlemen Prefer Blondes*. On screen and off, Russell seemed to play the role of understanding older sister, soothing Marilyn's anxieties and genuinely supporting Marilyn as she ascended to stardom.

Lucille Ryman (1906–2002): Married to actor John Carroll, and head of the talent department at MGM, Ryman believed in Marilyn's gift. Along with her husband, Ryman made a contract with the actress that guaranteed Marilyn a weekly income and that gave Carroll and Ryman the fees Marilyn earned. This business contract lasted for less than a year, after which Charles Feldman and others represented Marilyn's interests.

Hal Schaefer (1925–2012): Schaefer was a vocal coach who worked closely with Marilyn during the making of *There's No Business Like Show Business*. She became increasingly close to him, and they had a brief affair—which so unnerved Schaefer that he attempted suicide during her unhappy marriage to Joe DiMaggio.

Joseph Schenck (1878–1961): Schenck teamed with Darryl Zanuck to create Twentieth Century Fox. Marilyn relied on Schenck's wise counsel and on his efforts to secure employment for her. She often dined at his home and entertained his guests. She paid tribute to him in *My Story*.

Sam Shaw (1912–1999): One of Marilyn's principal photographers, Shaw helped her make a home in New York, introducing her to his friends—especially Norman Rosten and his wife, Hedda.

Frank Sinatra (1915–1998): Sinatra was one of Marilyn's favorite singers, her sometime lover, and her friend. She socialized with him, even though her psychiatrist, Ralph Greenson, believed that Sinatra and his retinue were harmful influences preventing Marilyn from concentrating on improving her mental outlook. Sinatra and his friends represented an unstable element in her life.

Sidney Skolsky (1905–1983): Hollywood columnist and Monroe confidant, Skolsky was responsible for helping her to create and manage much of her early publicity. Besides assiduously building up Marilyn's career, this gossip columnist often accompanied Marilyn to public events, especially when DiMaggio was unavailable or refused to attend such functions.

Emmeline Snively (1909–1975): As head of the Blue Book Modeling Agency, Snively gave Norma Jeane her start on a professional modeling career. Snively arranged for many photo sessions and work at trade shows. She was impressed with Norma Jeane's hard work and keen desire to improve.

Lee Strasberg (1901–1982): One of the principal proponents of the Stanislavsky school of acting, Strasberg exerted his influence through the Actors Studio, established by producer Cheryl Crawford, director Elia Kazan, and director Robert Lewis. The Studio had an enormous influence on American actors like Marlon Brando and James Dean, and Marilyn naturally gravitated to it in New York City since her earlier teachers—especially Michael Chekhov—had practiced their own versions of Stanislavsky's method. Under Strasberg, "The Method," as it came to be called, was closely aligned to a psychological approach to role playing, in which the actor or actress called upon his or her own experiences in relating to a character. Strasberg quickly made Marilyn a special case, giving her private lessons, including her in his family gatherings, and gradually introducing her into Actors Studio classes by preparing her for her classroom performances in important plays. He also advised Marilyn about roles she should play in Hollywood. Their plan for Strasberg to direct her in W. Somerset Maugham's *Rain* was abandoned when the television network would not hire Strasberg, citing his lack of experience in the medium.

Paula Strasberg (1909–1966): Lee Strasberg's wife served as a replacement for Natasha Lytess. Like Lytess, Paula was despised by directors who regarded her as a sycophant and a disruption on the set. Marilyn paid far more attention to her than to the director. But Marilyn may have become disenchanted with Strasberg. The actress was under pressure from her studio to jettison her coach when Marilyn resumed work on *Something's Got to Give*. Even so, Marilyn continued to confer with Paula. What Marilyn might have done about Strasberg if Marilyn had lived to complete the film is not clear.

Susan Strasberg (1938–1999): The daughter of Lee and Paula, Susan befriended Marilyn, who admired Susan's stage work and confided in Susan almost as if she were a younger sister.

Billy Travilla (1920–1990): Travilla was Marilyn's most important dress designer during the early stages of her stardom. He perfected a wardrobe that accentuated her figure and yet covered up just enough to satisfy censors. According to Travilla, he and Marilyn had a brief affair.

Walter Winchell (1897–1972): An influential syndicated columnist and radio personality, Winchell's early interest in Marilyn helped build her career, although she had no sympathy for his rabid anti-Communist politics.

Darryl Zanuck (1902–1979): Although studio head Zanuck had not been impressed with Marilyn's early performances, by the mid-1950s he realized she was a bankable star. He began making certain concessions, allowing Natasha Lytess on movie sets, for example, even when important directors like Jean Negulesco and Otto Preminger objected. But to Marilyn, Zanuck represented the studio system itself, a system she loathed because it limited her to playing stereotypes.

Timeline

1876

July 1: Della Mae Hogan, Marilyn's grandmother, is born in Brunswick County, Missouri.

1899

Della Mae Hogan marries Otis Elmer Monroe, Marilyn's maternal grandfather.

1902

May 27: Gladys Pearl is born to Della and Otis Monroe.

1908

Otis Monroe is admitted to Southern California State Hospital and diagnosed with general paresis (nerve damage and muscular weakness associated with partial paralysis and a disorder of the brain and central nervous system resulting in psychosis).

1909

July 22: Otis dies insane. His malady is not genetic, but instead probably results from living in unsanitary conditions in Mexico. But his family does not understand the aetiology of his condition.

1912

Della marries Lyle Arthur Graves, a violent alcoholic.

1913

Della leaves her husband in May.

1914

January 17: Della divorces Lyle Arthur Graves.

November 25: Joe DiMaggio, Marilyn's second husband, is born.

1915

October 17: Arthur Miller, Marilyn's third husband, is born.

1917

May 17: Gladys marries John Newton (Jasper) Baker, an abusive husband. She gives birth to their son, Robert.

1919

July 30: Berniece, Marilyn's half-sister, is born.

1920

Gladys becomes a film negative cutter at Consolidated Film Industries. She becomes friends with her supervisor, Grace Emma Atchinson McKee.

1921

April 12: James Dougherty, Marilyn's first husband, is born.
June 20: Gladys files for a divorce from Jasper Baker.

1923

Jasper Baker, Gladys's husband, takes custody of Berniece and Robert.

May 23: Gladys's divorce is finalized.

Gladys meets Stanley Gifford, a salesman at Consolidated Film Industries in Hollywood. Gifford has been identified in several sources as Marilyn's father, although no definitive evidence of parentage has been produced.

1924

Summer: Gladys meets Martin Edward Mortensen. She dies her hair red.

October 11: Gladys marries Martin Edward Mortensen, a meter man for the Los Angeles Gas and Electric Company.

1925

May 26: Gladys leaves Mortensen, and he files for divorce.
Autumn: Gladys becomes pregnant.

1926

March 20: Della leaves behind her pregnant daughter, Gladys, to join Charles Grainger—with whom she has lived off and on—in Borneo.

May 31: Gladys Mortensen goes into labor.

June 1: Tuesday, 9:30 a.m., Norma Jeane Mortensen is born at the Los Angeles General Hospital, delivered by Dr. Herman M. Beerman. The birth certificate misspells her last name as Mortenson. The father is identified as Edward Mortenson. His address is listed as "unknown." At the time, Gladys is separated from her husband. Gladys lists herself as Gladys Monroe (her maiden name), living at 5454 Wilshire Boulevard. Early accounts of Marilyn Monroe's life drop the final *e* from Jeane because Marilyn herself tended to do so. Gladys's friends pay the $140 cost of her hospital stay.

June 13: Gladys, a single mother, brings Norma Jeane to live with the Bolenders, an evangelical Christian family in Hawthorne, California, and they take care of the child while Gladys works.

September 8: Della arrives in San Francisco, returning from Borneo with malaria.

December 6: Norma Jeane is baptized at the Foursquare Gospel Church in Sister Aimee Semple McPherson's Angelus Temple in Los Angeles, where Della worships.

1927

February: Norma Jeane is learning to talk and is able to say "Mama."

June 1: Norma Jeane turns one.

July: Della Grainger, Norma Jeane's grandmother, purportedly tries to smother her with a pillow.

August 4: Della Grainger is diagnosed with manic-depressive psychosis and admitted to Norwalk State Hospital in Norwalk,

California. Her illness may be due to a cardiac condition whereby her brain, deprived of oxygen, provokes erratic behavior. Gladys, it seems, is depressed about her mother's mental state, and believes her family is prone to dementia—especially since Della's first husband, Otis Monroe (Gladys's father), died of the disease, perhaps as a result of contracting syphilis.

August 23: Della Grainger dies of a heart attack after a seizure in Norwalk State Hospital.

August 25: Della Grainger is buried in an unmarked grave next to her husband Otis Monroe at Rosedale Cemetery in central Los Angeles.

Gladys moves back to Hollywood and lives with a roommate, Grace McKee, but leaves Norma Jeane with the Bolenders.

1928

A divorce decree is granted to Edward Mortensen, who charges that Gladys "willfully and without cause deserted [him]."

Norma Jeane finds a playmate, Lester, one of the Bolender children who is her age. Photographs are taken of her and the family at the Santa Monica Beach.

June 1: Norma Jeane turns two.

1929

Gladys is promoted to section head at Consolidated Industries on Melrose Avenue in Hollywood.

Norma Jeane learns her first song, "Jesus Loves Me, This I Know." She continues to live with the Bolenders.

June 1: Norma Jeane turns three.

September: Norma Jeane attends the Hawthorne Community Sunday School.

1930

Gladys takes Norma Jeane on trolley trips to Sunset Beach for walks and picnics. In Venice, Norma Jeane is treated to ice cream and watches mimes, jugglers, and fire-eaters in St. Mark's Plaza. Gladys talks about movie stars such as Douglas Fairbanks, Mary Pickford, and Harold Lloyd, showing Norma Jeane the places where these Hollywood greats live. But these excursions are fitful, and Gladys's fluctuating moods make Norma Jeane uncertain of just who Gladys is. Compounding the confusion, the Bolenders believe Christian principles dictate no drinking, smoking, card playing, or any of the other amusements that appeal to Gladys.

April 1: Official census records list Norma Jeane as living with her mother and the Bolenders on Rhode Island Avenue in Inglewood, part of Los Angeles County.

June 1: Norma Jeane turns four.

September 28: Norma Jeane attends the Community Sunday School in Hawthorne, and is promoted to "Beginners Department" after successfully graduating from the "Cradle Roll Department."

1931

June 1: Norma Jeane turns five.

September 14: Norma Jeane starts school at the Ballona Elementary and Kindergarten School in Hawthorne, accompanied by her playmate Lester. Photographs of the two of them together show they were a good match and could have been taken for brother and sister.

1932

Norma Jeane learns to roller skate.

June 1: Norma Jeane turns six.

June 17: Norma Jeane's last day at the Ballona Elementary and Kindergarten School in Hawthorne.

Summer: At the Hollywood Bowl, Norma Jeane takes her place in a religious event among fifty children forming a living cross. Marilyn later recalled the day: "We wore white tunics under our dresses and, at the signal, we had to remove our dresses to change the black cross into a white one . . . I was bored. . . . I completely forgot and found myself the only black patch in a white cross. My family didn't forgive me ever."

September: Norma Jeane attends first grade at the Vine Street School at the corner of El Segundo Boulevard and Washington Street, long since obliterated by the Los Angeles International Airport. She likes recess, when she can get away from the strictures all too familiar from her days with the Bolenders. "I lived to play," Marilyn recalled later, "real drama, excessive adventures." She loved "to invent . . . I think more than the others—because at my foster parents' home, everything was so predictable."

1933

March: After the famous Long Beach earthquake, Norma Jeane briefly attends the Fifth Street School, where her teacher, Evelyn Gawthrop, perceives her as a "timid child who loved to sing."

Spring: Gladys takes off work to nurse Norma Jeane, who has whooping cough.

Norma Jeane's tonsils are removed.

June: A neighbor shoots Norma Jeane's dog, Tippy, for rolling in his garden. Gladys helps her daughter bury the dog.

Gladys removes Norma Jeane from the Bolenders and takes her to Hollywood to live with two British actors, George and Maude Atkinson. The Atkinsons teach Norma Jeane to dance the hula and to play cards. Norma Jeane prays for them.

Gladys takes Norma Jeane on an outing to Catalina.

Some days, Gladys parks Norma Jeane in movie theater palaces like Sid Grauman's Egyptian Theatre and his Chinese Theatre on Hollywood Boulevard.

June 1: Norma Jeane turns seven.

June 13: Taking advantage of the Roosevelt administration's program offering low-interest property loans, Gladys obtains a $5,000 loan from the Mortgage Guarantee Company of California and uses the money to purchase a six-room furnished house with three bedrooms at 6812 Arbol Street, in the vicinity of the Hollywood Bowl. In this house, Norma Jeane discovers the Franklin white piano she mentions in *My Story*, which becomes the lost token of her brief time with Gladys in their own home, when Norma Jeane could put into practice the piano lessons that she has taken from Miss Marion Miller at the Bolenders.

August 16: Gladys's son, Robert Baker, dies of tuberculosis of the kidney. She rails at Norma Jeane: "Why couldn't it have been you?"

August or September: Gladys and Norma Jeane move into their first home together. Gladys takes in renters, the Atkinsons, to help pay her mortgage. In this house Norma Jeane sees the picture of the man resembling Clark Gable and is told by Gladys that the man is her father. Meals at the house are often devoted to discussions of Hollywood and movie star gossip. And with the end of Prohibition, Norma Jeane is suddenly exposed to drinking, card games, perfume, dancing, and other indulgences that the Bolenders had banned. On weekends, Norma Jeane sees movies such as *Little Women* and *Grand Hotel* and gets to watch stars like Katharine Hepburn, Greta Garbo—and especially Jean Harlow. And yet, Gladys develops a religious mania and frequently quotes the Bible.

October: Gladys learns that her grandfather, Tilford Marion Hogan, has committed suicide, and she begins to suffer from hallucinations.

October 12: Sidney Skolsky, one of the creators of Marilyn stories, arrives in Hollywood to report on the world of motion pictures.

December: Norma Jeane starts listening to what becomes her favorite radio program, *The Lone Ranger*, which airs on Friday nights at 7:30.

1934

According to *My Story*, this is the year that eight-year-old Norma Jeane is sexually abused, although where this incident occurs and who fondled her have not been established.

Norma Jeane begins to stutter.

January: Gladys's erratic behavior becomes serious enough for the Atkinsons to contact Grace, who instructs them to call an ambulance. Norma Jeane remains in the care of the Atkinsons and Grace.

February: A listless Gladys returns home and resumes her work as a film cutter. Despite her religious scruples, Gladys lapses into drinking bouts and takes prescription drugs to alleviate her anxieties. She is hospitalized but then released.

June: Norma Jeane finishes the second grade at Vine Street School.

June 1: Norma Jeane turns eight.

Summer: Norma Jeane goes to see Claudette Colbert in *Cleopatra*.

Intermittent outings with Gladys disturb Norma Jeane, who finds it hard to make contact with her increasingly distant mother.

September: Norma Jeane begins the third grade at the Selma Street School.

October 21: Gladys's house is put up for sale at $4,500. An advertisement describes the dwelling as an English stucco house, with three bedrooms and three baths.

Gladys is hospitalized at least one more time near the end of the year. The Atkinsons move out and return to England, their home, and Grace, acting as Norma Jeane's guardian, temporarily places her with her sister Enid and Enid's husband, Sam Knebelkamp. Grace's aunt, Ana Lower, also takes care of Norma Jeane.

December: A report written by a senior consultant at the Los Angeles General Hospital describes Gladys's illness and notes her "constant religious concerns and with a deep depression and a big agitation. It seems that the illness has reached its chronic stage."

Christmas: In a letter dated August 15, 1962, Harry C. Wilson writes to Berniece Miracle about visiting Norma Jeane and her mother for Christmas 1935. (The date is a mistake, since Norma Jeane was then in an orphanage.) Wilson takes Norma Jeane to watch the Christmas Parade. "I lifted her onto my shoulder so she could see better. I remember something else about the evening after we came home from the Christmas Parade, and before I said good night to them. Gladys asked Norma Jean to sing for me. It was lovely. Gladys had a Christmas tree all decorated and Norma Jean stood between the tree and us and sang a pretty song. I was entranced by it and about everything else that seemed to have come into my life at the time. After Norma Jean left to go to bed I talked about it to Gladys. I told her I was very much in love with her and her little girl. It was less than a month later when tragedy struck. I almost lost my mind over it." (Wilson is referring to Gladys's incarceration in Norwalk Mental Hospital in early January 1935.)

1935

January 15: Gladys is declared insane and committed to the Norwalk Mental Hospital.

March 25: Grace McKee files a petition to become Gladys's legal guardian. As administrator of Gladys's property, Grace sells many items to satisfy Gladys's outstanding debts.

May 22: Grace pays twenty-five dollars to Nellie Atkinson for Norma Jeane's care.

Spring: Grace meets Erwin "Doc" Goddard, an aspiring movie actor.

June: Norma Jeane lives briefly with Harvey and Elsie Giffen, parents of Norma Jeane's best friend at school. She is treated well and likes the family.

June 1: Norma Jean celebrates her ninth birthday.

Norma Jeane finishes the third grade at Selma Street School.

June 12: Grace McKee Goddard sells the house Norma Jeane and her mother lived in.

July: Grace brings Norma Jeane to live with her.

August 10: Grace McKee marries Erwin "Doc" Goddard in Las Vegas, and the couple settles in at 6707 Odessa Avenue in Van Nuys.

August 15: Grace McKee writes to a friend that Gladys's doctor told her that Gladys's "type of insanity is the hardest case to do anything with. Her brain did not develop like an ordinary person's."

August 17: Norma Jeane becomes part of the Goddard household.

September: Norma Jeane begins fourth grade at the Vine Street School.

September 13: To make room for Doc Goddard's children by a previous marriage, Grace McKee places Norma Jeane in the Los Angeles Orphans Home. Norma Jeane finds herself among fifty or so children, some of them runaways, others abandoned, and still others taken from homes where their parents could not support them. Children are expected do light housework and chores and are paid small sums to bolster their sense of responsibility and discipline. In *My Story*, Marilyn presents this period in a darker, Dickensian light. In an orphanage report she is described as "healthy and normal, with good appetite and uniform sleep. She seems happy, doesn't complain and even says she loves her classroom." Grace visits on Saturdays and takes Norma Jeane for walks or lunch, or to the movies—including *Mutiny on the Bounty*, starring Clark Gable.

December 5: After a visit from Ida Bolender that upsets Norma Jeane, Grace McKee writes to Mrs. Sula Dewey, superintendent of the orphanage, requesting that no one be allowed to visit Norma Jeane unless they have Grace's written permission to do so.

Gladys escapes from Norwalk State Hospital but is captured and returned.

December 6: Mrs. Dewey writes to Grace asking for a list of people Norma Jeane is permitted to see. Mrs. Dewey notes that when Norma Jeane is "naughty she says, 'Mrs. Dewey, I wouldn't never want my Aunt Grace to know I was naughty.' She loves me very much."

December 25: Nearby RKO invites the orphanage children to visit the studio, eat ice cream and candy, and watch a movie.

1936

Norma Jeane learns to swim.

February 26: Grace McKee Goddard files papers to become Norma Jeane's legal guardian.

March 26: Grace's petition to become Norma Jeane's legal guardian is granted.

Spring: Gladys is moved to Agnews State Hospital near San Jose.

June 1: Norma Jeane turns ten.

June 21: Grace Goddard makes her last payment to the orphanage for Norma Jeane's care.

September: Norma Jeane begins fifth grade at Vine Street School. She joins the softball team.

October: Grace bleaches her hair and wears white in imitation of Jean Harlow, and tells Norma Jeane all about her favorite film star.

December: Without explanation, Grace misses several of her Saturday visits to the orphanage, and Norma Jeane becomes anxious.

1937

February 20: Orphanage report on Norma Jeane: "Sometimes she seems anxious and then she begins to stutter. Norma Jean [sic] is also prone to coughing fits and frequent colds . . . if she's not treated with much patience and constantly reassured, she is prey to panic attacks. I would recommend for her a strong and good family."

February 26: Grace signs documents to prepare for Norma Jeane's release from the orphanage.

June: Norma Jeane finishes fifth grade at the Vine Street School.

June 1: Norma Jeane turns eleven.

Norma Jeane is now five feet, three inches tall and a good athlete.

Grace loses her job as a film librarian.

June 7: Norma Jeane leaves the Los Angeles Orphans Home to live with Grace and her husband, Doc Goddard, at 6707 Odessa Avenue in Van Nuys.

Norma Jeane hears on the radio that Jean Harlow has died.

A drunken Doc Goddard evidently tries to fondle Norma Jeane, who complains to Grace about the abuse.

September: Norma Jeane begins sixth grade at Lankershim School.

November: Grace moves Norma Jeane to Oxnard, California, the home of Gladys's brother, Marion Monroe, and his wife, Ida Martin. Then Marion suddenly disappears (he is officially declared dead in 1939).

Norma Jeane feels unwanted and keeps asking what happened to Uncle Marion.

1938

Norma Jeane attends the Lankershim School in North Hollywood. She wins two first-place awards in the high jump and track and field events.

March: Norma Jeane is moved to the home of Ruth and Alan Mills, who live in the San Fernando Valley.

June: Norma Jeane is moved again to live with the Atchinsons (Grace's brother, Bryan, and his wife, Lottie), who take little interest in her. She finishes sixth grade at Lankershim School.

June 1: Grace celebrates Norma Jeane's twelfth birthday by buying her a dress for $11.74, spending another sixty dollars on hair styling, makeup, and a photograph taken by a professional photographer. To commemorate the event, Grace also gives Norma Jeane a photo album.

According to Donald Spoto, Norma Jeane is sexually assaulted by her thirteen-year-old cousin, Jack Martin.

August: Ida Martin receives her last payment for Norma Jeane's care.

August or September: Norma Jeane goes to live at 11348 Nebraska Avenue in West Los Angeles with Ana Lower, Grace's aunt, a devout Christian Scientist, who schools Norma Jeane in religious principles. Norma Jeane attends Christian Science services twice on Sundays and once during the week. She is taught to believe in mind over matter—that the spiritual world is more real than the physical world—an appealing, if confusing, notion to a child whose body and sexuality have already become issues for her.

Gladys writes Grace asking her to tell Norma Jeane that she has a half-sister, Berniece. Norma Jeane writes to Berniece.

Norma Jeane begins seventh grade at the Sawtelle Boulevard School. Mabel Ella Campbell, her natural sciences teacher, recalled that Norma Jeane seemed "a bit neglected. Her clothes made her different from the others. In 1938 she wasn't very physically developed. She was a kind girl, but introverted, not really radiant." Marilyn later remembered, "I was quiet and some kids called me the Mouse. During my first year in Sawtelle, I only had the 2 clean dresses of the orphanage. Aunt Ana had extended them because I had grown a little, but they didn't fit me. I mostly wore sneakers because they only cost 98 cents and Mexican sandals which cost less. I was certainly not among the most elegant girls and it can be said that I wasn't very popular."

1939

Grace joins the Christian Science church.

At Emerson Junior High School, Norma Jeane makes friends with Bob Muir, who is a grade ahead of her. They play monopoly and dance in his living room. They go for hikes in the Santa Monica Mountains.

Norma Jeane begins to menstruate. Her painful periods are difficult to deal with, because as a Christian Scientist, she is not supposed to use drugs.

Norma Jeane develops a crush on Harry Keel, an aspiring Hollywood actor, but he cannot reciprocate with a girl who is not yet sixteen, the legal age of sexual consent.

January 31: Norma Jeane is awarded a certificate "in recognition of the personal service rendered by her as a member of the [Sawtelle Boulevard] School Safety Committee."

June: Norma Jeane finishes seventh grade at the Sawtelle Boulevard School.

Norma Jeane travels by train with Grace to San Francisco, where Gladys is now hospitalized. Gladys looks well but says almost nothing to her child.

June 1: Norma Jeane turns thirteen.

Summer: Norma Jeane makes friends with Paul Johnsen, a schoolmate. He takes her skating, but at the end of the summer they part to attend different schools. She gives him a letter and photograph, which he kept, later saying, "Even before she became Marilyn, when she was barely more than a child, she apparently had the gift of making others feel appreciated."

September: Norma Jeane begins eighth grade at Emerson Junior High School.

Christmas: Grace McKee gives Marilyn a wind-up portable Victrola so that she can play Glenn Miller records.

Norma Jeane reaches her adult height of five feet five inches. She wears tight sweaters and skirts and attracts the attention of boys as she walks to school. At a time when the beauty industry was beginning to burgeon, she also has access to cosmetics.

1940

February: After Ana Lower's health begins to fail, Norma Jeane returns to live with Grace. Norma Jeane shares a spaniel with Bebe, Grace's daughter.

February 25: Norma Jeane's picture is taken during an outing with the Emerson Junior High School Glee Club to Green Valley Lake.

May: Neighbors take Norma Jeane on a picnic outing to the desert. Norma Jeane picks wildflowers for a bouquet. She tells Dorothy Muir, "No two flowers are alike. I never saw anything so lovely."

June: Norma Jeane joins friends at the Hi-Ho Drive-In restaurant on the corner of Wilshire and Westwood Avenues, not far from UCLA. She goes on her first dates with Chuck Moran, who takes her to dances and restaurant drive-ins.

June 1: Norma Jeane turns fourteen.

September: The dates with Chuck Moran end when he graduates and goes to a different school.

December: Because of Ana Lower's failing health, Norma Jeane returns to live with the Goddards in Van Nuys. She makes friends with Doc's daughter, Eleanor (called Bebe), who lived in as many as a dozen foster homes before returning to live with her father and stepmother. It is Bebe's story that Norma Jeane will borrow from when presenting her account of her own childhood. The two girls are the same age and look as though they are related. They share clothes and makeup.

1941

Norma Jeane is elected the "Oomph Girl" at Emerson Junior High School in West Los Angeles. She does well in journalism class and writes for the school newspaper, but she is shy and finds it hard to speak in public, sometimes lapsing into a stutter.

Norma Jeane develops an interest in Abraham Lincoln.

February 14: Chuck Moran sends Norma Jeane a Valentine's Day card.

June 1: Norma Jeane turns fifteen.

June 27: Marilyn graduates from Emerson Junior High School, completing the ninth grade.

September: Norma Jeane enters Van Nuys High School as a tenth grader.

October: Ethel Dougherty, Jim Dougherty's mother, asks him to drive Norma Jeane and Bebe to school. Jim, twenty and a Van Nuys High School graduate, is an athlete, student body president, and actor in school plays.

December 7: The Japanese attack Pearl Harbor, which leads the United States to declare war and enter World War II.

Grace makes plans to move to West Virginia, where her husband has been offered a job. Without a good home for Norma Jeane, Grace begins to think that Norma Jeane should marry Jim Dougherty.

December 25: At Grace's instigation and with Ethel Dougherty's approval, Jim Dougherty takes Norma Jeane to the company Christmas dance at Adel Precision Products, where Doc Goddard works.

1942

Norma Jeane attends University High School in West Los Angeles for a brief period and, because the Goddards are preparing to move to West Virginia, lives again with Ana Lower. She continues to date Jim Dougherty, whose mother, Ethel, agrees with Grace's idea that Norma Jeane marry Jim. He, too, agrees, bolstered by Norma Jeane's confidence in him and intrigued by her maturing body and personality.

February 14: Chuck Moran sends Norma Jeane a Valentine's Day card.

March: The Goddards leave for West Virginia. Norma Jeane has only the ailing Ana Lower and Jim Dougherty to rely on. She accepts Jim's marriage proposal.

Spring: Jim Dougherty takes Norma Jeane to movies, dinner, family picnics, and hikes. They listen to the radio and hear Frank Sinatra and songs such as "That Old Black Magic" and "Night and Day."

June: Norma Jeane leaves University High School before completing tenth grade.

June 1: Norma Jeane celebrates her sixteenth birthday.

June 7: Jim and Norma Jeane go looking for a home to rent and find a one-room bungalow on 4524 Vista Del Monte in Sherman Oaks. They sign a six-month lease.

June 19: Sunday at 2:30 p.m., Reverend Benjamin Lingenfelder of the Christian Science church marries Norma Jeane and twenty-one-year-old James Dougherty at the home of Mr. and Mrs. Chester Howell. Chester is an attorney and friend of Grace, who chooses the Howell home at 432 South Bentley Avenue in West Los Angeles because it has a spiral staircase that Norma Jeane uses to make a dramatic entrance. Ana Lower makes Norma Jeane's wedding gown and accompanies her to the altar. Norma Jeane has one bridesmaid, Lorraine Allen, a friend from University High School. No member of Norma Jeane's family is present, but the Bolenders make an appearance. It is the last time they will see her. After a modest reception at the Florentine Gardens in Hollywood, Norma Jeane and Jim go to their home in Sherman Oaks. Jim Dougherty later recalled that his wife held on to him the entire afternoon.

The young couple does not honeymoon but goes for a fishing weekend on Sherwood Lake.

On Sundays they attend the Sherman Oaks Christian Science church.

September: Norma Jeane writes to Grace, expressing excitement about setting up a new home.

Autumn: Norma Jeane attends a baby shower for Nellie Atkinson, the daughter of her former foster parents, and writes, "She got so many lovely things and I had such a nice time."

Norma Jeane spends time with her husband's sister, Elyda. Norma Jeane enjoys playing with Elyda's son, Larry, and Norma Jeane tells Elyda, "My first baby has to be a boy." When Elyda's second boy, Denny, is born, Norma Jeane helps to take care of the infant.

Winter: Both Jim and Norma Jeane are athletic and enjoy skiing together at Big Bear Lake.

Christmas: Norma Jeane most likely spends the holiday with the Doughertys. One family member recalled, "My grandfather played the fiddle, guitar, banjo and chorded piano, while my mother played the fiddle and a little violin and sang. Aunt Norma would just sit there with her eyes glued on Uncle Jim when he would sing a love song to her or some cute holiday song that was directed to her. She would occasionally join in and sing a little but as I recall would rather just watch."

1943

January: The lease on the Dougherty bungalow expires, and the couple moves in with Jim's parents at their house at 14747 Archwood Street in Van Nuys while he continues to work at Lockheed Aircraft.

Gladys discloses to Grace that Stanley Gifford is Norma Jeane's father. Grace tells Jim's mother, who tells Norma Jeane.

February 16: Gladys confirms to Norma Jeane that Stanley Gifford is her father. Norma Jeane writes to Grace that she plans to visit Gifford, who she assumes will be pleased to see her. "It's something I have to look forward to," she tells Grace. But he hangs up when she calls him, and Dougherty tries to console his distraught wife.

Spring: Norma Jeane and Jim move into a new house on Bessemer Street in Van Nuys. Norma Jeane falls in love with a cow (in a pen next door) that had "beautiful eyes." According to Jim Dougherty's nephew, "Norma Jeane used to stand by her pen and just stare at her, remarking at how pretty she was. Then the torrential rain came one night and the cow was standing by the fence and Norma Jeane apparently thought she wanted in so she opened the gate and was going to bring her into the house. After much conversation about the matter, Uncle Jim convinced her that she really belonged in her pen and Norma Jeane finally gave in and it was over, but she still thought that the cow would have been better off in the living room!"

June 1: Norma Jeane turns seventeen.

Summer: Norma Jeane begins to open up, relying less on Jim and making new friends, surprising and disconcerting her husband, who is protective and jealous of the males attracted to her vitality and charm—especially on the beaches of Santa Monica and Venice.

Norma Jeane adopts a collie named Muggsie.

August: Norma Jeane officially joins the Christian Science church.

September: Norma Jeane and Jim move into an apartment on Catalina Island, which has been turned into a military training camp. Jim has enlisted in the Merchant Marine. The couple lives in an apartment overlooking the bay side of the island. Norma Jeane makes friends with other military couples. She becomes interested in physical training and begins to work out with weights. Jim grows uneasy about her growing independence.

Late 1943: Norma Jeane writes a remarkable personal testimony, which is startling because it sounds like it issues from an older woman looking back on the early years of her marriage: "[M]y relationship with him was basically insecure from the first night I spent alone with him." She finds him attractive but unsure of his ability to please her. She wants to feel she belongs to someone and to follow the directives of her elders, who have encouraged the marriage. A part of her wants the marriage to work, but she also feels stifled, since she has not given up on her dreams of becoming a model and an actress.

Norma Jeane's adjustment to marriage and adulthood is complicated by what she describes as her introverted personality. She is shy and finds her greatest pleasure in reading. She questions her own motives. Is she in love, or just thrilled that her husband wants her? This awareness of her own weaknesses stimulates her desire to improve, even as she acknowledges that her failings debilitate her. She questions not only herself, but also those close to her—in this case making her wonder if her husband has been unfaithful. She also knows that too much self-examination can harm her: "Everyone needs a little conceit to carry them through & past the falls." This line, with its misspellings, is characteristic, and other parts of this message to herself reflect the shaky syntax of a high school dropout. But the introspective quality of this seventeen-year-old powerfully informs this six-page document.

Christmas: At a dance on Catalina Island, Jim becomes disturbed by his growing awareness of the interest Norma Jeane excites in other men.

1944

February: Norma Jeane writes to her half-sister, Berniece, inviting her to visit Catalina Island.

April: James Dougherty ships out to the South Pacific, leaving behind Norma Jeane, who feels abandoned. She moves in with Jim's mother, Ethel, at 5254 Hermitage Street in North Hollywood.

April 18: Ethel Dougherty finds a job for Norma Jeane as a typist at Radioplane, a munitions factory that makes drones. But at a speed of only thirty-five words a minute, she does not do well and is assigned to inspecting parachutes. She is paid twenty dollars per week. She works ten hours a day and tells Grace McKee it is hard work because she is on her feet most of the time. But the alternative, a job with the army, was worse because of all the "wolves."

April 19: Norma Jeane attends a picnic at Balboa Park with her fellow workers. Photographs show her with long curled hair, standing and sitting in the center of a lineup with four other women, posing for the camera.

June 1: Norma Jeane turns eighteen.

June 15: Norma Jeane writes to Grace McKee Goddard, "Of course I know that if it hadn't been for you we might not have never

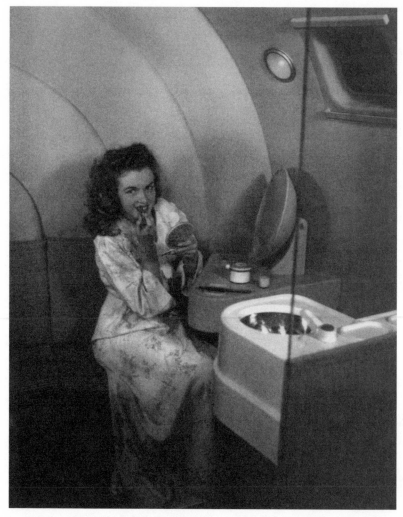

Norma Jeane before electrolysis, hair coloring, and plastic surgery

been married and I know I owe you a lot for that fact alone, besides countless others. . . . I love Jimmie in a different way I suppose than anyone, and I know I shall never be happy with anyone else as long as I live, and I know he feels the same toward me. So you see we are really very happy together, that is of course, when we can be together. We both miss each other terribly." Marilyn later suggested she was trying to please Grace.

Summer: Norma Jeane leaves California for the first time to visit Grace, who is working at a film laboratory in Chicago. She also visits Bebe Goddard in West Virginia.

July 15: *Radioplane Static* mentions that Norma Jeane has been crowned queen of the Radioplane picnic and awarded a fifty-dollar war bond.

August 31: *Radioplane Static* mentions that Norma Jeane won a gold button for making a good suggestion about improving plant operations.

October 23: Ana Lower writes to Norma Jeane during a visit to Norma Jeane's half-sister, Berniece, in Detroit. Ana, a devout Christian Scientist, tells Norma Jeane to "stop this nonsense about car sickness." Norma Jeane has to think lovely thoughts: "God's law never ceases to operate, and that is what governs your every minute day and night."

December: Norma Jeane changes jobs at Radioplane. She is now packing parachutes rather than spraying glue on airplanes (drones). She works hard and is given a certificate awarding her an *E* for excellence. She misses her husband and writes him a gloomy letter saying all she can see outside is fog.

During the holidays Norma Jeane visits Ana Lower.

As part of a project to promote the patriotism of pretty girls in commercial and military publications, David Conover, a member of the Army First Motion Picture Unit, photographs Norma Jeane working at Radioplane. He suggests Norma Jeane could make a success of modeling.

December 3: Norma Jeane writes to Grace, thanking her for a dress while also sending money to her former guardian.

Christmas: Jim comes home on a brief holiday leave.

1945

Norma Jeane becomes a member of the Westwood Public Library.

Norma Jeane works as a hostess at the Los Angeles Home Show in the Pan Pacific Auditorium for ten days at a rate of ten dollars per day.

Norma Jeane works as a hostess/model for the Holga Steel Company for ten dollars a day.

January: Jim returns to the South Pacific. Norma Jeane continues to work at Radioplane and to live with Jim's parents, but later in the month starts phoning in sick.

February 10: Norma Jeane sells her white piano to Ana Lower.

March 2: Norma Jeane sends a note to her half-sister, Berniece, thanking her for hankies that have been sent as a gift. She writes that she hopes Berniece will move to California.

March 15: Radioplane terminates Norma Jeane's employment, costing her a salary of fifty dollars a week.

Spring: Norma Jeane pursues modeling jobs and is praised by David Conover for her fresh, lively, and flirtatious treatment of the camera, as well as for her professionalism. She studies proofs and negatives, seeking to perfect herself in the camera eye. Conover begins to introduce her to other photographers, including William Carroll and Potter Hueth.

April: James Dougherty is assigned to the Far East. He writes to Norma Jeane, expressing disapproval of her modeling. "You can have only one career," he says, but she angrily rejects his command.

May 18: Norma Jeane poses in a bikini for photographer Lee Bush. Jim is upset and asks her again to stop modeling and start making a family.

June 1: Norma Jeane turns nineteen.

June 4: Norma Jeane sends Berniece a note saying that she is staying with Ana Lower. She hopes her mother can be released from the hospital soon, and that Berniece will join them in California.

Norma Jeane writes to Grace McKee Goddard, explaining she has not worked at Radioplane since January: "The first I know [the photographers] had me out there, taking pictures of me. . . . They all asked where in the H---l I had been hiding." Conover told her that the pictures "came out perfect." Conover mentions his contacts in modeling, and Norma Jeane reports, "I told him I would rather not work when Jimmie was here, so he said he would wait, so I'm expecting to hear from him most any time again. He is awfully nice and is married and is strictly business, which is the way I like it. Jimmie seems to like the idea of me modeling, so I'm glad about that."

June 26: David Conover photographs Norma Jeane for *Yank* magazine.

Summer: The Goddards return to California, and Grace is delighted with Norma Jeane's transformation.

July: Norma Jeane accompanies David Conover to a photo shoot in the Mojave Desert and Death Valley.

July 21: Norma Jeane writes to Berniece and sends her lipstick and rouge, telling her to get a good lipstick brush. She says that she misses her husband.

August: Gladys is released from Agnews State Hospital in San Jose. She is briefly united with Norma Jeane and Berniece, but then goes to lives with an aunt in Oregon.

Potter Hueth photographs Norma Jeane as a country girl with a straw hat, leaning on a bale of hay and carrying a basket of vegetables. He sends the photographs to Emmeline Snively at the Blue Book Modeling Agency.

August 2: Norma Jeane walks into the Blue Book Modeling Agency and is interviewed by Emmeline Snively. On the same day, she appears on the cover of *Stars and Stripes* in a photograph shot by David Conover. She pays twenty-five dollars to have her picture in the agency catalog, and one hundred dollars is deducted from her salary for lessons in makeup and fashion. She wears a size twelve, is five feet six inches in height, and weighs 120 pounds, measuring 36-24-34.

September: Ethel Dougherty criticizes Norma Jeane's behavior, saying a modeling career is incompatible with a happy marriage. Norma Jeane moves out, leaves Muggsie, and returns to Ana Lower's home at 1138 Nebraska Avenue in West Los Angeles.

September 2: Norma Jeane joins other models in a test shot at the Ambassador Hotel.

September 5: Norma Jeane gets her first booking, working as a hostess in a Holga Steel Files booth at an industrial show. She earns ninety dollars for ten days' work.

November: After three months of modeling, Emmeline Snively sizes up Norma Jeane as a "scared, pretty lonely little kid who wore mostly fresh white cotton dresses."

Andre de Dienes photographs Norma Jeane in a simple skirt and blouse standing, sitting, and reclining on Highway 101. Other shots show her with frizzy brown hair, sitting on a pile of pumpkins and sitting on a bed of leaves.

Jim Dougherty tries to contact Norma Jeane by phone when his ship docks in New York, but Ana Lower tells him that Norma Jeane is not home very often.

December: Norma Jeane spends the month in Death Valley, Yosemite, and Oregon on an Andre de Dienes photo shoot expedition. She is paid a $200 flat fee.

Norma Jeane agrees to bleach her hair for Raphael Wolff, who shoots a shampoo advertisement.

December 15: Norma Jeane sends Jim Dougherty a postcard from Death Valley, where she has been posing. She calls him "My Dearest Daddy" and signs herself "All My love, Your Baby."

December 25: Much to the displeasure of Ana Lower and Ethel Dougherty, Norma Jeane spends Christmas with photographer Andre de Dienes during their shooting trip to Washington state, making enough to repair her 1935 Ford. De Dienes takes her to visit Gladys, who says almost nothing and then frightens her daughter by blurting out, "I wish I'd live with you Norma Jeane." De Dienes could see Norma Jeane did not know what to make of this request from a mother she hardly knew and could only kiss and then leave, giving Gladys her address and phone number. In distress, Norma Jeane calls Ana Lower, then returns home to Jim, who delivers an ultimatum: Choose him or her career. She continues to work as a model.

1946

Norma Jeane appears in a color photograph on the back cover of *Allt* (Sweden) resting her right arm and hand on the trunk of a tree.

In a color shot (photographer not identified), Norma Jeane, still a brunette, wears a striped bikini. With the sea in the background, she is shown on a balcony shaking hands with a Great Dane mix, while the fingers of her left hand fall casually on a sculpture of a mythical beast that is a cross between a tiger and a lion.

Laszlo Willinger photographs Norma Jeane in a gold bathing suit for a calendar.

Bruno Bernard photographs her with a ship captain's hat and a starfish in his studio on the Sunset Strip. The photographer wrote in his journal, "I have never seen a model, beginner or pro, who is so at ease before the camera. Norma Jeane seems to have a sixth sense between the optical interplay of subject and camera. Concentration, projection, and synchronization are second nature to her." Bernard's daughter, Susan, has written that her father was quite taken with Norma Jeane's "fresh-faced wholesomeness" and showed a portfolio of her pictures to Ben Lyon, head of talent at Twentieth Century Fox. "At that time my father knew her as few did, becoming a close friend, confidant, and father figure. Later, as the world came to know her as Marilyn Monroe, she always remained Norma Jeane."

Norma Jeane appears in print advertisements for Lustre-Creme Shampoo, photographed as a bleached blonde by Raphael Wolff, and in Tru-Glo makeup and lipstick made by Westmores of Hollywood.

January: Jim Dougherty returns to service in the South Pacific.

Norma Jeane now lives with Ana Lower and begins to separate herself from Grace, whose erratic alcoholic behavior is disturbing.

Photographer William Burnside is intrigued by Norma Jeane's fluctuating moods, which sometimes change in the midst of a smile. David Conover is impressed with her enthusiastic and cooperative spirit. She remains, however, shy and prone to doubt her abilities. But her photographs exude just the opposite: a young woman entirely in possession of herself. Richard C. Miller photographs Norma Jeane for *True Romance*, featuring her as a young bride and another holding a prayer book.

January 1: Norma Jeane appears on the cover of *Douglas Air Review*. She is shown in an interior cockpit picture as one of four passengers. She is smiling and wearing a red hat. The photograph was taken in December 1945 in Santa Monica, California.

February: Norma Jeane has her hair straightened and bleached for the first time at Frank and Joseph's Salon. Sometime during this period, she is photographed as a blonde, with two other models on either side of her holding a life preserver that advertises Blue Book Modeling around her waist.

March: Norma Jeane has an interview with Paramount studios, but she is not offered a screen test or a contract.

Jim Dougherty returns home on leave from the merchant marine and finds that Norma Jeane is living with her mother at Ana Lower's home. He realizes his marriage is effectively over.

Gladys alternates between periods of lucidity and listlessness.

March 6: Emmeline Snively, head of the Blue Book Modeling Agency, sends Norma Jeane to Joseph Jasgur for test shots. In *The Birth of Marilyn*, Jeannie Sakol reports Jasgur's first impressions: "What he saw was not too encouraging. Her hips were too broad and would photograph even broader if he didn't take special pains. Her loose pink wool sweater and check pedal pushers only exaggerated the imperfections of her figure and emphasized her need to lose some weight. As for her hair, it was thick and wild and reddish brown, its natural curliness obviously impossible to control—although she had equally obviously tried to do just that with a saucy beret. The colour, Jasgur realized, was totally wrong for her blue eyes and peach blossom skin tones. If ever a girl should be blonde it was this girl who was so patiently enduring his professional scrutiny. . . . She didn't have a chance, he thought, until he looked into her eyes. . . . A lovely vivid blue, they gazed at him with a calm and quiet dignity, neither arrogant nor seductive. There was *something* there. Jasgur shakes his head with amazement that has never left him in forty-five years. 'I never thought that *something* would take her so far.'" He finds her shy and anxious. Other photographers report similar experiences with her. But in front of the camera, Jasgur remembered, "[S]he was relaxed, no trace of self-consciousness. Even in those formative days, I think she trusted the camera more than she trusted people."

March 9: Jim returns on shore leave, but Norma Jeane is not home. He leaves a note expressing the hope that they will be able to repair their marriage.

March 10: Norma Jeane poses for photographer Joseph Jasgur. She appears at his studio shy, breathless, anxious, and an hour late—and yet she is thoroughly professional. She poses in front of the Hollywood sign. Other shots show her on Zuma beach, drawing hearts and smiling in a color photograph of her in a two-piece swimsuit.

March 11: Norma Jeane signs a contract with the Helen Ainsworth Agency as part of her bid to become a movie star. Harry Lipton of that agency represents her.

Earl Moran, a calendar and magazine illustrator, hires Norma Jeane—soon to become Marilyn Monroe—as a model for ten dollars an hour. She continues to pose for him over the next four years whenever she needs ready cash.

March 12: Norma Jeane poses for photographer Richard Miller.

March 14: Norma Jeane writes to Jim Dougherty, apparently responding to his request that she not pursue a career. She declares she will "carry on," and she wishes him well, signing herself "Always lovingly, your wife."

March 16: Norma Jeane and Jim go to the Ambassador Hotel for lunch at the Coconut Grove, where they talk. Otherwise, he spends his two-day leave at his mother's home.

March 18–23: Norma Jeane works with Jasgur at Zuma beach. She is affectionate with the photographer. He does not take advantage of her, remembering, "We'd have popcorn and whisper in the dark. She'd nibble on my ear and kiss me on the cheek. And what she'd like best was to cuddle like a homeless kitten or puppy." She often appears in these shots as a working girl in a plaid shirt and jeans, playing with the camera on a tripod, and hamming it up with actors from *The Drunkard*, a melodrama in a local production.

April 26: Norma Jeane appears dressed as a farm girl with a baby lamb in her hands on the cover of *Family Circle*.

May: Norma Jeane appears on the cover of *U. S. Camera*.

Norma Jeane is treated for trench mouth (the result of an infection that sets in after extraction of her wisdom teeth) in Las Vegas General Hospital. She also has a short hospital stay after contracting the measles.

Norma Jeane has dinner with Roy Rogers and his film crew at the Last Frontier Hotel restaurant.

In Las Vegas, Norma Jeane meets Bill Pursel, a World War II veteran, but neither seems ready for romance. She meets his family and tells them that she likes to read Carl Sandburg's poetry.

May 14–July 10: Norma Jeane takes up residence in Las Vegas in order to get a divorce. She stays with Grace's aunt, Minnie Willette, at 604 South 3rd Street.

May 25: Norma Jeane writes to Emmeline Snively about meeting Roy Rogers and riding his horse, Trigger. Fans on the Roy Rogers movie set think she is a movie star and ask for her autograph. When she tells them she is not in pictures, "[T]hey think I'm just trying to avoid signing their books, so I sign them."

June: Norma Jeane appears in a color photograph on the cover of *Laff*. She is wearing a two-piece bathing suit and is identified as Norma Jean Dougherty [she dropped the *e* from her name].

Summer: Norma Jeane goes surfing with aspiring actor Tommy Zahn.

June: Norma Jeane appears on the cover of *Pageant*.

In Hollywood, Norma Jeane rents a room at the Studio Club. Uncertain of her appeal and of the way she dresses, she is encouraged by the openhearted actress Eleanor Powell, who befriends the Hollywood hopeful.

June 1: Norma Jeane turns twenty and spends her birthday in a rented room in Las Vegas.

Norma Jeane appears on the cover of the *Sunday World-Herald Magazine*, pictured sitting on the floor reading a magazine with two babies lying on a blanket in front of her.

June 26: David Conover photographs Marilyn for *Yank*.

July: Gladys is released from Norwalk Mental Hospital into the care of an aunt in Oregon.

Norma Jeane begins dating Bill Pursel and Ken Dumain, who encountered her at the Blue Book agency. Robert Slatzer claims to have first met her during this month on the Fox lot.

July 18: Norma Jeane leaves Las Vegas.

July 19: A Hedda Hopper column reports that Howard Hughes wants to sign Norma Jeane to a movie contract.

July 25: Through the efforts of Helen Ainsworth, an agent, Ben Lyon, talent director at Twentieth Century Fox, meets Norma Jeane for the first time and is impressed. He arranges for a contract to be issued and schedules a screen test for August 14.

July 29: A *Los Angeles Times* gossip column reports, "Howard Hughes is on the mend. Picking a magazine, he was attracted by the cover girl and promptly instructed an aide to sign her for pictures. She is Norma Jeane Dougherty, a model." Hughes does not sign Norma Jeane to a contract, but the story is evidence of her increasing visibility.

August: Norma Jeane appears on the covers of *Family Circle* and *Salute* (photograph by Laszlo Willinger).

In a second appearance on a *Laff* cover, she is identified as "Jean Norman," wearing a bikini with her hair falling to her shoulders in ringlets.

Jim Dougherty receives written notice of Norma Jeane's intention to divorce him and makes arrangements to stop the military pay sent home to her.

August 2: Norma Jeane joins the Blue Book Modeling Agency.

Norma Jeane auditions for *The Red House*, a Fox production, but is considered unsuitable to appear opposite the film's star, Lon Mc-Callister.

August 14: Norma Jeane's first screen test. She appears in a gown selected by Charles LeMaire, the head of wardrobe at Fox. She is made up by Whitey Snyder, who becomes her favorite makeup artist, and is shot by Leon Shamroy, who later said, "When I first watched her, I thought, 'This girl will be another Harlow!' Her natural beauty plus her inferiority complex gave her a look of mystery. . . . I got a cold chill. This girl had something I hadn't seen since silent pictures. She had a kind of fantastic beauty like Gloria Swanson . . . and she got sex on a piece of film like Jean Harlow. Every frame of the test radiated sex. She didn't need a sound track—she was creating effects visually. She was showing us she could sell emotion in pictures."

Berniece, Norma Jeane's half-sister, arrives for a long visit.

August 24: Norma Jeane's second screen test. She changes her name to Marilyn Monroe.

August 26: Norma Jeane signs her first contract with Twentieth Century Fox. She is accompanied by Grace McKee, who signs as Norma Jeane's guardian, since, legally, Norma Jeane is still a minor. The starting salary is seventy-five dollars a week. Her legal name is still Norma Jeane Dougherty.

Marilyn moves into the Studio Club and pays twelve dollars per week for rent.

September 5: Marilyn is mentioned for the first time in *Variety* in the "New Contracts" column.

September 13: Marilyn's divorce is granted at 2:00 p.m. in Las Vegas. Jim Dougherty is not present. She tells the judge that her husband's "extreme mental cruelty" has impaired her health: "My husband didn't support me and he objected to my working, criticized me for it and he also had a bad temper and would fly into rages and he left me on three different occasions and criticized me and embarrassed me in front of my friends and he didn't try to make a home for me." Marilyn and Jim never meet again.

As part of the property settlement, Marilyn gets Jim's 1935 Ford.

Marilyn celebrates the end of her marriage by going out for dinner with Grace, Ana Lower, and her half sister, Berniece, who is accompanied by her daughter, Mona Rae, and Grace's sister, Enid Knebelkamp.

Marilyn begins frequenting Schwab's Drugstore.

Gladys returns to Portland, Oregon.

Autumn: Marilyn does her first radio broadcast on KFI in Los Angeles. Photographer Leo Caloia is one of the first to photograph her at a time when she is still mainly a model. She is interviewed as one of Fox's starlets.

Marilyn is given no acting assignments at Fox, but she roams the studio, studying wardrobes and asking questions about lighting, camera work, and other technicalities of moviemaking.

December 30: Fox publicity chief, Harry Brand, issues a studio biography, calling Marilyn "a sort of junior Lana Turner."

1947

Tommy Zahn, a Fox contract player and a celebrated surfer, photographs Marilyn at a party for surfers.

Journalist Lloyd Shearer interviews Marilyn on the Fox lot and after her death reports in *Parade* (August 5, 1973): "She confided to us over lunch that she had been assaulted by one of her guardians, raped by a policeman, and attacked by a sailor. She seemed to me then to live in a fantasy world, to be entangled in the process of invention and to be completely absorbed in her own sexuality."

Marilyn poses for the *Jantzen Wholesale Swimwear Catalogue*, wearing a swimsuit called the "Double Dare."

In San Juan Capistrano, Andre de Dienes photographs Marilyn in an intense close-up, without makeup—a headshot, with her blonde hair glowing.

January: Marilyn sends Andre de Dienes a copy of *Science and Health*, a Christian Science publication. She marks the passage that reads: "Divine Love always has met and always will meet every human need."

In a Fox publicity shot, Marilyn, in a two-piece swimsuit, smiling and with her head resting on her left arm, lies on a beach towel with a springer spaniel.

January 1: Marilyn appears on the cover of *Laff* wearing a two-piece swimsuit, with her right arm behind her head, slighting reclining, so that her breasts are emphasized in a typical cheesecake pose.

January 4: *The Shocking Miss Pilgrim* is released. Marilyn's voice is heard briefly in the role of a telephone operator.

January 30: In the *Los Angeles Times*, Fox promotes the story that Marilyn had been discovered while babysitting for a casting director. She is shown diapering a baby and reading to a child. The article makes her two years younger than her actual age and says she is an orphan.

February: Marilyn's Fox contract is renewed at $150 a week.

Marilyn appears in studio publicity photos wearing a two-piece swimsuit, holding on to ski poles as if ready to glide over the sand dunes.

Marilyn works on *Scudda Hoo! Scudda Hay!* in a few crowd scenes and in a canoe. She has no discernible character to play, but can be glimpsed very briefly in a scene saying hello to "Rad" (June Haver), who answers, "Hi, Betty." In *Blonde Heat*, Richard Buskin includes a photograph of Marilyn in a canoe, dressed in a swimsuit, and with a paddle gripped in both her hands. Behind her is "June" (another starlet, Betty Townsend). The scene was cut from the film.

February 17: Andre de Dienes publishes a color photograph of Norma Jeane on the cover of *Parade*. He shoots her from her left side. She is wearing a green sweater and yellow-gold slacks in a strongly diagonal shot that shows her posed against a mountainside, her right and left hands touching a rock face, her right knee bent as though she is climbing. She is smiling and looking directly at the camera. Her sleeves are rolled up, and on her left arm is a lady's watch. The photograph was taken in Death Valley in 1945.

March 12: The continuity script for *Scudda Hoo! Scudda Hay!* reveals that originally Marilyn was to play a character named "Betty." She and "June" are described as "a couple of pretty bobby-soxers." In another scene, Marilyn has two lines addressed to "Stretch" (Robert Karnes).

Spring: While studying at Actors' Lab, Marilyn meets actress Dorothy Dandridge, who recommends her voice coach, Phil Moore. Moore later works with Marilyn.

April 15: Marilyn attends the annual ceremony and presentation of honorary colonels at the Hollywood Legion Stadium. She receives a badge of honor, as do seventeen other starlets.

April 26: Marilyn appears in a cast and crew photograph for *Scudda Hoo! Scudda Hay!* She is seated directly behind June Haver on the steps of a church.

May: Marilyn is assigned a very small role in *Dangerous Years*.

June: Fox sends Marilyn to study at the Actors' Laboratory, one of the country's best acting schools. She is exposed to actors and plays from the New York stage and later says she thought of the "far, faraway place called New York, where actors and directors did very different things than stand around all day arguing about a close-up or a camera angle." Phoebe Brand, who ran the Lab along with her husband, Morris Carnovsky, remembered that Marilyn "worked her scenes with care," but made no distinct impression.

Photographed by Richard Miller, Marilyn appears as Norma Jeane, wearing her actual wedding dress, on the cover of *Personal Romances*.

June 1: Marilyn turns twenty-one.

June 11: Now that Marilyn is twenty-one, she signs a document reaffirming the terms of her August 24, 1946, contract. She signs twice—as Marilyn Monroe and then as Norma Jeane Dougherty.

June 30: *Dangerous Years* is filmed. Marilyn plays Evie, a waitress who has to fend off the advances of a teen gang member in a juke joint. She is not the accommodating Marilyn of later fame. When one young tough says hi to her, she replies, "Hi, small change." To another suitor who asks if he will see her later that night, she responds indifferently, "If I'm not too tired." She works on the picture for about a week.

Summer: Marilyn lives at 131 South Avon Street in Burbank, close to the Warner Brothers Studio. She is housesitting for a couple on vacation.

July: Marilyn appears on the cover of *Personal Romances*, wearing a red striped blouse and ship captain's hat in a photograph by Bruno Bernard. At a time when she does not have the money for an extensive wardrobe, she often wears the same clothing in several photo shoots.

July 20: Marilyn appears at the Brentwood Country Club for Fox's Annual Golf Tournament.

July 26: Fox informs Marilyn that her option will not be renewed.

August: Marilyn attends the Cheviot Hills Country Club's annual golf tournament. Starlets act as caddies for the stars. Marilyn is photographed, with a golf club and high-heeled sandals, teeing up, with Henry Fonda next to her, bending with her and apparently giving instruction.

August 17: At another tournament, Marilyn caddies for actor John Carroll and his wife, Lucille Ryman, a talent scout at MGM.

August 25: Strapped for funds, Marilyn leaves the Studio Club to live with John Carroll and Lucille Ryman. The couple takes an interest in her ambition. Carroll and his wife decide to help groom her for stardom. They advance her money, and she lives with them for the next five months.

Marilyn's Fox contract is not renewed. Photographer Bruno Bernard writes in his journal: "There was another factor contributing to Marilyn's dismissal. It's Marilyn's bad luck that [Darryl] Zanuck [the studio head] is more receptive to exotic beauties than to blondes, which is my observation of his personal tastes."

August 31: Marilyn receives her last check, for $104.13, from Fox.

September: Marilyn appears on the cover of *True Experiences*, smiling while standing at the wheel of a boat. She is dressed in a red blouse and suspendered shorts.

Marilyn makes the cover of *Laff*, wearing a two-piece yellow swimsuit. She is shown on the diagonal, her left leg bent at the knee, which is resting on a blue velvet platform.

Marilyn appears on the cover of *Cinemonde* (France) standing in a two-piece swimsuit, photographed on her left side, her face turned toward the camera with a flower in her hair. The caption announces she will be appearing in *Scudda Hoo! Scudda Hay!*

Lucille Ryman introduces Marilyn to the owner of the Bliss-Hayden Miniature Theatre.

October: According to biographer Keith Badman, Marilyn takes her first tranquilizers before she does a brief walk-on that is later cut from *You Were Meant For Me*, starring Jeanne Crain and Dan Dailey.

October 12–November 2: Marilyn appears in *Glamour Preferred* at the Bliss Hayden Theatre, playing Lady Bonnie Towyn, "blonde, smartly dressed, and beautiful in a rather obvious way."

December: Marilyn moves out of the Carroll/Ryman residence and finds an apartment in Burbank, but she spends her weekends at the Carroll/Ryman ranch in Granada Hills in the San Fernando Valley.

December 1: Marilyn signs a three-month management agreement with Carroll and Ryman. She receives one hundred dollars a week, while Carroll and Ryman collect any fees she earns as an actress, less 10 percent owed to her agent, Harry Lipton.

December 8: *Dangerous Years* is released. Marilyn has her first close-up and speaking role as Evie, a waitress in a hangout for juvenile delinquents.

1948

Marilyn appears in a publicity still for *Sitting Pretty* alongside the star, Clifton Webb, who is a friend.

Marilyn auditions as a singer for the Benny Goodman band but does not get the job.

Marilyn is named "Miss Press Club," and serves as hostess at the Los Angeles Press Club's functions and meetings.

Marilyn does a screen test for the role of Billie Dawn in *Born Yesterday*. Garson Kanin, who wrote the film, reports in *Tracy and Hepburn*: "Those who saw it thought it was excellent. But Harry Cohn, head of the studio, did not trouble to take the six steps from his desk to the projection room to look at her."

Producer Sam Spiegel rejects John Huston's request to screen test Marilyn for *We Were Strangers*.

Laszlo Willinger photographs Marilyn in various exercise positions and bare breasted (her arms cover her nipples), bending over in tight shorts, bolero hat, and white calf-length boots.

J. R. Eyerman photographs Marilyn sitting on the floor, wearing fishnet stockings and a short sleeve sweater top, apparently mending her right stocking, with a dance shoe visible by her left foot.

Douglas White photographs Marilyn in a swimsuit sitting inside a giant heart, standing in a one-piece swimsuit with a heart below her left breast, and out in the open standing on turf while wearing the same costume.

January 16: *Dangerous Years* is previewed.

February: Marilyn writes to Berniece on stationary imprinted with her new name, but she signs the letter Norma Jeane. She mentions appearing in *Dangerous Years* and that she has not heard from her mother, still living in Oregon. Shortly afterward, Marilyn calls long distance to Berniece in Florida, telling her sister that Gladys has returned to Los Angeles and is doing housekeeping work. Grace takes the phone and explains that she and Marilyn have concocted a story about Marilyn being an orphan taken care of by foster families.

Marilyn appears at two jewelry stores in Salinas and Castroville, California, to promote diamond sales. She stays in the Jeffrey Hotel in Salinas for a week. In a notebook she writes about taking a Greyhound bus from Monterey to Salinas, traveling with "sixty Italian fishermen and I've never met sixty such charming gentlemen—they were wonderful. . . . Some could hardly speak english not only do I love Greeks [illegible] I love Italians. They're . . . warm, lusty, and friendly as hell—I'd love to go to Italy someday."

At a party, Marilyn meets Pat De Cicco, the inventor of bonbons sold in movie theaters. Through De Cicco she meets Joseph Schenck, former head of Fox, who lives in a Hollywood Renaissance palace at 141 South Carolwood Drive in Los Angeles.

Joseph Schenck asks Harry Cohn at Columbia Pictures to consider signing Marilyn to a contract.

February 8: On the cover of *V* (France), Marilyn appears in a three-piece ensemble, wearing a sailor's hat, a red-striped blouse that shows off her midriff, and darker red shorts, with her hands on her hips, and with a background picture of canoeing figures.

February 20: Marilyn is crowned California Artichoke Queen in Salinas, California.

Holiday features Marilyn poolside in swimsuits.

February 29: Marilyn's management contract with John Carroll and Lucille Ryman expires.

March: Columbia has Marilyn's hairline raised by electrolysis and changes her hair color from ash blonde to platinum.

March 9: With Schenck's help, Marilyn obtains a contract with Columbia Pictures for $125 a week. The studio puts her up at the Hotel Bel-Air.

Ed Cronenwerth shoots her in various exercise positions, toning and stretching her body. She is also shown seated on steps, her right elbow on her raised right thigh and her right hand on her chin next to the sign "Los Angeles City Limits." He also photographs makeup sessions. Marilyn applies lipstick, looking into a hand-held mirror, and is shot sitting while Helen Hunt styles her hair.

March 10: Marilyn meets Natasha Lytess, who will become her acting coach, and Fred Karger, her future voice coach and then her lover, for the first time.

March 11: *Scudda Hoo! Scudda Hay!* premieres in Sedalia, Kansas. Marilyn's brief scenes were cut, although some viewers have spotted her in at least one long shot.

March 14: Ana Lower dies.

March 18: Marilyn attends funeral services for Ana Lower.

April 14: Official release date for *Scudda Hoo! Scudda Hay!*

April 22–May 3: Marilyn works on *Ladies of the Chorus* under the supervision of Fred Karger.

Fred Karger arranges for Marilyn to see orthodontist Walter Taylor, who equips her with a retainer to fix her slightly protruding teeth.

May 26: With Mickey Rooney, Marilyn attends the premiere of *The Emperor Waltz*, directed by Billy Wilder.

May 28: On the cover of *New Screen News* (Australia), Marilyn is shown smiling and standing in high-heel sandals in a one-piece black-and-yellow swimsuit.

June 1: Marilyn turns twenty-two.

June 3: Marilyn moves into a double room at the Hollywood Studio Club. *Green Grass of Wyoming* is released, with Marilyn appearing as an extra in a square dance scene.

Summer: Marilyn is photographed with producer George Jessel at the Florentine Theatre Restaurant.

July: Photographs are taken of Marilyn at the Town House Hotel in Los Angeles, showing her with tennis racket in hand.

August 15: Marilyn appears in *Stage Door* at the Bliss-Hayden Theatre (her role has not been identified).

September 3 or 4: Marilyn attends a performance of *Madame Butterfly* at the Hollywood Bowl with Bill Pursel. The two first met in the late 1930s, and he later became her boyfriend. She continues to see him from time to time in Las Vegas and Los Angeles. She seem subdued during the Hollywood Bowl performance, and afterward confides to Pursel that she was remembering a pageant staged there in which she had forgotten her cue (see entry for summer 1932).

September 8: Columbia does not renew Marilyn's contract.

September 9: Marilyn's Columbia contract expires.

In *Hidden Hollywood,* author Richard Lamparski claims Marilyn worked briefly as a stripper at the Mayan Theatre in downtown Los Angeles. In *The Intimate Sex Lives of Famous People*, Anton LaVey claims to have had a two-week affair with Marilyn during this same period.

September 21: Marilyn is involved in a minor car crash on Sunset Boulevard. She meets photographer Tom Kelley, who lends her cab fare.

September 25: Andre de Dienes publishes a cover photograph in *Wereld-Kroniek* (Holland) of Marilyn, smiling and wearing slacks, with her hair drawn up into a bun, sitting with her legs drawn up.

November 16: Marilyn signs a contract with photographer Earl Moran, who shoots her in a variety of positions, including one color photo of her in a Hawaiian skirt wearing a lei that only partially covers her left breast. Another shows her topless with a bottom cushion covering her nipples. And still another shows her leaning over in a top that barely manages to conceal her nipples. In one pose, she is shown bare-breasted, leaning backward and using her arms for support. In the most playful and suggestive pose, she stands garbed in what looks like a matador's top, exposing her breasts and partially obscuring her face with a white mask.

Christmas: Marilyn purchases a $500 watch on the install-
ment plan as a gift for Fred Karger. She has the watch engraved
"12.25.48," and tells him, "You'll have some other girl to love. You
wouldn't be able to use my present if my name was on it."

December 31: At a Hollywood party attended by important directors such as Otto Preminger, John Huston, Henry Hathaway, and
Jean Negulesco (all of whom would eventually direct Marilyn), she
meets William Morris agent Johnny Hyde, who immediately takes
an interest in her and her career.

1949

A smiling Marilyn in a one-piece swimsuit emerging from a pool is
published on the covers of several Sunday newspaper supplements
across the country.

January 1: Marilyn is Johnny Hyde's guest at his Palm Springs
home.

Early January: Johnny Hyde buys Marilyn's contracts and begins
his campaign to make her a star.

January 8: Andre de Dienes publishes a cover photograph of Marilyn playing in the snow on Mount Hood. She is on her hands and
knees smiling directly at the camera, with a cap jauntily tilted on the
right side of her head. The photograph was taken in 1945.

January 24: Gossip columnist Earl Wilson interviews Marilyn at
the Sherry-Netherlands Hotel, dubbing her "the Mmmmmmmm
Girl."

February 10: *Ladies of the Chorus* is released. Tibor Krekes in the
Motion Picture Herald gives Marilyn her first review: "One of the
brightest spots is Miss Monroe's singing. She is pretty, and with her
pleasing voice and style, shows promise."

February 15: Marilyn appears on the cover of *Votre Sante* (France)
in a close-up. Her hair is somewhat shorter than in earlier 1940s
poses, but not yet perfected as the lighter, more subtly curled style
featured in the 1950s.

Marilyn in *Love Happy*

February 28: Marilyn's contract with Carroll and Ryman ends.

March 2: Johnny Hyde has Marilyn sign with the William Morris agency.

Johnny Hyde secures a walk-on part for Marilyn in *Love Happy*, a Marx Brothers movie.

To her line, "Men keep following me," Groucho, rolling his eyes, says, "Really? I can't understand why."

March 12: On the cover of *Kroniek Van De Week* (Holland), Andre de Dienes publishes a full-length shot of Norma Jeane, wearing a pinafore and holding a baby lamb.

March 13: Marilyn leaves the Hollywood Studio Club and moves into a one-bedroom suite in the Beverly Carlton Hotel.

March 16: *Riders of the Whistling Pines*, in which Gene Autry sings to a photograph of a rancher's dead wife, is released. The photograph is a shot of Marilyn Monroe.

March 26: The *Picture Post* cover is a close-up of Marilyn laughing as the wind blows back her hair, which flows into and out of the picture frame.

April: Phillipe Halsman photographs eight starlets, including Marilyn.

April 20: Grace McKee Goddard writes Marilyn telling her that Gladys has married John Stewart Eley, an electrician. Marilyn has been sending her mother money regularly for some time.

Spring: John Hyde leaves his wife, Mozelle Cravens, and their children. He persuades Marilyn to leave the Studio Club and live with him in a rented villa at 718 North Palm Drive in Beverly Hills. But he also rents a room at the Beverly Carlton Hotel so that she can have a business address.

May: Hyde takes Marilyn to plastic surgeon Michael Gurdin, who removes flesh from the tip of her nose to narrow it, and adds silicone to her lower jaw to make is more symmetrical. Hyde also outfits her with new clothes from Saks.

May 25: Tom Kelley calls Marilyn about a nude modeling job for a calendar.

May 27: Marilyn poses nude for Tom Kelley's calendar photographs while listening to Artie Shaw. She is given a fifty-dollar flat fee for signing a contract, using the name Mona Monroe. Altogether Kelley takes shots of twenty-four poses, although only two are published, titled "A New Wrinkle" and "Golden Dreams."

June: On the cover of *Opden Uitkijk* (Holland), Andre de Dienes publishes a photograph of brown-haired Marilyn leaning over a wooden fence in a country-girl pose.

June 1: Marilyn turns twenty-three.

June 21: Marilyn travels to Warrensburg, New York, where she delivers the keys to a new house won in a Photoplay competition.

June 27: Sidney Fields is the first columnist to write about Marilyn, commenting in the *New York Mirror*: "Marilyn is a very lovely and relatively unknown movie actress. But give her time; you will hear from her."

July 23: Andre de Dienes photographs Marilyn on Tobey Beach, Long Island, New York, walking in a swimsuit and holding a red polka dot umbrella near the surf. A close-up shot shows both her nose and jaw before plastic surgery made the nose narrower and the jaw symmetrical.

July 27: Earl Wilson interviews Marilyn for his newspaper column.

August: For the cover of *Glamorous Models,* Laszlo Willinger, in a low angle shot, shows Marilyn from the midriff up, crossing her arms just below her breasts and smiling with her head thrown back, in a pose that almost seems to be a laugh.

August 5: Marilyn appears for costume fittings for *A Ticket to Tomahawk.*

August 13: Marilyn appears on the cover of *Picture Post* squatting on the beach, both hands touching the sand with her finger tips, and smiling, her hair done up in an unusually compact style.

August 15: Marilyn begins work on *A Ticket to Tomahawk* in Durango, Colorado.

September: Marilyn concludes her work on *A Ticket to Tomahawk,* including a fundraiser for a local hospital. In front of packed bleachers she takes part in a baseball game, working out a gag that involves her turn at bat. During a run to first base, her blue jeans came undone, exposing her black lace panties and sending the crowd into an uproar.

Hit! uses a Laszlo Willinger portrait of Marilyn in a two-piece yellow swimsuit with golden hair and a very red-lipped smile.

September 25: Marilyn attends a party at the Mocambo Club.

Autumn: Marilyn appears wearing a cap and dressed in what looks like a leopard-skin coat on the cover of the *So-Rite* catalog.

October: Marilyn appears on the cover of a comic book, *Teenage Diary Secrets*, in a photograph taken by Bruno Bernard. She is wearing a red sweater with the caption "I Played Kiss and Run."

October 10: Philippe Halsman photographs Monroe for a *Life* article about Hollywood's aspiring stars.

Marilyn appears in "Eight Girls Try Out Mixed Emotions" in *Life*.

October 28: Marilyn calls gossip columnist Louella Parsons to announce she has won a role in John Huston's *The Asphalt Jungle*. She earns $350 a week for a total of $1,050. Marilyn plays Angela Phinlay, mistress of a corrupt lawyer.

December 28: Production ends on *The Asphalt Jungle*.

December 31: Marilyn spends New Year's Eve with Johnny Hyde at the Racquet Club in Palm Springs.

1950

Marilyn, accompanied by her vocal coach and lover, Fred Karger, performs at the Marine Corps Air Station El Toro in Anaheim. She sings "Do It Again."

Laszlo Willinger photographs Marilyn in color, wearing an orange hat, orange shorts, and white calf-high western boots. She is wearing no top, but her crossed arms cover her breasts. Another shot, published in *Das Magazine*, has her standing on the beach in a one-piece red swimsuit, arms at her sides, with her head swiveling toward the camera, smiling into the wind, which ripples through her hair.

Roman Magasinet (Denmark) features a cover shot of Marilyn in a seductive pose similar to Angela Phinley's in *The Asphalt Jungle*.

Marilyn appears in a television commercial for Royal Triton Oil.

Marilyn auditions for roles in the Players Ring Theatre, a new venue at 8351 Santa Monica Boulevard, but is not successful.

January 5: Marilyn begins work on *The Fireball*. She works with hairstylist Agnes Flanagan, who becomes a friend and works regularly for Marilyn.

January 20: Andre de Dienes's color photograph of Marilyn on Mount Hood is on the cover of *Vecko Revyn* (Sweden). She is wearing a snow cap and a red sweater, and snow covers her pants and left leg, which is bent in a kneeling posture as she smiles straight at the camera.

February: Marilyn ends work on *The Fireball*.

Laff publishes a Bruno Bernard cover photograph of Marilyn sitting in a kneeling posture, her arms covering her bare breasts, which are also covered slightly with a painted-on mesh-looking fabric. She is holding a light blue cosmetic sponge, and is wearing only lacy panties, as if she has been captured in the process of dressing.

February 16: *The Asphalt Jungle* is previewed at the Picwood Theatre in West Los Angeles. Audience appraisal cards refer to the "hot blonde" and request, "Let's see more of the blonde."

February–March: *Man to Man* publishes a Laszlo Willinger photograph of Marilyn in a black, revealing negligee, glancing up as she talks on the phone.

While browsing in a bookstore with Rupert Allan, a writer for *Look* introduced to Marilyn by Johnny Hyde, Marilyn purchases art books. Later, she tacks up reproductions of Fra Angelico, Dürer, and Botticelli in the kitchen and bedroom of the North Palm Drive house she shares with Johnny Hyde. On her bedside table is a photograph of the famous actress Eleonora Duse, whom Natasha Lytess loved.

Marilyn reads Rainer Maria Rilke's *Letters to a Young Poet* and purchases an edition of Vesalius's work on anatomy. Natasha Lytess has her reading Chekhov and Tolstoy.

March 8: *Love Happy* is released. Marilyn's total screen time is thirty-eight seconds—long enough for Groucho to respond to her slinking into his detective agency office with the question, "Is there anything I can do for you?" He promptly responds, "What a ridiculous statement." Marilyn tells him that men keep following her and sways out of camera range as Groucho comments, "Really? I can't understand why." Marilyn later recalled, "There were three girls there and Groucho had us each walk away from him. . . . I was the only one he asked to do it twice. Then he whispered in my ear, 'You have the prettiest ass in the business.' I'm sure he meant it in the nicest way." Groucho later said Marilyn was "Mae West, Theda Bara and Bo Peep rolled into one." Marilyn received $500 for her appearance and another three hundred to pose for promotional photographs.

Marilyn is sent on a promotional tour for a fee of one hundred dollars a week. She meets dress manufacturer Henry Rosenfeld in New York City, and they become lifelong friends. During this period she also does her famous Jones Beach photo sessions with Andre de Dienes. The tour takes her to Detroit, Cleveland, Chicago, Milwaukee, and Rockford, Illinois.

Marilyn attends a party at the Chicago nightclub Ricketts with Roddy McDowell.

Marilyn appears in print advertisement for Kyron diet pills, with accompanying text: "If you want slim youthful lines like Miss Monroe and other stars, start the KYRON Way to slenderness—today!"

Spring: Richard Miller photographs Marilyn at the Players Ring Theatre near Beverly Hills. She auditions for a role in Elmer Rice's *Street Scene* but is not cast in the production.

March 27: Marilyn wins the part of Miss Caswell in *All About Eve*.

April: Production of *All About Eve* begins.

April 21: *A Ticket to Tomahawk* is released. Marilyn plays Clara, one of four showgirls. She makes four appearances (with dialogue) in group scenes and musical numbers.

May: Marilyn appears in Richard Miller's color photograph on the cover of *Glance* in a two-piece swimsuit on a diving board, with her knees tucked toward her chest.

On the cover of *True Experiences*, a wholesome-looking Marilyn appears in a tight close-up, her left shoulder showing, asking readers to "read my Cinderella story on page 22." She portrays herself as a lonely child who stayed at home reading books and watching movies until she won a part in a school play. At the time she was only eight, portraying a prince disguised as a beggar. She was thrilled with her teacher's compliments, calling the episode the first time she seemed to matter. She wanted to become an actress.

May 11: Johnny Hyde negotiates a new seven-year contract for Marilyn at Fox. She is to be paid $500 a week, beginning in 1951, with semi-annual increases not to exceed a total of $1,500 a week.

May 17: Photographer Earl Leaf shoots Marilyn in Johnny Hyde's garden at his home on North Palm Drive.

Marilyn wins a lead role in a gangster film, *Cold Shoulder*, but Fox studio head Darryl Zanuck stops production.

May 27: In *Revue* (Germany), Andre de Dienes publishes a cover photograph of brown-haired Norma Jeane in a three-quarter pose, turning toward the camera, looking over her shoulder, and shot from the waist up.

May 23: *The Asphalt Jungle* is released (with a world premiere at Grauman's Egyptian Theatre), and the film and Marilyn get good reviews.

May–June: On *Gala's* cover, Marilyn appears in an Andre de Dienes photograph taken at Tobey Beach, near New York City, in 1949. She wears a one-piece bathing suit and bends over while standing on her toes, with her arms extended diagonally holding on to a beach umbrella turned upside down.

June 1: Joe Schenck celebrates Marilyn's twenty-fourth birthday with the gift of a Chihuahua. She is photographed feeding the dog, which jumps up off the ground as she leans over to offer a treat. In another shot she puckers her lips while holding the dog slightly away from her face.

June 20: *Look* publishes "The Girls in the Asphalt Jungle."

Summer: Marilyn sees Bill Pursel for the last time, telling him she is breaking off their relationship, which comes as a surprise to him, since they seemed closer than ever.

July 18: Louella Parsons plugs Marilyn in a column, saying she "packs the same punch Lana Turner did in her early days. . . . Marilyn didn't have a big role in *Asphalt Jungle* but what she did was so punchy that 20th brought her back home at many times what she had received before. I'm told she is excellent in *All About Eve*, which is whispered to be a honey."

July 20: Marilyn visits a marine base and is given the title of "Miss Morale of the Marine Corps."

August: Production of *All About Eve* ends.

Marilyn vacations in Palm Springs with her drama coach, Natasha Lytess. They now share the same apartment.

Ed Clark photographs Marilyn for *Life*. The photographer shoots her in Griffith Park, reading poetry and a script. She takes off her blouse, revealing a bikini top. But the magazine rejects the shots, calling them "over-developed."

August 13: With Johnny Hyde, Marilyn attends a party at Danny Kaye's home. Vivien Leigh is the honored guest, having arrived for her work with Elia Kazan on *A Streetcar Named Desire*. Marilyn meets Kazan and Olivier (a meeting Olivier will not remember).

August 27: Philip K. Scheuer writes one of the first feature-length articles about Marilyn for the *Los Angeles Times*.

September: Marilyn meets photographer Milton Greene.

September 2: Louella Parsons writes a column saying Marilyn should get the role of Lorelei Lee in *Gentleman Prefer Blondes*.

September 12: Gossip columnist Sheilah Graham reports that Marilyn has been seen on the beach with Peter Lawford.

Autumn: Marilyn attends ten weeks of Tuesday evening classes on literature and the history of art at UCLA.

September 28: Fox gives permission to the LeGallion Perfume Company to use Marilyn's name and image for "Sortilege Perfume" advertisements.

October 1: Marilyn stores some of her personal belongings at the Janis Van and Storage Company.

Marilyn writes a check for ten dollars to Grace Goddard, who acts as her assistant.

October 7: *The Fireball* is released. Marilyn plays Polly, a roller derby groupie.

Marilyn sleeps on a sofa bed at Natasha Lytess's apartment, a two-room duplex at 1309 North Harper Avenue in West Hollywood. Marilyn sometimes takes care of Natasha's daughter, Barbara, and Marilyn's Chihuahua, named Josefa. Marilyn sees less of Johnny Hyde during this period and more of Joe Schenck.

Marilyn meets gossip columnist Sidney Skolsky at Schwab's Drugstore, where he maintains an office. Skolsky becomes a friend and a key promoter of Marilyn's career.

November 5: Marilyn writes a forty-dollar check to a Dr. Seligman for an undisclosed treatment.

November 7: Louella Parsons mentions in her column that Johnny Hyde has the flu, although the real problem is his heart.

November 10: Marilyn poses for Fox's Thanksgiving Day publicity and is shot in a pilgrim costume holding a firearm pointed at a turkey.

November 14: *Right Cross* is released. Marilyn's appears as a model, Dusky Ledue, in a few scenes playing opposite Dick Powell (Rick Gavery).

November 15: Marilyn writes a forty-dollar check to Dr. Seligman for an undisclosed treatment.

November 22: *All About Eve* is released. Marilyn plays Miss Caswell, an aspiring actress lacking both talent and intelligence.

December: On a shopping trip in Tijuana, Mexico, Marilyn buys Natasha Lytess a gold-framed ivory cameo brooch.

December 2: Marilyn appears next to the fuselage of a new Mexican Airlines plane to promote the first direct Los Angeles-Mexico City flights. In two shots she stands with an artist's palette painting what looks like a map of Mexico, while a pilot and three suited executives gather around her.

December 5: Johnny Hyde secures a three-year contract with the William Morris Agency for Marilyn.

December 7: Johnny Hyde calls to tell Marilyn that she is scheduled for a sound test with Richard Conte for the film *Cold Shoulder*. (A still from the test is included in Richard Buskin's *Blonde Heat*.) Richard Conte praised her intensity, but the picture was never made.

December 10: Marilyn shoots her screen test with Richard Conte. She plays a gangster's girlfriend.

December 16: Johnny Hyde goes to Palm Springs for a vacation.

December 17: Johnny Hyde suffers a massive heart attack and is rushed back to Los Angeles.

December 18: Johnny Hyde suffers a fatal heart attack at Cedars of Lebanon Hospital in Los Angeles.

December 19: Marilyn attends Johnny Hyde's funeral, dressed in a black suit she purchased from I. Magnin's for $146.41. Hyde's son, James, recalled her screaming his father's name at the funeral. Even more lurid accounts have her throwing herself on Hyde's casket and sobbing, "Johnny, Johnny!"

December 24: Marilyn receives a mink stole that Johnny Hyde had bought for her.

December 25: Marilyn gives Natasha Lytess an antique cameo broach with a note that reads, "I just want you to know that I owe you much more than my life." According to Lytess, she saved Marilyn from overdosing with sleeping pills.

December 31: *Stars and Stripes* crowns Marilyn "Miss Cheesecake" of the year.

1951

Soldiers in the Aleutians vote Marilyn "The Girl Most Likely to Thaw Alaska," the Seventh Division Medical Corps votes her

"The Girl Most Wanted to Examine," and the All Weather Fight Squadron, based in San Diego, salutes her as "The girl they'd like to arrest."

Marilyn visits the USS *Benham*, representing the *Los Angeles Daily News* as a hostess. She wears a glamorous black gown shown in shots of her that also show sailors and officers. In one crowd scene, she wears jeweled earrings and is surrounded by a ring of adoring sailors that is reminiscent of the "Diamonds Are a Girl's Best Friend" number from *Gentlemen Prefer Blondes*.

Marilyn initiates her first sessions with a psychoanalyst, Dr. A. Gottesman, at his Los Angeles clinic, paying $200 per visit.

Marilyn is photographed lying on the grass reading Walt Whitman's *Leaves of Grass*.

Larry Barbier Jr. photographs Marilyn, dressed in short shorts and holding a baseball bat, held by player Gus Zernial. This is the pose that caught Joe DiMaggio's attention.

John Florea photographs Marilyn lying on a bed reading *How to Develop Your Thinking Ability* by Kenneth Keyes, and in a sultry pose lying on a fur, the little finger of her right hand just touching her lower lip.

Bruno Bernard photographs Marilyn in a lacy negligee sitting atop a large globe.

Marilyn is photographed with Joe Schenck at the El Moroco. She wears a strapless gown and long black gloves.

January: Sometime this month, Marilyn begins an affair with Elia Kazan. They meet in her room at the Beverly Carlton Hotel or at the home of his agent, Charles Feldman, who begins to represent Marilyn, although she is still legally bound to the William Morris Agency.

January 1: Marilyn appears in "Apprentice Goddesses" in *Life*.

January 16: Arthur Miller arrives in Hollywood to work on a screenplay with his friend, director Elia Kazan.

Marilyn meets playwright Arthur Miller on the set of her film, *As Young as You Feel*.

January 26: Kazan asks Miller to escort Marilyn to a party that Charles Feldman is hosting in honor of Miller. Miller and Marilyn spend time together visiting bookshops and going on a picnic. He watches her delight in reading an e.e. cummings poem.

January 27: Marilyn and Kazan drive Miller to the airport. He is returning home to work on a screenplay for Kazan. Miller is obviously smitten with Monroe, but also determined to save his marriage. She is clearly taken with him and is hoping that at some time they can renew their relationship.

February: Marilyn sells one of Johnny Hyde's gifts to her for $1,000, which she gives to Natasha Lytess to help her purchase a small house in Hollywood.

February 7: Harry Brand, Fox publicity chief, issues a studio biography playing up Marilyn's experience as an orphan, her reliance on Ana Lower, her early "immature" marriage, Howard Hughes's interest in her, her struggles to be recognized as an actress, and her featured roles in *The Asphalt Jungle* and *All About Eve*.

February 15: Marilyn accompanies Kazan and Miller to Santa Barbara for a preview of *A Streetcar Named Desire*, directed by Kazan.

Marilyn moves out of Natasha Lytess's apartment and into another apartment with Shelley Winters.

March: On the Fox lot, Marilyn generates huge interest as she walks barefoot six blocks from the wardrobe department to the photo studio, wearing only a sheer negligee.

At a lunch with Spyros Skouras, Marilyn persuades him to speak with Darryl Zanuck, head of production at Fox, about casting her in every role at the studio that requires a blonde.

March 29: Marilyn presents an Academy Award at the Pantages Theatre, 6233 Hollywood Boulevard. She presents the award for best sound recording to Thomas Mouton for his work on *All About Eve*. She is photographed wearing a low-cut mull (cotton) dress borrowed from the Fox wardrobe.

April: According to Shelley Winters, Marilyn meets the poet Dylan Thomas at a dinner party. While Thomas engages in bawdy humor with Winters, he is gentle and respectful with Monroe and does not make a pass at her.

April 5: Marilyn appears for costume fittings for *Love Nest*.

Marilyn enrolls at UCLA in a "Backgrounds of Literature" course.

April 12: Marilyn appears for another costume fitting for *Love Nest*.

April 18: Marilyn begins work on *Love Nest*.

May 2: Sidney Skolsky reports in his column that Marilyn had undressed to do a shower scene for *Love Nest*. As the crew watched, the "electricity was palpable," Skolsky reported.

May 5: Natasha Lytess asks Marilyn to pay a $1,000 debt owed to a dentist. The request upsets Marilyn, but she agrees to pay the dentist $200 a week. Lytess agrees to pay Marilyn back in weekly installments of twenty-five dollars.

May 7: Marilyn accompanies Elia Kazan to a party at the home of powerful Hollywood agent Charles Feldman.

May 11: Marilyn signs a new seven-year contract with Fox.

Hometown Story is released. Marilyn plays Iris Martin, a voluptuous secretary.

Marilyn begins work on *Let's Make It Legal*.

May 15: Marilyn and John F. Kennedy meet briefly during a party in Beverly Hills at the home of designer Elsie de Wolfe and her husband, diplomat Sir Charles Mendl.

June 1: Marilyn turns twenty-five.

June 2: In *Wereld-Kroniek* (Holland), Andre de Dienes publishes a cover photograph of Marilyn smiling, dressed in rolled-up slacks, her hair drawn back with a hairband, and bent over, dragging her left hand through the surf on a California beach.

June 6: In a *Los Angeles Daily News* column, Ezra Goodman identifies Marilyn as a rising new talent.

June 14: Marilyn does a sound test with Robert Wagner, who stars with her in *Let's Make It Legal*.

June 15: *As Young as You Feel* is released. Marilyn plays Harriet, a conniving secretary.

June 17: Marilyn appears on the cover of *Confidenze* (Italy), relaxing on a chaise longue, a short sweater exposing her midriff. Her arms are folded behind her hand, emphasizing her breasts, and her calves tucked up tight against her thighs. Her feet are clad in laced-up pumps.

July: *Movieland* reports that Marilyn spends too much on her clothes and other accessories and has not learned to budget her expenses.

July 18: *Hometown Story* is released. Marilyn plays Iris Martin, a sexy secretary.

August 4: Marilyn is photographed in Hollywood at the Farmers Market wearing a chef's hat and a swimsuit, as she stands bending over a four-layer cake, revealing a good deal of cleavage. In another shot, she holds a ceremonial sword over the cake while standing next to Polish diplomat Michael Gaszynski, who is celebrating his American citizenship.

August 21: Fox agrees to loan Marilyn to RKO for *Clash by Night*. Paul Douglas, starring in the film, is not pleased with the attention Marilyn receives, referring to her as a "blonde bitch." A good deal of Marilyn's dilatory behavior can be attributed to nerves. She vomits and breaks out in blotches, but her unsympathetic director, Fritz Lang, bans Natasha Lytess, Monroe's source of support, from the set.

September: Marilyn, photographed by John Miehle, appears in a close-up in a yellow knitted sweater on the cover of *True Romance*, her hair blown against her face as she looks upward, smiling with her mouth half open.

A Laszlo Willinger cheesecake photograph, with Marilyn leaning forward in a revealing two-piece swimsuit, makes the cover of *Your Money Maker*.

September 8: *Collier's* publishes "1951's Model Blonde," the first major national magazine profile of Marilyn Monroe.

Autumn: On the recommendation of actor Jack Palance, Marilyn enrolls in Michael Chekhov's acting class. She plays Cordelia to his Lear and comments, "This is what I find out exciting about acting. The illusion that becomes reality. Mr. Chekhov *is* Lear."

Marilyn appears in a print advertisement for Rayve Shampoo. She is quoted as saying, "Get a tube or jar of Rayve Creme Shampoo today. . . . See how it makes even a tired wave *want* to curl!"

For Saks department store, Marilyn is photographed wearing a white mink coat, a conservative dark suit—complete with a veil and feather atop her hat—and an elegant white chiffon dress. The caption for the shots reads, "This she must have for her big date at dusk . . . perfect for starlight allure in a favorite spot."

October 23: Marilyn appears on *Look*'s cover and in an article, "Who Says Hollywood is Dying?"

October 25: Marilyn attends the Hollywood Foreign Correspondents annual event at the Mocambo. She is photographed in the center of a group of men welcoming Zachary Scott.

October 26: Marilyn receives medical treatment, perhaps for endometriosis. She writes a check to Dr. A. Gottsman for $200.

October 31: *Let's Make It Legal* is released. Marilyn plays Joyce Mannering, another predatory temptress. Macdonald Carey, one of the film's stars, remembers "she was riding the coat-tails of Joe Schenck at that time and she was late for everything. One day I was in make-up, and there was Marilyn being made up too. She was pleasant enough, but when it was time to go to the set they sent a big limo for her . . . and a Jeep for me! She only had a few lines to say." When the director, Richard Sale, complained about her tardiness, Marilyn told him to take it up with Mr. Schenck. But Sale said he would notify Darryl Zanuck, as Marilyn walked off the set. She returned a short while later and apologized, even thanking the director for "straightening her out."

November: Marilyn travels to Hemet, California, and tries to contact Stanley Gifford, the man she thinks is her father. According to her, he refuses to see her.

According to Shelley Winters, she and Marilyn shared a $227-a-month apartment on Holloway Drive in Hollywood for several months.

November 5: Marilyn receives medical treatment, perhaps for endometriosis.

November 9: Marilyn receives medical treatment, perhaps for endometriosis, and writes a check for fifty dollars.

November 14: *Love Nest* is released. Marilyn plays Roberta Stevens, a voluptuous ex-WAC who complicates the life of her friend Jim Scott (William Lundigan), who has to contend with his jealous wife, Connie (June Haver).

November 19: *Quick*, a weekly news magazine, puts Marilyn on the cover and calls her "the new Jean Harlow." Inside, she poses three times as Harlow.

November 30: RKO studio issues a biography by Perry Lieber that declares, "From lonely orphan to sought after motion picture star is the true life Cinderella story of Marilyn Monroe." The focus is on RKO, which Norma Jeane visited when in the orphanage, and on *Clash by Night*, an RKO picture. Ana Lower's role is emphasized, as is Marilyn's dedication to acting and roles in *The Asphalt Jungle* and *All About Eve*. The biography ends, "The return to RKO studios ended a cycle in Marilyn's life and opened the doorway to another one in which the heartaches of the past will be remembered only as inspiration for the future."

December: Marilyn begins work on *Don't Bother to Knock*.

Marilyn moves in with Natasha Lytess at 611 North Crescent Drive in Beverly Hills.

Marilyn is photographed on the floor with her legs crossed, working with Lytess, who reclines in an armchair observing her pupil. In another shot, Marilyn stands with her hands clasped, looking up in an aspirational pose, while Natasha stands, right hand on her hip, watching with intensity.

Focus puts Marilyn on the cover and devotes an article inside to her: "Marilyn Monroe: She Breathes Sex Appeal."

December 6: Marilyn appears for costume fittings for *Don't Bother to Knock.*

Christmas: Marilyn appears in a pin-up pose released on Christmas Day. She is standing on a stool in front of a fireplace in a long body stocking, with a holiday wreath in the background behind her head.

December 31: Marilyn calls Associated Press journalist James Bacon, saying, "I don't want to stay at home alone on New Year's Eve, Jim. Can I go to a party with you?" Bacon, who claims in *Hollywood is a Four-Letter Town* to have had a sporadic affair with Monroe, declines, saying his wife would not approve. "I understand," Marilyn says as she hangs up.

1952

Marilyn receives five thousand fan letters a week.

Stars and Stripes crowns Marilyn "Cheesecake Queen of 1952."

The Artists Institute of America rejects Marilyn as the pin-up of 1952, stating that her legs are too short and her derriere too sloped.

Marilyn wins the *Look Achievement Award* for "Most Promising Female Newcomer."

Marilyn appears in print advertisements for Louis Creative Hairdressers.

Marilyn poses in a potato sack for photographer Earl Theisen.

Lucille Ryman refuses Marilyn's offer to pay back all the money that Ryman and her husband spent on Marilyn during her period of struggle. Ryman suggests that Marilyn could use the money to help another actress in need.

Marilyn presents an engraving of Abraham Lincoln to Michael Chekhov with the inscription, "Lincoln was the man I adored most of all through school. Now that man is you."

Marilyn is photographed in the garden of the Hotel Bel-Air in Los Angeles: lying down with an open book beside her bent right knee; reading Heinrich Heine during the making of *Niagara*; and standing next to several shelves of books reading Arthur Miller's *Death of a Salesman*.

George Hurrell, perhaps the greatest of the Hollywood portrait photographers, shoots a series of pictures with Marilyn in his studio. He later commented: "She did the same routine Harlow did. [She arrived] wrapped in something and, all of a sudden, let it fall. I presume the idea was to get you going. Well, they were exhibitionists."

Cheese Cake: An American Phenomenon features an Anthony Beauchamp photograph of Marilyn in a yellow bikini and the headline, "A Pictorial Report on the Impact of the Female Form from September Morn to Marilyn Monroe." The French work *Matinée de Septembre*, by Paul Émile Chabas, created a scandal when it was first exhibited in Chicago in 1912. It depicts a nude woman, bending over, her right arm crossing her breasts and touching her left arm as she gazes at the morning light and a background of hazy clouds and mountains, while standing in water that rises to her calves. The picture can be seen as a forerunner of all cheesecake—especially cheesecake with the theme of the self-aroused woman touching herself.

Marilyn is photographed in a romantic clinch with ventriloquist Edgar Bergen and his dummy, Charlie McCarthy.

Marilyn lives briefly in a small, furnished house at 1121 Hilldale Avenue in West Hollywood.

January: *Movieland* features an Ed Clark photograph of Marilyn on its cover, which shows her reclining, wearing a black gown and gloves.

January–February: Marilyn works on *We're Not Married*.

January 5: "I want you to talk with this girl. We're grooming her— or maybe I should say she's grooming herself—to be the sexiest thing in pictures since Jean Harlow," says Harry Brand, Fox publicity director to columnist Hy Gardner. Gardner remembers the day shortly after Marilyn's death (*New York Herald Tribune*, August 8, 1962).

January 7: Marilyn records the song "Do It Again."

January 11: Marilyn appears for costume fittings for *We're Not Married.*

Inez Melson replaces "Doc" Goddard, Grace's husband, as Marilyn's business manager.

January 26: Marilyn is invited to attend the Foreign Press Association's First Annual International Film Festival at the Club Del Mar in Santa Monica and creates a sensation by wearing an Idaho potato burlap bag designed for her by Billy Travilla.

February: Marilyn in a black negligee and femme fatale pose is featured on the cover of *Silver Screen.*

Pic features an Earl Theisen head shot, with Marilyn tilting her head down while opening her eyes wide in a tempting, provocative manner.

February 2: Marilyn attends a party at Romanoff's to celebrate the release of *The African Queen.*

Marilyn attends a UCLA "junior prom" and is photographed with tuxedoed young men presenting her with a corsage. Other shots show her looking at a campus map, studying in the library, examining a stuffed toy with "UCLA" printed on it, and sitting at a lunch room table with college students who are drinking cartons of milk.

February 5: *The Los Angeles Herald and Express* publishes "Studios Push Beauties in Glamor Derby," subtitled "All Want Queen Marilyn's Crown." Marilyn is called Fox's "M-bomb."

February 8: She wins the Henrietta Award as "The Best Young Box Office Personality" at the Del Mar Club at 1910 Ocean Front Avenue in Santa Monica.

February 26: Marilyn begins work on *Monkey Business* with director Howard Hawks. As usual, she is late to the set, but Ginger Rogers, in a starring role, said Marilyn always knew her lines. Billy Travilla, her dress designer, admitted she hated the beige jersey wool dress with pleated full skirt that is her ensemble in the picture's opening scenes.

She writes a check to the Carlton Hotel for $150.

March 1: Marilyn makes an appointment at Cedars of Lebanon Hospital, complaining of appendicitis, but director Howard Hawks insists that she return to the set of *Monkey Business*, and her operation is delayed until the end of production.

Marilyn in *Monkey Business*

March 6: Marilyn attends the *Look* awards party at the Beverly Hills Hotel. She is photographed with Ginger Rogers.

March 8: Marilyn is supposed to meet Joe DiMaggio for the first time and have dinner at the Villa Nova Restaurant. DiMaggio shows up at 6:30, but Marilyn does not arrive until after 8:00. Mickey Rooney, a baseball fan, comes over to their table to talk to Joe, not Marilyn.

March 13: Columnist Aline Mosby breaks the story about Marilyn posing for a nude calendar.

March 17: Marilyn is photographed watching DiMaggio play baseball for the one and only time. Sidney Skolsky breaks the story that she is dating Joe DiMaggio.

March 19: Marilyn and DiMaggio dine alone.

March 20: In *Zondagsvriend* (Holland), Andre de Dienes publishes a cover photograph of Norma Jeane holding up a baby lamb and smiling.

Spring: Nico Minardos, an aspiring actor at Fox, has a seven-month affair with Marilyn, according to biographer Anthony Summers. Minardos characterizes her as bright and sensitive. He claims Marilyn could never have a climax. She tells him her childhood rape story. He believes she was "acting in her real life. She knew what reality was but she acted things out because she loved the drama. . . ."

March 26: *Okinawa* is released, with a clip of Marilyn singing "Every Baby Needs a Da-Da-Daddy" from *Ladies of the Chorus*.

April 4: Marilyn performs for ten thousand marines at Camp Pendleton, California, singing "Do It Again" and "Somebody Loves You."

April 7: Marilyn first appears on a *Life* cover, photographed by Phillipe Halsman. Inside she is featured in "Hollywood Topic A-Plus."

April 14: *Estampa* (Argentina) features a still from *The Asphalt Jungle*, displaying Marilyn from the bust up in a rather sophisticated pose, wearing a lavender-colored suit and the alluring expression of a femme fatale.

April 18: Fox renews its option, and Marilyn is paid $750 a week.

April 22: "I'm a bookworm and proud of it," Marilyn tells columnist Erskine Johnson.

April 23: John Stewart Eley, Gladys's husband, dies of heart disease. Shortly afterwards, Gladys writes to Marilyn, "Please my Dear daughter, I wish to hear from you. Here I just have problems and I'd like to leave as soon as possible. I'd rather have my child's love than her hate. Tenderly, your mother." The note upsets Marilyn, who cannot bear to visit her mother and be reminded of the traumas of her childhood.

April 28: Marilyn's appendix is removed at Cedars of Lebanon Hospital. Marilyn tapes a note to her surgeon: "*Most important* to Read Before *operation*. Dear Doctor, *Cut as little as possible*. I know it seems vain but that doesn't really enter into it—the fact that I'm a *woman* is important and means much to me. Save please (can't ask you enough) what you can—I'm in your hands. You have children and you must know what it means—*please Doctor*—I know somehow you will! thank you—thank you—for Gods sakes Dear Doctor No *ovaries* removed—please again do whatever you can to prevent large *scars*. Thanking you with my all *heart*. Marilyn Monroe." She is photographed in bed, smiling and holding a pamphlet titled "No More Appendix." Whitey Snyder does her makeup for the series of hospital photographs.

Joe DiMaggio sends her two-dozen roses. Dan Dailey sends her a tulip tree with singing toy canaries on every limb.

May: On the cover of *True Story* (Japan), Marilyn appears as a robust sweater girl, raising her right arm and bending it at the elbow over her head so as to tilt the whole composition to the right, as she looks out dreamy-eyed and with a big, red-lipped smile.

May 3: Responding to reports that she is not an orphan and that her mother is alive, Marilyn issues a statement through Erskine Johnson in the *Los Angeles Daily News*: "My mother spent many years at the hospital. Through the Los Angeles County, my guardian placed me in several foster families and I spent more than a year at the Los Angeles Orphanage. I haven't known my mother intimately, and since I'm an adult, and able to help her, I have contacted her. Now I help her and I want to keep helping her as long as she needs me."

May 4: Hedda Hopper publishes "The Blowtorch Blonde" in the *Chicago Sunday Tribune Magazine*: "Marilyn Monroe who has zoomed to stardom after a three-year stretch as a cheesecake queen is easily the most delectable dish of the day. . . . She is fast supplanting Sam Goldwyn as a source of anecdotes and every producer at Twentieth is bidding for her as box office insurance."

May 6: Marilyn shies away from public appearances, living quietly at the Beverly Carlton Hotel, where DiMaggio visits her. She does, however, appear in publicity shots taken at the hotel.

May 21: Marilyn reports to Fox for color and wardrobe tests for *Niagara*.

May 25: On the front cover of the *Chicago Sunday Tribune* magazine, photographer Ernest Bachrach presents an elegant Marilyn, wearing jeweled earrings and with her hair closely curled against her head, creating a startling reversal of her typical glamour shots. She projects a much more commanding and restrained persona, dignified by a dress that fully covers her neck and shoulders and arms in a gauzy black silken fabric, below which she wears a black-and-white lacy dress. She is leaning back, sitting on a piece of furniture, her arms in back of her for support. She casts her eyes downward as though lost in thought.

Late May: Marilyn rents a luxurious suite with a pool and terraced garden at the Hotel Bel-Air for $750 a month. Publicity shots show her leaning against a wall in a swimsuit and talking on the phone, as well as leaning backward on her arms as she stands in the shallow end of a pool.

May 26: Filming of *Niagara* begins.

June: *Redbook* features Marilyn in "So Far To Go Alone." To Jim Henaghan she gives a detailed account of her period in the orphanage. She portrays herself as shy and scared and sitting alone at Christmas without presents or a parent to love her.

The cover of *Movie Pictorial* (Japan) portrays the Marilyn of *Clash by Night*, a very down-to-earth looking—if teasing—working girl.

Marilyn reads Mabel Elsworth Todd's *The Thinking Body*, Rilke's *Letters to a Young Poet*, and Khalil Gibran's *The Prophet*.

Rumors begin to spread that Marilyn is going to marry Joe DiMaggio.

June 1: Marilyn learns on her twenty-sixth birthday that she has been chosen for the role of Lorelei Lee in *Gentlemen Prefer Blondes*. She orders a steak at the Bel-Air Hotel and dines alone. Later that night, Jo DiMaggio phones her.

June 2: Filming of *Niagara* begins in Buffalo, with Marilyn playing Rose Loomis, the femme fatale murdered by her co-star, Joseph Cotten. Marilyn stays at the General Brock Hotel in Niagara Falls.

Joseph Cotten arranges a cocktail party for cast and crew in his hotel room. Marilyn arrives in a terry cloth robe and drinks orange juice. When a guest observes that "Sherry Netherlands Hotel, New York" is embroidered on the robe, Marilyn replies, "Oh, that. I thought I had stolen this robe, until I paid my bill." Cotten is amused with her and calls her a "pretty clown, beguiling and theatrically disarming." On this occasion she is charming.

On weekends Marilyn goes to New York City to be with DiMaggio.

June 3: Marilyn appears on the cover of *Look* and in "The Tragedy of West Point's Class of '50."

June 5: Photographer Jock Carroll has lunch with Marilyn Monroe to prepare for an article about her in *Weekend Magazine*, a Canadian publication. She tells him, "I can't eat fish. When I was a child, I couldn't even eat chicken. I would look at a leg, then I would imagine the whole animal and I just couldn't eat. I think I'll have a salad and maybe a sherbet." She talks about attending night classes in college and mentions reading Mabel Elsworth Todd's *The Thinking Body*. She cheerfully signs autographs for those interrupting her lunch, but confides to Carroll, "I look forward to the day when I'll be free of all this. And perhaps free of depression." Carroll's interview notes quote her as saying, "Henry [Hathaway] is very positive. He knows exactly the way he wants things. And everyone obeys."

June 8: Marilyn flies to New York for dinner with Joe DiMaggio at Toots Shor's and makes an appearance as well at the Stork Club. She sends a note to Sidney Skolsky about her trip.

June 10: Sydney Skolsky devotes his entire column to Marilyn's life and career.

June 12: The Pacific Telephone and Telegraph Company sues Marilyn for unpaid telephone bills totaling $168.

June 16: *Clash by Night* is released. Marilyn is making $500 a week. Marilyn's name appears above the title, suggesting her growing star power, even though she plays a supporting role as Peggy, a fish cannery worker. Her co-star, Keith Andes, who played her boyfriend, remembers Marilyn's appearances at a military base not far from Monterey, where the picture was filmed: "[Man] did she work those crowds. She'd pout that mouth and kind of rub up against them with her tits, and these guys would go crazy! It was great! What a doll."

June 18: *People Today* places Marilyn in a cheesecake pose in a two-piece swimsuit, climbing a ladder and thrusting her left leg out so that her derriere tilts upward.

June 26: Filming of *Niagara* is interrupted when Marilyn testifies in court against two men who are convicted of using her name and doctored image to sell nude and indecent pictures. She is photographed outside the courthouse and also inside of what looks like a judge's chambers.

June–July: Canadian photographer Jock Carroll shoots Marilyn standing beside the *Maid of the Mist* boat at Niagara Falls; talking to a sailor; seated by the railing near the falls, leaning forward exposing cleavage; and smoking in bed.

DiMaggio asks Marilyn to think about giving up her movie career.

With Keith Andes in *Clash by Night*

July: *Movieland* uses a Bruno Bernard photograph of a well-toned Marilyn, raising her arms as a kind of frame around her head, and wearing a satiny blue top and ribbon around her neck with a jeweled brooch. The caption reads, "I Dress for Men Says Marilyn Monroe." Inside, she speaks of running around the block to keep in shape and spending her nights on exercises with Lotte Goslar, the famous mime.

Marilyn in red-tinted hair leans forward, her cleavage barely visible through her red-and-black lacy negligee, on the cover of *See*.

J. W. Richardson shoots Marilyn in a series of glamour-girl poses in a low-cut dress for *Leatherneck*.

Marilyn rents a small house at 11121 Hilldale Avenue in West Hollywood for six months, but then changes her mind and returns to the Hotel Bel-Air.

July 14: Marilyn writes a check to the Hotel Bel-Air for $133.

July 23: *We're Not Married* is released. Marilyn is now making $750 a week. Marilyn plays "Mrs. Mississippi," who learns that owing to a judicial error, she is not married. David Wayne, her co-star, said, "Marilyn had no concept of camera technique. I'll never forget one scene we did . . . where I was standing opposite her, and the camera was shooting over my shoulder, with her key light coming over my shoulder as well. She kept backing away, and of course my shadow completely blacked her out, and so finally what I had to do was lean and hold onto the door so that she couldn't back across my arm and go into black. That's how naïve she was."

July 25: Marilyn writes a check to the Hotel Bel-Air for $1,000.

July 30: *Don't Bother to Knock* is released. Marilyn plays a deranged babysitter in this, her first major dramatic role.

August: *Screenland* publishes a color photograph of Monroe that is reminiscent of her character Angela Phinlay in *The Asphalt Jungle*, with the headline: "Marilyn doesn't believe in hiding things."

Incom Illustrata (Italy) puts a photograph of Marilyn on its cover. She is pictured examining an envelope, part of the evidence presented in court on June 26 in a case against two men engaged in a nude photo mail order business that used her name in its advertising.

August 3: Marilyn is photographed meeting Lassie (jumping at and eyeing Marilyn's cleavage) at a party hosted by musician Ray Anthony. Marilyn arrives by helicopter and is entertained by Mickey Rooney playing the drums. Ervin Drake and Jimmy Shirl composed a song simply titled "Marilyn" for the party.

August 5: Columnist Erskine Johnson publishes "Marilyn Inherits Harlow's Mantle" in the *Los Angeles Daily News*.

August 9: *Weekend Picture Magazine* (Canada) uses a photojournalist's picture of Marilyn, dressed in a red blouse and white skirt with matching red shoes, and sitting on a rock wall with crossed legs, smiling—a pose that was part of the publicity for *Niagara*.

Publicity still

August 11: *Time* publishes its first article about Marilyn, "Something for the Boys."

August 29: Columnist Dorothy Kilgallen mentions Robert Slatzer as a "dark horse in the Marilyn Monroe romance derby." It is likely that Kilgallen, Slatzer's friend, planted this item for him.

August 31: Marilyn appears in *Statement in Full*, her first radio drama, on *Hollywood Star Playhouse*.

September: The *Los Angeles Mirror* publishes three articles, "Wolves I Have Known," a collaboration between Marilyn and columnist Florabel Muir.

On its cover, *Focus* puts what looks like an illustration of golden-haired Marilyn, with only the scanty top of a two-piece golden swimsuit showing, next to the headline, "A Psychiatrist Looks at Marilyn Monroe."

I Confess displays on its cover a golden-blonde, bejeweled Marilyn in a black strapless evening dress.

September 1: United States Army photographs of Marilyn, used as part of a recruitment drive, are withdrawn because of complaints that she is showing too much cleavage.

Marilyn poses with Miss Alabama at a press conference.

September 2: World premiere of *Monkey Business* at Atlantic City's Stanley Theatre.

Marilyn is grand marshal of the Miss America pageant.

Marilyn is photographed visiting a children's hospital, where she autographs pictures of herself and plays with the children.

Marilyn is photographed in New York City at the Sherry-Netherland Hotel, posing for a Sunday newspaper magazine layout that shows her front and back in a white dress, looking by turns coy and surprised. Another shot shows her looking at herself on the cover of *Look*.

September 3: Marilyn returns to Los Angeles.

September 7: In the *Sunday Mirror* (magazine section) Marilyn is shown mirroring Marilyn, with the caption, "Who Needs Talent? Marilyn Monroe has other assets."

September 9: Marilyn appears on the cover of *Look* and inside in "Yea, Georgia Tech! Marilyn Monroe." She is wearing a cheerleader's uniform. She is quoted on her desire to learn, to read books, and to study art.

September 14: Marilyn attends an "I Am an American" party at the Hollywood Bowl.

September 15: Marilyn moves to 2393 Castilian Drive in Los Angeles, renting a house with DiMaggio.

Marilyn takes part in a charity baseball game at Gilmore Field in Los Angeles.

September 18: Robert Slatzer uses Dorothy Kilgallen's column to describe his first meeting with Marilyn in 1947, when they were both employed at Twentieth Century Fox. They were both fired and did not see one another again until her work on *Niagara* in June.

O'Henry's Full House is released. Marilyn plays a streetwalker in a brief cameo with Charles Laughton.

September 27: *Ciune Mundo* (Spain) presents a smiling, almost demure Marilyn in a publicity photograph for *As Young as You Feel*.

October: *Coronet* publishes "The Story Behind Marilyn Monroe."

Movieland puts Marilyn on the cover in a particularly provocative yellow swimsuit, with the headline "Why Women Hate Marilyn Monroe."

Movie Pix shows Marilyn in a typical glamour pose, with dreamy eyes and half-open mouth, with the headline "Marilyn Monroe the body is paid for."

Marilyn spends time in New York promoting *Monkey Business*.

October 1: Joe DiMaggio introduces Marilyn to his pal, the comedian Lou Costello.

Monkey Business is released. Marilyn plays Miss Laurel, a secretary who is so dumb she does not know the difference between "punctual" and "punctuation."

October 3: Lydia Lane interviews Marilyn for the *Oakland Tribune*. Marilyn describes her yoga sessions and other exercises intended to firm her body and lift her breasts.

Cine Revue (France) includes a shot from *Monkey Business* (Cary Grant in thick glasses looking at Marilyn's "acetates"—she has pulled up her skirt to show him the stockings he has invented).

October 4: This is the date Slatzer says he went with Monroe to Mexico for a marriage that Fox insisted be annulled. But, as biographer Michelle Morgan reports, Monroe was with Natasha Lytess that day on Wilshire Boulevard, "shopping as the cheques she wrote show, and nowhere near Mexico." Marilyn purchases Jax slacks, blouses, and other accessories.

Marilyn is on the cover of *The Photoplayer*, wearing a red, one-piece, strapless swimsuit with matching high-heeled red sandals, and holding on to a palm tree with her left hand while her right hand rests comfortably on her hip—a picture of elegant, sexy cheesecake in an ensemble from *Monkey Business*.

October 17: Marilyn signs a check for $300, payment for lessons with Natasha Lytess.

October 18: Marilyn records an episode of the weekly radio program, *The Charlie McCarthy Show*.

October 21: Marilyn does a costume fitting for *Gentlemen Prefer Blondes*.

October 26: Marilyn's appears on ventriloquist Edgar Bergan's radio show, announcing that she is engaged to his dummy, Charlie McCarthy.

October 31: Marilyn does more costume shots for *Gentlemen Prefer Blondes*.

November: Marilyn crashes the reception at Chasen's Restaurant for Fred Karger and Jane Wyman, extending her congratulations to the newly married couple.

On its cover, *Eye* features a sultry-looking Marilyn, wearing a two-piece swimsuit that looks identical to the one on the cover of the September 1952 issue of *Focus*.

Marilyn is on the cover of the British edition of *Photoplay*, reclining with her breasts apparently wrapped in fur.

November 1: Marilyn appears for color tests for *Gentlemen Prefer Blondes*. She is photographed at the piano with Jane Russell; again with Russell, conferring on the script; and meeting with Jack Cole, their choreographer.

November 8: Marilyn appears for hairdressing tests for *Gentlemen Prefer Blondes*.

November 12: Marilyn does costume shots for *Gentlemen Prefer Blondes*.

November 16: The *American Weekly* publishes "The Truth About Me," by Marilyn as told to Lisa Wilson. Marilyn explains that even though she had always refused to pose nude, she agreed to do so for Tom Kelley because she needed rent money. Kelley and his wife told her no one would recognize her. She still refused, until she received an eviction notice. She received fifty dollars for her work and celebrated with a quiet dinner at home.

November 24: Marilyn tells Aline Mosby, Hollywood correspondent for United Press, that she has not dated anyone but Joe DiMaggio since meeting him in March. Mosby quotes Lytess's claim that Marilyn will win an Academy Award. "I think tragic roles are her forte," Lytess declares. "There is a strangeness about her . . . an unreal quality." Marilyn tells the reporter, "I'm trying to find myself now, to be a good actress and good person. Sometimes I feel strong inside but I have to reach in and pull it up. You have to be strong inside way deep inside of you. It isn't easy. Nothing's easy as long as you go on living."

Thanksgiving: Marilyn takes Nico Minardos to dinner at Fred Karger's home.

Minardos parts company with Marilyn, not wishing to become "Mr. Monroe."

December: Elyda Nelson (James Dougherty's sister) publishes "The True Life Story of Marilyn Monroe" in *Modern Screen*.

Screen Fan angles Marilyn to the left in a diagonal shot that shows her in a black, strapless gown and jeweled earrings and necklace.

In a *Movie Fan* cover photograph by Bruno Bernard, Marilyn leans forward exposing her breasts in a low-cut red dress next to the headline "You've Gotta Stop Kickin' This Girl Around!"

Marilyn is making $1,000 a week.

December 3: Marilyn attends an auction of the manuscripts of Max Reinhardt, a famous German theater producer whose work had been introduced to Monroe by Natasha Lytess. Marilyn purchases 178 items for $1,335 and then sells them to Reinhardt's son, Gottfried, who in turn sells the material to a university.

Marilyn appears with a cigarette in her right hand, which she holds close to her mouth in a Rose Loomis/*Niagara* pose for the cover of *People Today*.

December 25: Marilyn attends a Fox studio party. Then she spends her first Christmas with Joe DiMaggio.

1953

Andre de Dienes photographs Marilyn eating an ice cream sundae.

Marilyn receives twenty-five thousand fan letters a week.

Walter Winchell interviews Marilyn on ABC radio.

Marilyn and Jane Russell perform at the Hollywood Bowl in a benefit for underprivileged children at St. Jude's Hospital in Memphis, Tennessee.

Marilyn is photographed standing on a library ladder with a book about Goya in her hands, and in a bookstore wearing long white gloves and reading an Avon paperback titled *Big Brokers*, "by the author of *The Amboy Dukes*."

Edward Clark photographs Marilyn on the set of *Gentlemen Prefer Blondes* rehearsing a dance number with Gwen Verdon.

Gene Trindl photographs Marilyn sitting in front of a mirror, smiling slightly. On her right is hairstylist Gladys Rasmussen, standing and working on Marilyn's hair, while Marilyn stretches out her left arm and touches photographer John Florea in an affectionate gesture.

Bert Reisfeld photographs Marilyn in a swimsuit and high-heeled sandals holding on to a hanging rope while suspending herself in the air. Another shot puts her on a stairway beside tall, lighted fire-crackers with her fingers in her ears.

In *Me Naiset* (Finland), Andre de Dienes publishes a color cover photograph of Marilyn, wearing her reddish-brown hair tied back with a head scarf, and dressed in a pink sweater and black-and-white checked slacks. She is smiling and raises her left arm to the branch of a pine tree. He also shoots Marilyn at the Hotel Bel-Air in Beverly Hills seemingly in mid-dance; standing on an ottoman, script in hand and a pencil in her mouth with her back reflected in a mirror; eating dessert at an outdoor café; resting against a tree looking exhausted; and in black-and-white close-ups that show her looking distraught, perhaps even fearful.

Alfred Eisenstaedt photographs himself with Marilyn, with his right arm around her neck and posing in a rather aggressive stance. Her arms are swung back behind her head and she wears a challenging yet playful expression that has her bringing her hands to the sides of her head in mock surprise.

Harold Lloyd takes color shots of Marilyn in a red swimsuit and high-heeled sandals, walking the length of a swimming pool and lounging poolside.

Ben Ross photographs Marilyn in a black blouse and striped pants, looking especially meditative, perhaps even sad.

Marilyn Monroe Pin-ups is published, its contents devoted exclu-sively to photographs of her.

That Girl Marilyn! by Jane Russell is a magazine devoted exclusively to Monroe.

Motion Picture and Television features a headshot of Marilyn, smiling with a white fur around her shoulders, and the headline "Wolves I Have Known." Inside she tells the story of a policeman who followed her home and tried to enter her room. She escaped and he was later apprehended.

For new subscribers, *Photoplay* includes a photograph of Marilyn in a silvery garment that just barely registers the impression of her nipples. The caption reads: "Marilyn Monroe's Beauty Secrets."

Screen Annual publishes a cover of Marilyn looking very much like a *Playboy* bunny. The back cover features a calendar with Marilyn's picture on it.

Joe Franklin and Laurie Palmer publish *The Marilyn Monroe Story*.

January: Marilyn records George Gershwin's "Do It Again." She studies voice with Phil Moore and Hal Schaefer.

Laff publishes a cover shot of Marilyn at the beach in a very red two-piece swimsuit, with her hands trailing backward in the sand.

Marilyn appears on the cover of *NAS* (Naval Air Station) magazine, which honors her election as "Miss NAS."

Filmland features a shot of a glowing Marilyn, dressed in a very low-cut halter top, looking up with a wide-open smile next to the headline "Marilyn Monroe Writes her Sensational Success Story."

John Florea photographs Marilyn for *Life*. She is wearing in a one-piece, strapless bathing suit and lying on what looks like animal fur, with her head tilted toward the camera and one of her fingers just barely touching her mouth.

Bert Reisfield takes novelty shots of Marilyn climbing a rope, Marilyn under an umbrella, and Marilyn next to a huge firecracker bearing a July 4 sign.

January 1: Marilyn joins the CinemaScope party at the Coconut Grove in the Ambassador Hotel, along with Donald O'Connor (who will co-star with her in *There's No Business Like Show Business*), Cole Porter (photographed seated next to her), and Joe DiMaggio (photographed in a sedan with Marilyn).

January 2: Marilyn has more costume fittings for *Gentlemen Prefer Blondes*, directed by Howard Hawks. She models a jewel-encrusted

Marilyn in Niagara

outfit, with a tiara, huge choker necklace, bands of diamonds on
her arms, wrists, and waist, and a tapering bikini-like belt of jewels
covering her pubic area. This costume was never worn in the film
owing to public protests over Marilyn's public exposure of herself

and over her provocative performance in *Niagara*. Designer Billy Travilla later created the pink and much more modest silky gown used in "Diamonds Are a Girl's Best Friend," which actually enhances Marilyn's appeal as both an innocent and a sexy blonde.

January 6: Max Reinhardt's son purchases his father's collection from Marilyn, who wishes it to become available to drama students.

January 23: *Niagara* is released, making Marilyn a star. She plays Rose Loomis, a femme fatale. The picture features her 116-foot walk to the falls.

January 23–29: Marilyn appears on the cover of *TV Guide*.

January 26: The Independent Theater Owners of Arkansas confer on Marilyn the "State's Most Popular Movie Actress" award.

January 29: A buxom Marilyn, arching her back so that her breasts are especially prominent, appears in a gold dress on the cover of the *Australasian Post*.

February: Marilyn is named "The Most Advertised Girl in the World" by Advertising Association of the West.

John Florea's teasing photograph of Marilyn, bending her backside closer to a roaring fireplace in a low-cut pajama-like garment, makes the cover of *Eye*.

Marilyn makes her first appearance on a *Photoplay* cover in Gene Kornman's photograph, which emphasizes her rather hooded expression reminiscent of a femme fatale. Cropped to show only her head and neck, the emphasis on her body and her carnality seems less important than her attitude, as reflected in the magazine's headline: "Is Hollywood Carrying Sex Too Far?"

February 2: *Time* features Marilyn in "Go Easy."

February 6: Marilyn chooses Roger L. Provost, an eighteen-year-old seaman aboard the USS *Taconic*, as "The Boy with Whom She Would Most Like To Be Cast Adrift."

February 9: Gladys enters Rockhaven Sanitarium. Marilyn pays $250 a month to support her mother.

Marilyn is honored as "A Rising Star" at the Photoplay Awards Dinner at the Crystal Room of the Beverly Hills Hotel. Sidney Skolsky accompanies her after Joe DiMaggio refuses to do so. Her gold lamé dress causes a sensation. Columnist Florabel Muir writes that the dress seems painted onto Marilyn's body and is so striking (photographs of it are often reproduced) that Joan Crawford and Lana Turner were hardly noticed at the event.

February 12: Marilyn meets with agent Charles Feldman but does not sign a contract with him. He continues to promote her in the hopes that she will sign on with him for future projects.

February 14: Marilyn is photographed with Sidney Skolsky attending the wedding of gossip columnist Sheilah Graham, who appears in several two-shots with Marilyn.

February 24: Marilyn appears on the Martin and Lewis Show performing a skit, "So Who Needs Friends."

February 27: *Cine Revue* (France) features Marilyn and Jane Russell dressed like bridesmaids in a publicity shot for *Gentlemen Prefer Blondes*.

March: James Dougherty publishes "Marilyn Monroe Was My Wife" in *Photoplay*.

Marilyn is shown on the cover of *Follie!* wearing a red-and-white hairband and a two-piece red and yellow swimsuit, shaded by a beach umbrella.

Show shows Marilyn in a fetching pose arrayed on a cushion, one of her shoulder straps falling down her left arm. The feature article reports that her salary has been raised from $750 a week to $2,500.

Redbook puts Marilyn on its cover, announcing its fourteenth annual movie awards.

March 1: Marilyn sends a check to Grace Goddard for $851.04 to pay for Gladys's care.

March 3: Associated Press columnist Bob Thomas reports Joan Crawford's comments on Monroe's appearance at a *Photoplay* awards dinner: "It was like a burlesque show. Someone should make her see the light; she should be told that the public likes provocative personalities but it also likes to know that underneath it all the actresses are ladies." Marilyn replies via Louella Parsons's column in the *Herald Examiner*: "What hurts me more is what Miss Crawford said, is that I have always admired her to be such a wonderful mother—to have adopted 4 children and have given them a family. I'm well-placed to know what it means not to have a house when you're a child."

March 4: Marilyn in white fur and opera gloves attends the premiere of the Fox musical *Call Me Madam*, starring Ethel Merman. Ken Murray interviews Marilyn in front of the theater. "Tell the audience how we met," he says to her. "Once you *almost* gave me a job," she said, without any apparent rancor.

March 6: Marilyn completes work on *Gentlemen Prefer Blondes*. She is now making $1,250 a week. Jane Russell tells Richard Buskin, "I used to stop by her dressing room and say, 'Come on, it's time to be there,' and she'd get up and come with me. I think if there had been someone to do that on a lot of other films she would never have been late. She was just scared." By all accounts Marilyn worked hard and remained focused on her role, especially during the shooting of "Diamonds Are a Girl's Best Friend."

During the making of the film, according to biographer Anthony Summers, Marilyn is reported to have affairs with Billy Travilla, her dress designer, and Edward G. Robinson Jr., a "pill freak" who introduces her to drugs such as Benzedrine and other barbiturates.

March 9: Filming of *How to Marry a Millionaire* begins.

March 18: Marilyn moves to an apartment on 882 North Doheny Drive in Beverly Hills. Jane Russell and interior designer Thomas Lane help Marilyn decorate. She gets her piano out of storage and has it painted white.

Spring: Marilyn studies with Lotte Goslar, a famous mime, after watching Goslar's production of an Anton Chekhov play.

Marilyn meets actor John Gilmore, who later will write one of the better memoirs about her. He calls her "shadowed and strange; dif-

Marilyn with Jane Russell in *Gentlemen Prefer Blondes*

fident yet vivacious, determined while fearful. She was intense and funny at the same time, and was very, very far from being 'dumb.'"

April: *Imagenes* (Spain) publishes a close-up of Marilyn reclining on a large blue pillow, her brilliantly blonde hair flowing up and out of the frame. Shot from the left and on the diagonal, her eyes look out to the right as if at something also outside the frame.

Movie Pix's cover shows Marilyn in Ernest Bachrach's photograph in a red-and-white lacy negligee.

In *Movieland*, Marilyn is pictured sitting in a silky blue skirt with her hands on her thighs. The spread of her lower body forms a triangle that dominates the lower half of the cover. She is wearing a lacy black negligee top, with gauzy material enveloping her arms. To the side of her face, with its determined expression, is the headline "How Marilyn Changed Hollywood." It is a rare, early tribute to her that emphasizes her power. Inside, Louis Calhern, who in *The Asphalt Jungle* played the lawyer whose mistress (played by Marilyn) betrays him, is quoted saying, "We all thought she was dumb when she made *Asphalt Jungle*, and when I saw her in *We're Not Married*, her façade was one of utter stupidity, but I sensed that she was no jerk. Nobody was putting anything over on her."

April 7: With Betty Grable, Marilyn attends a birthday party for columnist Walter Winchell.

Marilyn signs a contract with Famous Artists Agency.

April 11: Marilyn attends costume fittings for *River of No Return*.

April 13: Jean Negulesco, director of *How to Marry a Millionaire*, is upset with Natasha Lytess, to whom Marilyn defers during several takes, and bans the acting coach from the set.

April 14: Marilyn does not show up for work, complaining of bronchitis. Charles Feldman, her agent, issues a memo saying Marilyn cannot do the picture without Lytess, who is hired back and given a higher salary. Lauren Bacall later commented, "I couldn't dislike Marilyn. She had no meanness in her—no bitchery. She just had to concentrate on herself and the people who were there only for her."

Marilyn is hospitalized and treated for endometriosis.

April 16: Andre de Dienes photographs Marilyn on the side of a rock face, in a green sweater and golden yellow slacks. It is a companion piece to the same pose published on the cover of *Parade* (February 17, 1947), except that this shot is taken from Marilyn's right side.

April 18: *Tempo* (Italy) features a John Engstead color photograph of Marilyn in her Miss Caswell mode from *All About Eve*. Her genial smile makes her look less predatory than the character she plays in the film.

End of April: Marilyn completes work on *How to Marry a Millionaire*.

May: Marilyn makes the cover of *Cosmopolitan*.

Charles Feldman, Joe DiMaggio, and Lloyd Wright (Marilyn's new attorney) all advise her on renegotiating her Fox contract. Her current salary of $1,250 is not commensurate with her value to the studio.

Marilyn is photographed at home writing in a notebook.

A 1949 photograph by Laszlo Willinger, a close-up of an open-mouthed Marilyn, showing only her face and the top of her swimsuit, appears on the cover of *I Confess*.

Pic shows Marilyn in a one-piece black swimsuit with straps tied around her neck and the headline "In DiMaggio's Shoes."

The *American News* publishes an Andre de Dienes photograph of Marilyn purchasing a book at Walter Martindale's Book Shop in Beverly Hills.

May 11: Marilyn reaches her salary cap of $1,500 a week.

May 20: Marilyn visits the Louella Parsons radio show.

May 25: "Marilyn Takes Over as Lorelei" is published in *Life*.

Settimo Giorno (Italy) shows a seductive Marilyn, bent forward—a publicity shot for *Gentlemen Prefer Blondes*.

June: Marilyn appears on the cover of *Regal* (France) in a bikini, exposing a lot of cleavage in a typical cheesecake pose photographed by Laszlo Willinger.

On the cover of *Screen* (Japan), Marilyn reclines to the left, with hooded eyes and a suggestive leer on her seductive red lips. The picture looks painted rather than photographed, as if made for a lobby card.

Marilyn, photographed by Ernest Bachrach, is sultriness personified, enveloped in black lace that emphasizes her cleavage on the cover of *Cinelandia* (Brazil).

On the cover of *Screen Fan*, Marilyn appears in one of her costumes from *Gentlemen Prefer Blondes*, posing with that fey, wondering look associated with Lorelei Lee. The article inside quotes Natasha Lytess calling Marilyn "just a lost child," and Henry Hathaway announcing that she is the "best natural actress and greatest natural talent I ever directed."

RCA sells seventy-five thousand recordings of "I'm Gonna File My Claim," one of Marilyn's songs in *River of No Return*.

June 1: Marilyn celebrates her twenty-seventh birthday with Grace Goddard. Marilyn calls Gladys at the Rockhaven sanitarium. "I don't remember giving birth to you," Gladys tells her daughter.

June 6: Marilyn attends costume fittings for *River of No Return*.

June 7: A glamorous two-shot of Marilyn and Richard Widmark, a publicity still for *Don't Bother to Knock*, is on the cover of *La Domenica Della Donna* (Italy).

June 8: Marilyn attends still more costume fittings for *River of No Return*.

June 9: Grace helps Marilyn sort through material sent to her from her fans.

June 13: A Fox publicity man visits Marilyn and Grace and has Marilyn sign photographs and personal notes to important people.

June 17: Marilyn is photographed with Ronald and Nancy Reagan at Charles Coburn's birthday party at the Beverly Hills Hotel, and then is interviewed by Earl Wilson.

June 19: On the cover of *Motor World*, Marilyn sits sort of side-saddle on the left fender of a Singer sports car, wearing her dress from *How to Marry a Millionaire*.

June 26: Marilyn places her hands and feet in cement outside Grauman's Chinese Theatre at 6774 Hollywood Boulevard. Jim Dougherty, now a Los Angeles policeman, is assigned to the detail holding back crowds outside the theater. DiMaggio does not attend the event, but joins Marilyn's party at Chasen's restaurant.

June 27: *Collier's* publishes "Gentlemen Prefer Monroe."

June 30: Marilyn appears on the cover of *Look* and inside in "Monroe, Bacall, and Grable: Take on a New Dimension."

July: The Jewelry Academy names Marilyn "The Best Friend a Diamond Ever Had."

Marilyn appears in a yellow bikini on the cover of *Photo*.

Estudio (Portugal) uses a publicity shot from 1950, neither femme fatale nor dumb blonde, but appearing rather more sophisticated in a low-cut gown, reclining so as to emphasize her beautiful neck, flowing blonde hair, and the wistful expression on her face, tilted upward.

The color cover of *Motion Picture Times* (Japan) uses a John Engstead publicity still from *All About Eve*, cropped so as to show only Marilyn's face and upper body. Her breasts are obscured by her right hand, which is gripping her upper left arm. It is a taunting, slightly smug pose.

July 4: Grace writes to Berniece about helping Marilyn go through ten cartons of fan mail.

July 8: Marilyn receives the "Best Friend a Diamond Ever Had" award from the Jewelry Academy.

July 10: Marilyn attends Danny Thomas's gala for St. Jude's Hospital in Memphis, Tennessee, which is held at the Hollywood Bowl and features Jane Russell, Robert Mitchum, and Danny Kaye.

July 11: Marilyn goes shopping at Beverly Silks and Woolens.

July 25: Marilyn flies to Canada for work on *River of No Return*. She is photographed arm-in-arm with two Canadian Mounties.

July 28: Marilyn begins work on *River of No Return*. She stays at the Banff Springs Hotel in the Canadian Rockies.

July 31: *Gentlemen Prefer Blondes* is released. Marilyn plays a gold digger, Lorelei Lee.

August: Marilyn appears in a yellow bikini on the cover of *Eye*.

The cover of *Theme* (a magazine devoted to music and records) puts Marilyn, Jane Russell, and Dan Dailey on the cover, with all three wearing stovepipe hats.

August 5: Charles Feldman advances $5,000 to purchase the screenplay, *Horns of the Devil*.

August 8: Marilyn refuses to meet with director Otto Preminger after he bars Natasha Lytess from the set of *River of No Return*. Marilyn asks Charles Feldman to work on reinstating her drama coach. Feldman meets with Darryl Zanuck. For the first time, Zanuck sides with Marilyn, and Preminger is forced to accept Lytess's return to the set.

August 15: *Picture Post* (England) features a jolly scene with Charles Coburn (wearing a monocle) sitting in an armchair and flanked on either side by Jane Russell and Marilyn in a publicity shot for *Gentlemen Prefer Blondes*.

August 20: Marilyn sprains her knee on location when she slips on a pier, although in her autobiography Shelley Winters claims Marilyn faked the accident as a way of enlisting sympathy from an otherwise obdurate director. But producer Stanley Rubin insisted Marilyn slipped on a rock and injured herself, and that no time was lost in production since they were able to shoot around her.

Joe DiMaggio arrives to lend his support and is photographed in an intimate shot leaning into Marilyn as they sit in front of a window. Several shots show him animated and unusually relaxed. He has been hunting and fishing and looks comfortable in his outdoor clothing. Marilyn is photographed in a leg cast, with golf club in hand addressing the ball. DiMaggio evidently instructed her in the basics of the game.

End of August: Shooting of *River of No Return* ends.

September: During a party at Gene Kelly's house, Marilyn meets photographer Milton Greene, on assignment for *Look* magazine, for the first time.

Stag uses for its cover what looks like a publicity photograph shot around the time Marilyn was working on *Don't Bother to Knock*.

Movie World puts a close-up headshot of Marilyn on its cover with the headline "Is Marilyn More Than SEXY?" According to *Marilyn Monroe: Cover to Cover*, she was receiving a hundred requests a week for public appearances.

September 1: Marilyn flies from the Banff set to Los Angeles to complete work on *River of No Return* at the Fox studios.

DiMaggio spends time with Marilyn at her apartment at 882 North Doheny Drive.

September 10: Marilyn rehearses for her appearance on *The Jack Benny Show*. Natasha Lytess is in attendance, as is Whitey Snyder, who does her makeup, and Gladys Rasmussen, who does Marilyn's hair.

September 13: Marilyn appears on *The Jack Benny Show* and accepts a new black Cadillac convertible as her fee, since her Fox contract forbids her to earn money from performances outside the studio. She performs in a sketch, "Honolulu Trip," and sings "Bye, Bye, Baby" from *Gentlemen Prefer Blondes*.

Marilyn attends a benefit at the Hollywood Bowl for St. Jude's Children's Hospital.

September 28: Grace Goddard, dying of liver cancer, takes a Nembutal overdose and commits suicide, upsetting Marilyn.

October: Marilyn signs a recording contract with RCA Records.

Marilyn is photographed with columnist Walter Winchell at Ciro's for a Damon Runyon Cancer Fund benefit. Among the guests are Sheilah Graham, Louella Parsons, Darryl Zanuck, and Joe Schenck.

On the cover of *Movieland*, Marilyn sits on the edge of a high stool, wearing a two-piece swimsuit and covered in a red gauzy material she flings upward with both arms. "What Women Can Learn from Marilyn Monroe," is the headline in this issue, which also quotes her saying, "As long as there is a boy in Korea who wants a pinup of me, I'll go on posing for cheesecake."

Posing for the cover of *Movie Stars Parade* in jeweled earrings and necklace, Marilyn smiles more broadly and openly than usual in this otherwise typical glamour shot. The magazine reports she is anemic and under a doctor's care.

In *Eiga No Tomo* (Japan) Marilyn is shown on the cover in a John Florea photograph, her head thrown back with an open-mouthed smile and half-closed eyes, showing off a good bit of her breasts, which are enveloped by a white fur stole.

Marilyn's interview with Sidney Skolsky is published in *Motion Picture*. The feature includes Bob Beerman's photographs of Marilyn, fully made up, with a book about Goya in hand as she stands by bookshelves; combing her hair in bed, lying under the covers in a sultry pose; smiling provocatively as she sits at a piano, her hands on the keys; and in a halter top dress, pen in her right hand, seated at a round table, with a piece of paper in her left hand, apparently answering correspondence.

Milton Greene shoots several pictures for *Look*, including the two of them on a bale of hay, and a stunning black-and-white shot of Marilyn kneeling, dressed in a one-piece sweater dress, split open at the middle in one long vertical line intersected by the fingers of her right hand, suggesting a more vulnerable, complex woman. These photographs are his proof that he can portray her far more subtly than her earlier photographs and films have done.

Marilyn begins to pull away from Natasha Lytess, whose demands on Marilyn for both money and attention prove to be burdensome and an irritant to Joe DiMaggio.

October 1: Marilyn arranges Grace's funeral. "I feel an anchor is gone," she tells her half-sister, Berniece.

October 10: Marilyn accompanies Joe DiMaggio to meet his family in San Francisco. They stay in Joe's house on Beach Street. She learns how to make his favorite spaghetti sauce.

October 11: Joe and Marilyn attend a baseball game, and then she appears at the premiere of *The 5,000 Fingers of Dr. T* starring Tommy Rettig (he played Robert Mitchum's son in *River of No Return*).

October 16: *Collier's* publishes "Marilyn on the Rocks."

October 21: *A Cena Muda* (Brazil) uses one of Frank Powolny's studio portraits. Marilyn is posed lying back on a large, velvet-like green pillow, wearing a dark red dress and jeweled earrings and necklace. She is framed so that her head and the upper part of her body are shot on the diagonal tilting left, giving the picture a superior dynamic.

October 29: *How to Marry a Millionaire* premiers in New York City.

October 30: Marilyn interviews Inez Melson for a position as her business manager. Marilyn makes Inez a cup of tea and hires her on the spot. Inez said, "I loved her from the moment I met her. She seemed like a fluffy toy."

November: Marilyn appears on the cover of *See* in a classic gold lamé gown in Frank Powolny's photograph.

The cover of *Cinelandia* (Brazil) uses an Earl Theisen photograph from the set of *How to Marry a Millionaire*, featuring a fully-dressed Lauren Bacall center stage, flanked by Betty Grable on the left—

How to Marry a Millionaire with Betty Grable and Lauren Bacall

showing off her famous legs in a blouse and short shorts—and Marilyn on the right in a one piece red swimsuit, leaning toward Bacall.

Screen Life's cover pictures Marilyn in a one-piece bathing suit holding out a beach umbrella and carries the headline "You'll Never Guess Marilyn Monroe's Secret Beauty Formula."

On the cover of *TV Starland*, Marilyn and columnist Walter Winchell are shown dancing. The photograph was taken at a party given in Winchell's honor by the Los Angeles Press Club at Ciro's, a popular Hollywood nightclub.

Motion Picture & Television Magazine puts Marilyn, dressed in a gold, strapless, one-piece swimsuit, in the center of its cover, posing with her arms brought straight up and bent at the elbow toward the back of her head, smiling. The headline reads, "Marilyn Monroe— Loveable Fake."

November 4: Los Angeles premiere of *How to Marry a Millionaire* is attended by Marilyn, Lauren Bacall, Humphrey Bogart, screenwriter Nunnally Johnson, and his wife. Joe DiMaggio does not join the group. Marilyn wears a strapless, flesh-colored crepe de Chine gown embroidered with sequins and with a long white velvet train. To this dress, previously worn on *The Jack Benny Show*, she adds a white fox fur stole and muff, long white gloves, and assorted jewelry, including diamond earrings borrowed from Fox. She joins Bacall and Bogart, who jokes with her, saying she should tell the press, "You came to see how I loused up the picture." In this classic Hollywood scene, searchlights pierce the night sky, five blocks of traffic has to be re-routed, and newsreel cameras record the arrival of stars and Hollywood notables such as Cecil B. DeMille, Mitzi Gaynor, Debbie Reynolds, Shelley Winters, Clifton Webb, Robert Mitchum, and Rock Hudson. "This is just about the happiest night of my life," Marilyn says to the radio microphones, as fans call out to her. She links arms with Bacall, Bogart, and Nunnally Johnson. Marilyn walks along the barricade and signs photographs. Photographer Earl Leaf describes the event in the April issue of *Movie Spotlight*: "On some feminine faces you could see a look of green envy, or something that passed for supercilious contempt, but the collective face that turned toward Marilyn Monroe was tinged more with swoonery than snobbery."

Marilyn is photographed with director John Negulesco at his party.

November 6: *Hjemmet* (Denmark) presents Marilyn in her flaming *Niagara* dress, leaning against the rock wall that separates her from the falls, but she is smiling without the menacing look she could muster as Rose Loomis.

November 14: Marilyn meets King Paul and Queen Fredericka of Greece at the Fox Studios.

November 17: Marilyn appears on the cover of *Look* and in "Marilyn Monroe: Photographs."

Marilyn works on retakes for *River of No Return*.

November 21: DiMaggio meets with Lloyd Wright, Marilyn's attorney, about renegotiating her contract with Fox. DiMaggio asks Wright to convey to Fox her position, a series of demands for script and director approval, for example, that would put her in charge of her own career.

November 23: *Voir* (France) shows a rear-end view of Marilyn in blouse and skirt, looking back fetchingly, as if beckoning the viewer to follow her.

Thanksgiving: Marilyn spends the holiday in San Francisco with DiMaggio and his family.

November 30: *Time* features Marilyn in "Portrait."

December: The first issue of *Playboy* appears, with Marilyn as the centerfold. On the cover is a September 1952 shot of Marilyn riding in a convertible as the grand marshal of the Miss America pageant.

Photoplay publishes one of the most popular three-quarter profile poses of the dreamy-eyed Marilyn, with half-open mouth, adorned with a silver-black necklace and clothed in white fur.

Marilyn attends the "Toys for Tots Campaign" sponsored by the United States Marine Corps. She is photographed with two marines in their dress uniforms.

Marilyn begins working with talk show host Joe Franklin on an autobiography, but then halts the project because of negotiations with Ben Hecht, who will help to write her story. Franklin continues to work on the book as a biography.

December 1: Marilyn decides to refuse all Fox assignments until she has a new contract.

December 2: Marilyn, dressed in a one-piece swimsuit, hugs a white Greek column on the cover of *People Today* alongside the caption "Marilyn Monroe: More 'n' More."

December 4: Marilyn returns to Los Angeles and is photographed at a charity event with Jack Benny and Bob Hope.

December 5: Marilyn answers the phone and is told she must report to the studio to begin work on *The Girl in Pink Tights*. She manages to get off the phone without agreeing to show up for work. But Natasha Lytess calls, urging Marilyn (at Darryl Zanuck's request) to return to work. Marilyn regards Lytess's call as a betrayal.

December 7: At Zanuck's insistence, a producer calls Marilyn again, relaying the studio head's message that the studio had made her a star, and that *Pink Tights* had been written expressly for her. This time Marilyn adamantly refuses to report for work.

December 10: Zanuck orders Marilyn to come to the studio to complete work on a song for *River of No Return*. Marilyn sends him word that she cannot come in.

December 11: More calls issue from the studio, requesting Marilyn come in for retakes of *River of No Return*. She returns to work hoping to avoid an encounter with Zanuck and continues to work on the picture until December 23.

December 12–13: Charles Feldman drafts a document that includes Marilyn's three key demands: more money; fewer films; and approval of director, script, and cinematographer.

December 13: Marilyn and Joe attend a party at Bob Hope's house.

December 15: Marilyn again refuses to report for work on *The Girl in Pink Tights*.

December 17: The role of Vicky is created for Marilyn in the script for *There's No Business Like Show Business*, and she is assigned to do the "Heat Wave" number.

December 23: Marilyn flies to San Francisco for a period of rest at the DiMaggio family home on Beach Street.

December 24: Marilyn attends the DiMaggio Christmas Eve dinner.

1954

Marilyn uses the name Norma Baker when she checks into a Westwood motel.

Marilyn is spotted at the Crescendo Club dancing with Jacques Sernas, a European film action hero under contract to Warner Brothers.

Marilyn discovers that she does not have a suitable passport picture, and she rushes out with Joe DiMaggio to have one taken at a coin-operated arcade.

Marilyn is photographed with composer Irving Berlin on the set of *There's No Business Like Show Business*.

The cover of *Quick* features Marilyn in a John Florea photograph, placed against a red background of stars, wearing an aqua-blue evening gown and beckoning the viewer to her with the same hand gesture used in publicity photographs for *Gentlemen Prefer Blondes*.

January: Marilyn appears on the cover of the pocket-sized *Prevue* in a Gene Kornman photograph showing her only from the neck up, with a kind of wondering, even lost look that would not be out of place in *Don't Bother to Knock*.

3-D Hollywood Pin-Ups features a side view of Marilyn, dressed in a one-piece blue swimsuit, with her right arm aligned across her torso and hand on her upper thigh, while her left hand is drawn back to her head as she smiles seductively at the camera.

Now shows Marilyn in a dress similar to the one she wore in *The Seven Year Itch*. She is seated at a table with Joe DiMaggio, who appears uncharacteristically relaxed and open to the camera, with a slight smirk on his face and eyes that seem to express his amusement.

January 1: Marilyn receives the "Award of Achievement" from the *Motion Picture Herald* as one of the top ten moneymaking stars of 1953.

January 2: Marilyn has her first meeting with Ben Hecht to discuss her autobiography.

January 4: When Marilyn does not show up for the first day of filming, she is suspended without pay for refusing to work on *Pink Tights*. Marilyn and Joe cancel plans to get married at the Hotel El Rancho in Las Vegas.

January 11: Charles Feldman informs Marilyn that she is facing a month or more of suspension while he negotiates with Fox.

January 12: At a birthday party for Joe DiMaggio's brother Tom, Marilyn accepts Joe's marriage proposal.

January 14: At 1:46 p.m. Marilyn marries Joe DiMaggio. She gives Harry Brand, publicity director at Fox, only one hour's notice, but one hundred reporters still manage to make it to the lobby and corridor of San Francisco's Town Hall, where the marriage takes place. Only a few of Joe's friends and family are present. Marilyn brings no guests to the three-minute ceremony. Photographs show Marilyn wearing a dark brown woolen suit with an ermine collar, holding three orchids in her hand. By the time the ceremony ends, an estimated two hundred photographers and three hundred fans crowd around Joe and Marilyn as the couple jumps into Joe's night blue Cadillac. The couple spends their wedding night at the Hot Springs Hotel in Paso Robles, California.

January 15–16: Marilyn and Joe spend the first two days of their honeymoon at the Clifton Motel in Paso Robles. DiMaggio pays $6.50 a night for a room with a television.

Marilyn's lawyer, Lloyd Wright, tells her the studio is going to lift her suspension.

January 16: Fox lifts Marilyn's suspension.

January 16–24: Marilyn and Joe spend the next ten days outside Palm Springs, in a house owned by her lawyer, Lloyd Wright.

January 17: *Epoca* (Italy) publishes John Florea's cover shot of Marilyn leaning out of the back seat of a car, dressed in her dance-hall girl outfit from *River of No Return*.

January 20: Marilyn fails to return to the studio on the day Fox has stipulated.

January 24: Marilyn and Joe return to Los Angeles, and she finds a script of *The Girl in Pink Tights* that has been sent to her Doheny Drive apartment.

January 25: *Life* publishes "Merger of Two Worlds."

Newsweek publishes "Mr. And Mrs. Joe DiMaggio."

Time publishes "Storybook Romance."

Marilyn's lawyer tells the press that she has read the *Pink Tights* script and rejects it.

January 26: The studio suspends Marilyn again.

January 28: Marilyn arrives in San Francisco the day before embarking for Japan, where DiMaggio has been invited to make appearances. She breaks her thumb, although a DiMaggio relative said Joe was responsible for her injury. He seems to have been taken by surprise when she came up behind him, and he instinctively grabbed her hand and bent back her thumb.

Dr. Clifton Bennett vaccinates Marilyn for her trip.

January 29: At the San Francisco airport on the way to Honolulu, Marilyn, her thumb in a splint, tells the press she bumped it.

January–February: *Rosso E Nero* (Italy) uses for its cover a publicity still from *Love Happy* showing Marilyn, golden haired and in a yellow-gold dress, sitting atop a red velvet-covered pedestal, flexing her right leg, with her hands clasped just under her knee.

Se (Sweden) features a cover shot of Marilyn, dressed in the high collar Joe DiMaggio preferred and seated next to him. His hand on her arm suggests a proprietary interest.

February: *Screen Stars, The Magazine for Young Moderns*, features Gene Kornman's photograph of Marilyn smiling and looking straight ahead, with her body cropped at her bustline, so that her breasts flare out to the right and left.

Marilyn appears on the cover of *Movieland*, leaning back on a red backdrop in the jewel-encrusted dress she also wore for *Mundo Uruguayo* (November 5, 1953). She speaks of her responsibility as a star, mentioning the letters from servicemen and her public appearances, which have "opened up a new world."

Seduction (Italy) exploits an especially self-absorbed image of Marilyn in her dreamy, sexy role as Rose Loomis in *Niagara*, although this is not a film still, but a publicity shot by Bruno Bernard.

Marilyn, her hands griping a necklace with a single diamond, projects a wide open smile verging on laughter for the cover of *Movie Time*.

Picture Life has Marilyn holding out the red top of her bathing dress and smiling, with the caption "Marilyn Monroe's 'Cheaters.'"

February 1: Marilyn and Joe fly from San Francisco to Honolulu, a stop on the way to Japan, where he is supposed to appear at the beginning of the baseball season.

February 2: Marilyn and Joe arrive in Japan. Two hundred policeman form an escort for her triumphal progress to the Imperial Hotel (designed by Frank Lloyd Wright), where she is photographed on a balcony, her right arm raised in a salute to her fans.

February 3: DiMaggio looks happy in the photographs taken at Marilyn's press conference, but is rumored to be upset at all the attention his wife attracts.

February 4–15: The couple visits holy places, Osaka, Mount Fuji, Yokohama, and the Izu Peninsula. Marilyn looks especially comfortable among a group of women dressed in traditional Japanese clothing. In some shots she wears a hat and a modestly cut suit.

In Korea to entertain the troops

Marilyn accepts the Japanese emperor's gift of a natural pearl necklace.

General John E. Hull invites Marilyn to entertain American troops in Korea. A disturbed DiMaggio opposes the invitation, but Marilyn accepts it.

Marilyn writes photographer Bruno Bernard from Japan: "I'm so happy and in love. . . . I've decided for sure that it'll be better if I only make one or two more films after I shoot *There's No Business Like Show Business* and then retire to the simple good life of a housewife and, hopefully, mother. Joe wants a big family. He was real surprised when we were met at the airport by such gigantic crowds and press. He said he never saw so much excitement, not even when the Yankees won the World Series."

February 5: Marilyn visits the Tokyo Army Hospital.

February 7: At Tokyo Army Hospital Marilyn signs autographs and poses for photographs. One soldier remembers that she "did a little skip—a kind of dance—with quick motions and a little song and came down the line to greet us." When Marilyn linked arms with the soldier, he asked about DiMaggio: "She told me he was playing baseball and seemed disgusted by that. I got the feeling she felt he should have been up there with her."

February 8: Marilyn and Joe visit Fukuoka, Japan's oldest city, and tour an ancient castle. She also visits the U.S. base at Gannosu.

February 9: Marilyn visits the Brady Airbase and is photographed with several women. She fits right in with her attire, which is like the conservative high-collar fashion displayed by the women who are pictured with her.

February 16: Marilyn flies to Seoul, South Korea, to begin entertaining the troops at ten different sites. Her outfit for her performances includes a skin-tight, low-cut, plum-colored crepe cocktail dress, with bugle beads and thin spaghetti straps, and high heeled sandals, with a matching long-sleeved bolero jacket she only wears when not on stage. Other than hoop earrings and a diamond brooch and bracelet, she wears no jewelry. Between performances, she covers over two hundred miles, wearing a flight jacket and combat boots. Neither snow nor sub-zero temperatures seem to impede her enthusiastic shows.

February 17: Hanson Baldwin of the *New York Times* reports: "On two occasions troops rioted wildly and behaved like bobby-soxers in Times Square, not like soldiers proud of their uniform."

February 20: Bob Alden writes from Korea on *New York Times* stationery to Stan (not otherwise identified): "The girl was just wonderful out here. She put every ounce of herself into everything that she did and won the hearts of a hundred thousand smitten G.I.'s. I doubt if any of them from General on down to Private will ever be the same again. Maybe we could send Marilyn up into North Korea to win over the Communists."

Alden writes a similar letter to Marilyn.

February 23: Marilyn and Joe fly to Hawaii on the first leg of their trip home to Hollywood.

February 24: Marilyn and Joe return to the mainland.

February 25: Mr. and Mrs. Rupe write to Marilyn about their son's reaction to her Korean trip. They quote his letter to them: "When she appeared on the stage, there was just a sort of gasp from the audience—a single gasp multiplied by the 12,000 soldiers present, was quite a gasp. . . . She is certainly making a lot of friends here . . . unlike the other entertainers . . . after the show she autographed, chatted, and posed for pictures. Then thru all the trucks and jeeps she rode perched on top of the seat of her jeep, smiling and waving. . . . She came to the divisions that have been so long on the line, and by-passed the easy duty in Seoul, Inchon, and the sunshine cities." One of the soldier's parents adds, "You are a real soldier. I know what the trip cost you. But you didn't disappoint those boys."

February 27: *Muncher Illustrierte* (Germany) displays Marilyn and Jane Russell in showgirl costumes, holding black top hats above their heads.

February 28, 11:38 p.m.: Marilyn writes a love letter to DiMaggio, who has departed for work in New York City: "I want someday for you to be proud of me as a person and as your wife and as the mother of the rest of your children. (Two at least! I've decided.)"

March: *Eiga No Tomo* (Japan) publishes one of many similar photographs to appear on the cover of the country's magazines. This one shows her hair curled tightly to her face just below her ears and showing only the top half of her body, her cleavage barely visible where her white fur stole drops down to her breasts.

March 1: *Life* publishes "Pin-up Takes Shape."

Newsweek publishes "This is Competition."

Movie Life puts Marilyn on the cover, holding a white cat close to her.

March 5: Marilyn flies from San Francisco to Los Angeles for the Photoplay Awards dinner. Joe flies to New York on business.

March 8: Marilyn wins the *Photoplay* award for her performance in *Gentlemen Prefer Blondes*. Sidney Skolsky escorts Marilyn, still under suspension, on stage, where she appears on the dais just a few seats away from Fox studio head Darryl Zanuck. She tells a reporter that she has no idea when she will return to work.

Mi Vida (Chile, August 3, 1962) puts on its cover the red, strapless dress that caused a stir at the awards. The bold red contoured dress features elaborate corded cups that flare out and emphasize her cleavage, while at her knees the dress flares out into a mermaid-like skirt.

March 9: Marilyn appears on a CBS radio program.

March 11: Fox decides not to make *Pink Tights*.

March 15: Marilyn and Joe, who returns from New York, meet with Charles Feldman in his office. Feldman reports that Darryl Zanuck has agreed not to do *The Girl in Pink Tights*, but the studio head refuses to consider giving Marilyn approval of script, director, and cinematographer.

March 18: Marilyn signs an agreement with Ben Hecht for up to three magazine articles about her life, stipulating that they are not to be published in book form. All material has to be presented for her approval: "This magazine article shall be signed either by me as the author or by you as the author as I may at my option elect."

Oggi (Italy) shows a smiling Marilyn among a group of soldiers during her Korean campaign.

March 21: A Frank Powolny photograph appears on the cover of the *Sunday Mirror*, showing Marilyn dressed in a lacy black top and looking over her shoulder at the camera with an inviting, open-mouthed expression. The headline reads, "Marilyn DiMaggio: Will It Last?"

March 23: Marilyn, decked out in a green velvet costume for *River of No Return*, is featured on the cover of the *Australasian Post*.

April: Marilyn and Joe rent an Elizabethan cottage on Palm Drive in Beverly Hills, not far from where she used to live with Johnny Hyde, but the couple makes frequent trips to San Francisco and stays at the DiMaggio home on Beach Street.

Sir! shows Marilyn off in a red low-cut dress, leaning forward and smiling seductively. The headline reads: "The Real Reason Joe Married Marilyn."

April 3: *Le Ore* (Italy) publishes a photograph of Marilyn showing the cement on her hands after putting them in wet cement outside Grauman's Chinese Theatre.

April 9: Marilyn meets with Ben Hecht to collaborate with him on her autobiography. According to Hecht's widow (interviewed by Anthony Summers), Marilyn "laughed and cried and expressed herself as 'thrilled.' She said she never imagined so wonderful a story could be written about her, and that Benny had captured every phase of her life." Hecht himself doubted the veracity of certain stories, but not Marilyn's passionate belief in them.

Marilyn records "I'm Going to File My Claim," a song from *River of No Return*.

April 13: Fox lifts Marilyn's suspension. She meets reporters to say details of her contract remain to be worked out.

In *River of No Return*

April 14: Marilyn returns to the Fox studios after her suspension is lifted.

April 15: Marilyn holds a press conference in her dressing room at Fox. She is photographed smiling in a high-necked dress, with a photograph of DiMaggio placed right behind her. She is also photographed in a scene with singing coach Hal Schaefer at the piano, and sitting atop an armchair, cigarette in hand.

She is presented with the "National Poll Award" for best actress of 1953.

April 23: Marilyn is upset by a negative review in the *Hollywood Reporter* criticizing her acting in *River of No Return*.

April 29: Fox holds the world premiere of *River of No Return* in Denver.

April 30: *River of No Return* opens in New York City.

End of April: Hecht finishes a draft of Marilyn's memoir.

May: A 1949 photograph of Marilyn in a very skimpy two-piece bathing suit, wearing her blonde hair quite long in the 1940s style, appears on the cover of *Male* (Australia).

Marilyn works with Milton Greene on several shooting sessions that present a more elegant and mysterious Marilyn Monroe.

May 1: Marilyn, driving a 1952 Cadillac convertible, rear ends Bart Antinora's MG. Antinora sues Marilyn and Joe DiMaggio (her passenger) for $3,000 each. The case is later settled out of court for $500.

May 5: Feldman calls Marilyn to say Fox has prepared the first draft of her contract. She is shocked to discover the studio has not given her any creative control over her pictures.

River of No Return is released and premieres in Los Angeles.

May 8: Feldman calls to say he will produce *The Seven Year Itch* with Fox's approval. But Marilyn angrily accuses him of not negotiating with the studio in her best interests.

May 9: The London tabloid *Empire News* publishes Marilyn's account via Ben Hecht of child abuse. What happened exactly is not clear, although apparently she was fondled, and then stammered when she tried to tell a foster mother what happened and was not believed. Journalist Jack Rosenstein, in *Hollywood Closeup* (May 17, 1974), quotes Marilyn saying later, "It did happen. But I didn't run out of the room crying or screaming. . . . I knew it was wrong, but to tell the truth I think I was more curious than anything else. . . . [N]obody ever told me about sex, and frankly, I never did think it was all that important or that it was wrong."

May 19: Work is interrupted on the autobiography and never resumed, and Hecht drops out when a portion of the book is published without his permission in *Empire News*.

May 20: Marilyn is encouraged by talks with photographer Milton Greene, who urges her to set up her own production company—thus cutting out Feldman, who did not yet have a contract to represent her.

May 28: Shooting begins on *There's No Business Like Show Business*. Marilyn's director, Walter Lang, does not seem to know how to handle her. Donald O'Connor, Marilyn's love interest in the film, recalls that the director was afraid to ask her to take her shoes off in a scene because her bouffant hairdo and high heels made her look taller than O'Connor. Lang wants the actor to stand on an apple box. O'Connor goes to Marilyn and tells her, "[T]his idiot's afraid to ask you to take off your shoes, but I'd feel very strange working with you, standing on an apple box." Marilyn says, "Oh Christ, the guy's nuts," kicks off her shoes, and "everything was fine," according to O'Connor.

May 29: *Revue* (Germany) puts on its cover an elegant, black-and-white picture of an upright Marilyn, wearing a necklace with a single jewel, and smiling confidently and calmly.

June: *Pic* catches Marilyn in mid-performance in a tight-fitting blue dress, singing to the troops in Korea. The shot bears the headline "The Real Story of Marilyn and Joe DiMaggio."

Sidney Skolsky publishes *Marilyn* under her auspices.

June 1: Marilyn turns twenty-eight.

June 15: Marilyn agrees to Feldman's compromise offer to Fox. She will demand only the right to choose her drama coach and choreographer. But the studio does not accept her offer.

June 18: Marilyn meets with Spyros Skouras, president of Fox, in the hope that he will take her side. He makes no commitment.

June 20: Marilyn learns directly from Skouras that her appeal to him has failed.

June 25: Spyros Skouras sends Marilyn a telegram: "DEAR MARI-LYN: TRIED TO REACH YOU ON THE PHONE BUT THERE WAS NO ANSWER TO SAY GOODBYE AND HOPE YOU FEEL BETTER. YOU KNOW HOW MUCH I RESPECT YOU AND OF MY HIGH REGARD. WHATEVER I SUGGESTED PLEASE BE-LIEVE ME WAS MEANT FOR YOUR BEST INTEREST."

Summer: The cover of the British magazine *Holiday Clubman* shows Marilyn made up and costumed for *River of No Return*.

Ted Baron photographs Marilyn, an occasional smoker, dressed in a horizontally striped dress, in a sultry pose (half-closed eyes, half-open mouth), with a cigarette delicately held in her left hand.

July: *Movie Fan*'s cover features a typical shot from the period, except that it is less revealing, cropped so as to show only Marilyn's head and shoulders, which are partially covered in white fur. The caption reads, "All My Glamour is for Joe!"

Song Fan features Marilyn and Robert Mitchum cheek-to-cheek in a publicity shot for *River of No Return*.

July 7: An armed forces representative presents Marilyn with a trophy and plaque for her morale-raising efforts in Korea.

July 8: Zanuck agrees to Marilyn's compromise offer.

July 9: *Collier's* publishes "Marilyn Monroe Hits a New High."

July 19: Marilyn, still stalling, tells Fox she will sign her contract by the end of the week.

July 20: Milton Greene, wishing to avoid Joe DiMaggio, who wants Marilyn to settle with Fox, wires Sidney Skolsky to set up a call to confer with Marilyn.

July 22: In a meeting with a Feldman associate, Marilyn gets an-gry, accusing Feldman of selling her out to Fox.

July 27: Hal Schaefer, Marilyn's vocal coach, attempts suicide by drinking typewriter fluid and cleaning fluid, and swallowing over a hundred pills. Despondent about Marilyn, with whom he was having an affair—but also about the course of his life—Schaefer barely survives.

July 28: Marilyn visits Schaefer in the hospital and continues to see him during his recuperation.

Feldman invites Marilyn and Joe to his house, hoping Joe will convince Marilyn to sign the Fox contract.

July 30: Feldman is surprised when Marilyn greets him warmly when he visits her dressing room at Fox.

August: *Night and Day*'s cover portrays a typical sex siren: Marilyn with her head thrown back, her eyes closed, her smile seeming to evoke pleasure with herself as she raises her left arm and touches the back of her head with her hand.

Movie Life shows Marilyn in a John Florea photograph, with her hands bringing down a strap as though she is about to take off her one-piece red swimsuit.

Marilyn meets Paula Strasberg on the set of *There's No Business Like Show Business*. Strasberg tells her she is welcome to visit the Strasbergs and the Actors Studio any time Marilyn is in New York.

Marilyn gives an interview to columnist Drew Pearson and is quoted as saying, "Not being a born actress, not a singer, not a dancer, I still pinch myself when I'm going to the studio in a very beautiful car, and sing, and dance, and perform a dramatic part."

Marilyn is photographed with Marlon Brando, dressed as Napoleon for *Désirée*.

August 27: Joe DiMaggio becomes upset while watching Marilyn perform the "Heat Wave" number in *There's No Business Like Show Business*. Hedda Hopper reports that fifty-two visitors watched in a kind of open house organized by the studio. To Susan Strasberg, Marilyn seems to "[f]licker like a flame giving off a nimbus of light. . . . I thought it was trick lighting until I stood next to her." Marilyn falters under Joe's disapproving gaze, but is cheered by Strasberg's presence. Marilyn tells her she would like to study with her father one day.

Late August: Marilyn finishes work on *There's No Business Like Show Business*.

August 30: Invited by Drew Pearson to write a guest column during his vacation, Marilyn notes, "I've been lucky and a lot of my fellow Americans have cheered from the sidelines as a little girl without much background found success and happiness the hard way."

September: The United States Post Office bans Fire Gem Company from selling drinks coasters featuring Marilyn's nude calendar photograph. On appeal, the company is allowed to market the coasters, owing to Judge William M. Byrne's ruling that the items are not obscene.

A brassy Marilyn, wearing long jeweled earrings and with a big, almost taunting smile, appears on the cover of *Cinelandia* (Brazil) in a photograph by John Florea.

A tentative Marilyn, wide-eyed and wearing jeweled earrings, appears on the cover of *The Eiga Story* (Japan).

Piff, a Swedish men's magazine, displays a nearly full-length shot of Marilyn decked out in a *River of No Return* dancehall costume, complete with a huge shock of feathers on her head.

September 1: Filming of *The Seven Year Itch* begins on the Fox lot.

September 3: For RCA, Marilyn records "A Fine Romance" and "She Acts Like a Woman Should."

September 8–9: Marilyn leaves Los Angeles and flies to New York City to work on *The Seven Year Itch*.

September 9: Marilyn does interviews with Earl Wilson and others, holds a press conference at the St. Regis Hotel, and meets Irving Berlin, composer of the songs in *There's No Business Like Show Business*. She stays at the Hampshire House Hotel.

September 10: Marilyn poses for Milton Greene at his Lexington Avenue studio. He shoots her in color, wearing a ballerina dress.

September 11 or 12: Sam Shaw shoots a series of candids, with Marilyn dressed casually and appearing by turns reflective and tired, apparently nodding off.

September 11: DiMaggio arrives in New York and joins Marilyn at the St. Regis Hotel in an eleventh floor suite.

The Seven Year Itch with Tom Ewell

Marilyn attends a performance of *The Pajama Game* at the St. James Theatre and is afterwards photographed by Milton Greene in the dressing room of actress Carol Haney. Marilyn wears a strapless black gown and black fur stole and seems to be enjoying the conversation.

September 12: Milton Greene photographs Marilyn and Joe having a good time at the El Morocco.

September 13: Billy Wilder shoots the first outdoor scene of *The Seven Year Itch* at 164 East 61st Street, with an estimated one thousand onlookers. Marilyn leans over an apartment balcony railing in a terry cloth robe.

During breaks in the filming, Bob Henriques, a Magnum photographer, shoots Marilyn studying her script, relaxing, and apparently thinking over her work. Sam Shaw is also present, taking photographs along with Elliot Erwitt.

Sidney Skolsky and Ben Lyon also visit the set, and columnist Earl Wilson is photographed with Marilyn and Italian actress Gina Lollobrigida on his left and right, respectively.

In the evening, Marilyn and Joe go to a performance of *Teahouse of the August Moon*, starring her friend and Actors Studio veteran Eli Wallach.

September 15: At midnight, Billy Wilder begins shooting Marilyn in the famous skirt-blowing scene that outrages Joe DiMaggio. The outdoor sequence takes five hours, with Marilyn positioning herself again and again over a subway grating as her dress is lifted by the wind generated by a passing train. The entire performance is for publicity purposes, since the noise of the city and the crowd makes the sequence unusable in the film. The scene is re-shot in a studio, where Marilyn's skirt is raised only a modest degree. Later that night, Marilyn and Joe have a violent quarrel that signals the end of their marriage.

September 16: The next day on the set Whitey Snyder covers up Marilyn's bruises with makeup.

Marilyn meets one of her biggest fans, James Haspiel.

Marilyn works on a photo shoot with Richard Avedon.

Marilyn flies from New York to Los Angeles.

September 27: *Life* publishes "Marilyn on the Town."

Marilyn consults with Mary Karger Short (Fred Karger's sister) about her plan to divorce DiMaggio.

October 2: DiMaggio consults Sydney Skolsky, hoping to find some way to avoid a divorce, but Marilyn has DiMaggio barred from the Fox lot.

October 4: Joe DiMaggio is served with divorce papers. At 2:45 p.m., Marilyn's attorney, Jerry Giesler, and Fox head of publicity Harry Brand issue a statement to the press.

Marilyn calls Billy Wilder to say she is too ill to work.

October 5: Marilyn officially separates from DiMaggio.

October 6: A distraught Marilyn, unable to talk, and assisted by Sidney Skolsky, appears before the press. This performance, carefully prepared by Jerry Giesler, goes according to plan.

October 7: Will Sykes, a nephew of Ana Lower, writes to Marilyn saying he is sorry hear about her divorce, and adds, "[B]ut as Aunt Ana used to say a C.S. [Christian Scientist] and a C. [Catholic] could never hit it off together very long."

Marilyn reports to the set of *The Seven Year Itch.*

October 17: Marilyn testifies in court about her husband's mental cruelty.

October 18: *Life* publishes "Last Scene: Exit Unhappily."

Newsweek publishes "Parting."

Time publishes "Out at Home."

October 25: In a dream sequence that is later cut from *The Seven Year Itch*, Marilyn plays a gun moll, Tiger Lil.

October 26: DiMaggio appeals one more time to Sidney Skolsky in an effort to change Marilyn's mind about the divorce.

October 27: Marilyn is granted a divorce. At the Santa Monica courthouse she tells the judge: "My husband was sometimes in so dark a mood that he didn't talk to me at all for 5 days, even 7 days in a row. Sometimes even more. I asked him: 'What's wrong?' No answer. . . . He forbade me to have some visits; in 9 months, I've only received my friends 3 times. . . . Most of the time, he only showed me coldness and indifference." Inez Melson testifies that she saw DiMaggio "pushing her away and telling her to leave him alone." DiMaggio puts up no defense.

October 28: *Cineromanzo* (Italy) used an intense blue and red cover photograph of Marilyn leaning forward, showing plenty of cleavage, and with an open-mouthed smile, a classic glamour shot.

November: Marilyn resides for a month or so at a luxurious duplex on 8336 DeLongoré in West Hollywood.

Marilyn helps Ella Fitzgerald get a nightclub engagement at the Mocambo, keeping her promise that she will sit at a front row table every night of Fitzgerald's performances.

Screen Stars advertises "Things They Never Told About Marilyn" with a cover shot of her in close-up, a jeweled bracelet on the right hand, which is held alongside her neck. She is described as reading von Clauswitz's *On War* when the photographer arrives.

Movieland's cover shows off Marilyn against a deep red background, shot on the diagonal and smiling like her brightly shining jeweled earrings, illustrating the caption, "Meet the *New* Marilyn Monroe."

See puts Marilyn on its red cover, dressed in a *River of No Return* low-cut dancehall costume, staring suggestively at the camera.

November 4: Marilyn completes principal photography on *The Seven Year Itch*.

Fox informs Marilyn that her next role will be in *How To Be Very, Very Popular*.

Marilyn attends a preview of *There's No Business Like Show Business*. She is photographed in the same row with Milton Greene and Alfred Eisenstaedt.

November 5: Marilyn records the song "There's No Business Like Show Business" with her singing teacher, Hal Schaefer.

DiMaggio, Sinatra, and detectives they hired, break into an apartment where Marilyn is supposedly carrying on an affair with Hal Schaefer, but the intruders enter the wrong residence.

In a shot reminiscent of "Diamonds Are A Girl's Best Friend," *Mundo Uruguayo* displays Marilyn armored with jewels: earrings, two bracelets, and a necklace that is contoured to her shoulder straps and travels down the front of her ensemble, emphasizing her cleavage and ending at her waist.

November 6: Marilyn attends a party held in her honor at Romanoff's restaurant. Billy Wilder, Humphrey Bogart, Claudette Colbert, William Holden, James Stewart, Doris Day, Susan Hayward, Clark Gable, Clifton Webb, Loretta Young, and other stars as well as studio moguls Darryl Zanuck, Jack Warner, and Sam Goldwyn attend. She dances with Webb, Bogart, Tom Ewell, and then Clark Gable.

November 8: Marilyn undergoes another gynecological operation.

Lucille Ball impersonates Marilyn in an episode of *I Love Lucy*.

"Inside Story of Marilyn's Divorce" is the headline above a cover shot of her smiling and wearing the kind of provocative, low-cut dress she wore in *Niagara*, while projecting an almost predatory joy in her staring, open-mouthed confrontation with the camera.

November 12: Marilyn leaves the hospital. Newsreel photographers record a pale, unsteady Marilyn, turning her face away from them.

November 19: Marilyn and Sidney Skolsky see Ella Fitzgerald perform at the El Mocambo, where Marilyn is photographed enjoying herself in the singer's company.

November 21: Beverly Hills patrolman H. P. Swantek issues Marilyn a ticket for driving without a license.

Marilyn and singer Johnny Ray are featured on the cover of *Sorrisi e Canzoni* (Italy) in a publicity still from *There's No Business Like Show Business*.

November 22: Marilyn leads Feldman to believe she will remain his client, even though she has not signed a contract with him. He shows her a copy of Terence Rattigan's play *The Sleeping Prince*, and proposes buying it for her.

November 25: Marilyn has dinner with DiMaggio at the Villa Capri to celebrate his fortieth birthday.

November 29: Milton Greene's lawyer notices that Fox delayed too long to renew Marilyn's 1951 contract, rendering it null and void and releasing her from any commitments to the studio.

Life publishes "*Life* Goes to a Select Supper for Marilyn."

Marilyn chats with Charlie Farrell at the Racquet Club in Palm Springs. The former actor had become the city's mayor.

Garry Winogrand photographs Marilyn for *Pageant*.

A photograph of Marilyn taken in September 1952, acting as grand marshal of the Miss American parade in Atlantic City and waving from the back seat of a convertible, is on the cover of *Playboy*.

Joulu Iso Kalle (Finland) displays Marilyn in a side view. She is dressed in a lacy undergarment, sitting quite erect, her knees bent, with her head turning toward the camera in a pose that is a provocation.

December 2: Marilyn attends a party hosted by Jess Rand, Sammy Davis Jr.'s publicist, and is photographed with Charles Feldman, Milton Greene, Davis, and Mel Tormé.

December 4: Marilyn is photographed with Charlie Farrell, owner of the Palm Springs Racquet Club, and with Charles Feldman and Milton Greene.

December 6: Marilyn attends Sammy Davis Jr.'s birthday party and is photographed with Tony Curtis.

December 8: Feldman pitches the idea of a picture about Jean Harlow (a project Sidney Skolsky wants to do with Marilyn) to Darryl Zanuck. Feldman schedules a meeting with Skolsky, who cancels.

December 10: For RCA, Marilyn records "You'd Be Surprised," "Heat Wave," "Lazy," and "After You Get What You Want You Don't Want It."

December 11: Feldman has lunch with a cheerful, agreeable Marilyn, who seems to have no complaints. She agrees to have lunch with him again in two days.

December 13: Marilyn cancels lunch with Feldman. She fires him and tells Fox it must do business directly with her, or with Milton Greene's attorney, Frank Delaney.

Marilyn goes into hiding with her friend Anne Karger at the Voltaire Apartments in West Hollywood.

December 23: Marilyn appears on the cover of *Settimo Giorno* (Italy) in a painted photograph with a color scheme (gold, red, and deep mauve) that makes her look cartoonish. It is the kind of work that might have inspired Andy Warhol.

December 25: *There's No Business Like Show Business* is released.

Marilyn spends Christmas with Milton and Amy Greene and their two dogs, a setter and a Kerry blue terrier.

Arthur Murray creates the "Marilyn Monroe Mamba" after watching her "Heat Wave" number. Columnist Ed Sullivan deplores the bad taste of her performance in the same number.

Louella Parsons writes a column explaining Marilyn's break with Hollywood.

1955

Marilyn helps Jane Russell in supporting WAIF, an organization that places abandoned children in homes.

Sam Shaw publishes *Marilyn Monroe as The Girl: The Candid Picture-Story of the Making of "The Seven Year Itch."*

Gardner Cowles, publisher of *Look*, approaches Marilyn about the possibility of marrying Prince Rainier of Monaco.

Marilyn owns a white Persian cat named Mitsou.

Marilyn appears incognito in the Broadway production of *Teahouse of the August Moon.*

Marilyn is photographed reading *To The Actor*, by Michael Chekhov, and dancing with Truman Capote at the Ambassador Hotel.

Phillipe Halsman shoots Marilyn in a series of photographs of her jumping.

Earl Theisen's 1952 potato sack photograph appears on the cover of *Flix*.

The Showgirl (England) uses a 1952 Bruno Bernard photograph that shows Marilyn in an intense blue halter-like garment and crops her figure at her bust line.

Ricu Ritas (Argentina) publishes on its cover a publicity still of Marilyn in a two-piece white outfit, sitting on the lap of a stupefied Tom Ewell, as she cradles his face in her left arm.

January 1: "Don't Blame Yourself, Marilyn," by Nanette Kutner, is published in *Photoplay*, offering Marilyn consoling advice after her breakup with DiMaggio.

Lilla Anderson's "The Girl You Know as Marilyn" is published in *Photoplay*. The piece organizes Marilyn's life into a three-act drama: act 1, the struggle amidst much discouragement to be a star; act 2, fame, love, and marriage; and act 3, which finds Marilyn still on stage, this time as a "bewildered, hurt young woman heartbroken over her failed marriage to DiMaggio."

January 3: Marilyn attends a board of directors meeting for Marilyn Monroe Productions. Greene, named vice-president, and his accountant, Joe Carr, and lawyer, Frank Delaney, meet to discuss film and television projects, plus a book of Greene photographs of Monroe.

January 7: "The new Marilyn Monroe" is introduced to the press, saying she would like to play the female lead in *The Brothers Karamazov*. She announces that her contract with Fox is void, according to her legal advisor (Frank Delaney).

After the press conference, Frank Sinatra takes Marilyn and Milton and Amy Greene, to dinner at 21. At a party afterward, Marilyn is photographed wearing a white satin dress designed by Norma Norell. Among the guests are Tony Curtis and Janet Leigh, Marlene Dietrich (photographed in hat and veil), and composer Richard Rodgers. Marilyn also attends Sinatra's performance at the Copacabana Club.

January 8: The *Los Angeles Times* runs a headline: "New Marilyn Same as Old—And That's Plenty."

"Elsa Maxwell and Marilyn meet at party to hail 'the new Monroe,'" announces the *New York Daily News*.

January 9: Marilyn appears for retakes for *The Seven Year Itch*.

January 11: Marilyn and Milton Greene attend Sammy Davis Jr.'s show at Ciro's on Sunset Boulevard.

January 12: Marilyn works on shots for *The Seven Year Itch*, but then is called upon to do costume fittings for *How To Be Very, Very Popular* the next day.

January 13: Marilyn shows up at the studio for still shots, but then departs not wanting to be present for a discussion of her next production with screenwriter Nunnally Johnson.

January 15: Marilyn flies to New York, and Fox suspends her again.

Joe DiMaggio also flies to New York.

January 19: Joe DiMaggio and photographer Sam Shaw help Marilyn move into the Gladstone Hotel on East 52nd Street near Park Avenue.

January 19–22: Marilyn works with Milton Greene in his Lexington Avenue studio on an all white series, with poses in fur and terry cloth.

January 23: DiMaggio drives Marilyn to Boston to meet with Henry Rosenfeld, a dress manufacturer and potential investor in Marilyn Monroe Productions. Rosenfeld declines to become a major contributor, although Greene secures some funds to support Marilyn at the Gladstone, to which she and DiMaggio return the same day.

January 24: *Time* publishes "Dostoyevsky Blues."

January 25: Marilyn sends a telegram to Darryl Zanuck saying she has received the script for *Pink Tights*: "AM EXCEEDINGLY SORRY BUT I DO NOT LIKE IT. SINCERELY MARILYN MONROE."

Marilyn has dinner in Wellesley, Massachusetts, where Dominic, DiMaggio's brother, has a home. She asks Joe for advice on handling Fox.

January 26: Journalist George Carpozi Jr. interviews Marilyn at the Gladstone Hotel. He is accompanied by photographer George Miller, who accompanies Marilyn, dressed in a dark fur coat, on a walk through Central Park.

She drives with DiMaggio to Cooperstown, New York, to see his induction into the Baseball Hall of Fame. They also visit his brother Dominic and Dominic's wife Emily, who are living near Boston.

February: *Movie Secrets* pictures a smiling, flirtatious Marilyn, her head turned toward her right shoulder so that she is looking back at the viewer. The headline in the top right corner reads, "Exclusive: What Made Joe Go? Six pages of sensational pix."

The *National Police Gazette* features the most famous photograph ever taken of Monroe, the Sam Shaw shot of her with her white skirt flaring around her.

February 1: Photographer Sam Shaw escorts Marilyn to a party at the home of Paul Bigelow, an assistant to Broadway producer Cheryl Crawford, an original member of the Group Theatre, where Kazan, Harold Clurman, Lee Strasberg, and other important theater professionals made their mark in the 1930s. Crawford invites Marilyn to accompany her to the Actors Studio, formed some years after the dissolution of the Group Theatre.

February 2: Judge Charles J. Griffin issues a warrant for Marilyn's arrest when she fails to appear in court after being cited for driving without a license.

February 4: Marilyn attends her first session at the Actors Studio. Elia Kazan introduces her to Lee Strasberg, who agrees to give her private lessons. On Strasberg's advice, she also sees a psychiatrist, Dr. Margaret Hohenberg, who has been analyzing Milton Greene for several years. They work on her childhood traumas, fear of abandonment, and inability to commit to long-term relationships.

February 14: *Tempo* features Marilyn in a swimsuit she wore in *We're Not Married*. Here she stands with her arms resting on a heart (almost as large as she is) with a cupid's arrow running downward and diagonally across the page. "Marilyn's New Career" is the headline for an article reporting her refusal to do the dumb blonde role in *How To Be Very, Very Popular*.

February 15: Inez Melson, Marilyn's business manager, writes a memo about her conversation with Jo Brooks regarding Marilyn's offer to host a party for Ella Fitzgerald, but Fitzgerald's opening occurs when Marilyn is out of town, and Marilyn is not able to host the party.

Mid-February: Marilyn establishes a routine of attending Strasberg's workshop on Tuesdays and Fridays, and then working with him alone three evenings a week, staying afterward to have dinner with his family. Her work on "sensory memory" is closely tied to her sessions with Dr. Hohenberg.

During this period, James Haspiel, one of Marilyn's devoted fans, shoots candids of her on the street, in her convertible, and on her way to do some shopping.

Meetings with Arthur Miller are still furtive, since he is still married, and she is trying to avoid public exposure of her affair with the playwright.

February 26: *Picture Week* features a smiling Marilyn in black-and-white, dressed casually in a loose blouse, resting the right side of her face on her hands and her upper body on her elbows. "A Glimpse into Marilyn's Future" is the promising headline.

Joe DiMaggio takes Marilyn to a birthday party for Jackie Gleason at Toots Shor's restaurant. Marilyn is photographed signing autographs, laughing with Gleason and DiMaggio, and with a very satisfied looking Milton Berle. She gets a splinter when she sits on a wooden chair, and actress Audrey Meadows removes the splinter with a straight needle sterilized with a cigarette lighter.

February 28: Marilyn meets with Irving Stein, working for Marilyn Monroe Productions, about negotiating tactics with Fox. She tells him she has to get Joe DiMaggio's advice.

March: Marilyn is offered a lucrative contract to perform at the New Frontier Hotel in Las Vegas, but the deal is never closed.

Marilyn attends a tea at the St. Regis Hotel, which Tennessee Williams hosts in honor of his mother.

A shot of Marilyn as the ingenuous hatcheck girl turned performer in *There's No Business like Show Business* graces the cover of *Jours de France*.

A Weegee photograph of Marilyn in her *Seven Year Itch* clothing appears on the cover of *Modern Man*.

March 5: Natasha Lytess tries to see Marilyn at her agent's house, but is turned away and never sees her protégé again.

March 9: Marilyn and Marlon Brando are celebrity ushers at a fundraiser for the Actors Studio during the premiere of *East of Eden*, directed by Actors Studio member Elia Kazan.

March 14: Fox sends three checks to Marilyn for weeks worked prior to her suspension, but her lawyers, not wishing to recognize the validity of the studio contract, send the money back.

March 24: With Milton and Amy Greene, Marilyn attends the opening of a new Tennessee Williams play, *Cat on a Hot Tin Roof*, at the Morosco Theatre in New York City. Afterwards, they dine at the El Morocco.

March 24–30: During this week, photographer Ed Feingersh shoots candids of Marilyn that will be published in *Marilyn 1955*. She is photographed atop the Ambassador Hotel leaning over a parapet, crossing her arms, holding a cigarette in her right hand, and looking down wistfully at the Manhattan street below. Another shot shows her inhaling, another looking up and smiling. Feingersh also captures her arranging her hair, applying makeup, perfuming herself with Chanel No. 5, and looking in the mirror, applying lipstick. She is shown seated at the El Morocco, looking up and concentrating on Greene, who is standing next to her. Many of the shots suggest their close collaboration and intimacy, such as when he looks over her shoulder as she reads the playbill. She is photographed bent over signing an autographed picture using one of her shoes as a flat surface. In another picture she appears almost a blur, on her way to a dinner party at the El Morocco. At the restaurant, she is shown bending her head to listen to Milton Berle, who whispers in her ear, and later in the evening she seems asleep, covered in a fur stole next to a fireplace. Feingersh shoots her reading a book, curled up on a sofa in Milton Greene's Connecticut home. She also reclines and reads *Motion Picture Daily*. Back in New York City, she is photographed standing in a white cloth coat in the subway, with the sign above her head pointing to the uptown local track in Grand Central Station. Like any other subway rider, she stands peeking along the track for the arriving train. Aboard a subway car, she clutches the sports section of the *New York Post*, and in another shot she stands, just another straphanger. Low angle shots capture that evanescent wondering look, but without the usual studio gloss, as she walks up the subway stairs to the street. She tilts her head in another informal pose, holding a cigarette in her right hand. In Costello's restaurant, she glances up from her chair, apparently amused by the James Thurber drawings on the wall. Back at the Ambassador, she seems utterly relaxed, giving way to a pensive pose, her hand to her mouth like Rodin's *The Thinker*. Her moods change rapidly. Her left hand goes to her throat, as she lifts her head in laughter. Feingersh accompanies Marilyn in sunglasses, dressed in a black dress and black fur, to Elizabeth Arden. Back in her hotel suite, she models a terry cloth robe with "Ambassador" monogrammed on the back. In another shot, she looks over her shoulder with one of those patented Marilyn Monroe smiling, fetching looks. The photographer is also present for her costume fittings, a kind of dancehall getup she will wear atop a pink elephant. She consults with Milton Greene about her ensemble, checking her fishnet stockings as Greene, a costume fitter, and three other males observe. Feingersh captures the multiple Marilyns in mirror photographs by two other photographers (over two hundred would be present at the Madison Square Garden). "The pinning, poking, and pawing," as Bob LaBrasca puts it in *Marilyn 1955*, is shown in a series that depicts Marilyn trying out various movements to see how well her costume works. She seems, at one point, to be overwhelmed with all the preparation, bowing her head, putting her left hand to her brow, and pressing the fingers of her right hand to her breasts. And yet other shots show her in a slip, apparently enjoying peek-a-boo with the photographer, as he records her fixing her stockings. It is a remarkable sequence of Marilyn Monroe equipment, so to speak. It is work, then it is pleasure, as Marilyn stands and smiles back at the woman helping her with the straps on her dress. In a limousine on the way to Madison Square Garden, Marilyn appears in half-shadow, smiling and listening to her companion, and then she emerges out into the public, showing that familiar expression of half-open eyes and mouth that makes her so instantly recognizable. The façade fades as she waits backstage, about to enter the dressing room where she will don her sequined costume for her elephant ride. The next shot of her seems to be after she has mounted the elephant. She is sitting on it in a sort of sidesaddle position before swinging forward and tucking her knees around the elephant's neck.

March 30: In front of an audience of eighteen thousand people, Marilyn rides a pink elephant in a star-studded benefit performance of the Ringling Brothers and Barnum & Bailey Circus in Madison Square Garden. The elephant's hide chafes her thighs. Afterward, she attends a party at Costello's restaurant.

Amy Greene commissions Norman Norell to design a black silk dress for Marilyn's appearances.

March 31: Marilyn attends a party with USS *Benington* sailors at the Astor Hotel grand ballroom.

Spring: Marilyn, in the company of photographer Sam Shaw, visits poet Norman Rosten and his wife, Hedda, in their home in Brooklyn. Marilyn writes a thank you note to Norman, mentioning her liking for poetry, including a book of his own that he gave her, and that she has written poetry, "but usually when I'm depressed." She begins sending him her poetry.

April: The cover of *Bild Journalen* (Sweden) shows Marilyn, dressed in a strapless lacy dress, waiting with closed eyes and open mouth for a brush-up from her favorite makeup artist, a smiling Whitey Snyder.

Marilyn becomes friendly with the "Marilyn Six," a group of fans who keep track of her comings and goings.

"Ten Years of Monroe" appears in *Photoplay*, a compilation of photographs of her as model, starlet, and star, accompanied by Sidney Skolsky, Joe DiMaggio, and Clifton Webb.

April 3: *Piccolo* uses a publicity still from *There's No Business Like Show Business*. In a two-shot with Donald O'Connor, Marilyn smiles in that half-waking mood that makes for a conventional pairing with a co-star with the bland looks shared by many of her early leading men.

April 4: In an issue of *Sports Illustrated*, DiMaggio hand writes a set of notes to himself about his effort to reconcile with Marilyn, including injunctions not to be critical: "[F]orget ego & pride . . . Be warm, affectionate, & Love . . . Be patient no matter what." He cautions himself not to be jealous: "Remember this is not your wife. She is a fine girl and remember how unhappy you made her. Happiness is what you strive for—for HER. Don't talk about her business or her friends. Be friendly toward her friends. Don't forget how lonesome and unhappy you are especially without her."

April 5: On the cover of the *Australian*, a beaming Marilyn is shown in an evening dress, wearing gloves that go up past her elbows. Her head is thrust upward and she is smiling broadly, but the camera angle makes her neck look quite thick, and her eyes are reduced to slits. Like many magazines, this one does not provide a headline other than her name.

April 6: Judge Griffin issues a new arrest warrant when Marilyn again fails to appear to answer the charge of driving without a license.

April 8: Marilyn appears on Edward R. Murrow's television show, *Person to Person*, and seems shy and inarticulate next to the well-spoken Amy Greene.

Dave Garroway interviews Marilyn for his radio show, and she ends her day with an interview with *Family Weekly*.

April 10: *Der Stern* (Germany) shows Marilyn backstage at Madison Square Garden, costumed and ready to ride her elephant. Her smiling image (she is sitting with hands on her hips) is replicated by a mirror showing her images back-to-back, and by another mirror projecting a half-dozen reflections of her, stretching out seemingly ad infinitum.

April 26: Marilyn attends the Newspaper Public Convention luncheon at the Waldorf Astoria. She is photographed with Hedda Hopper and J. Edgar Hoover.

April 29: Marilyn attends the funeral of Constance Collier, a British actress who gave Marilyn acting lessons. Truman Capote, who introduced Collier to Marilyn, sits next to her at the funeral.

May: *Man to Man*'s cover features a far less attractive, low-angle shot of the skirt-blowing scene from *The Seven Year Itch*. Marilyn's dress flies up to her neckline, revealing her panties and legs in a rather awkward position.

May 5: The extent of Marilyn's commitment to centering her life on the East Coast is apparent in the inventory of sixty items of apparel shipped from Los Angeles. Among the items is a purple sheath dress and jacket, trimmed in bugle beads, that is probably the outfit she wore for her performances in Korea. The wardrobe includes items that reflect the "new Marilyn Monroe," president of Marilyn Monroe Productions—such as a beige Don Loper suit—but also more glamorous items: a white fox fur stole, black fur stole embroidered with "MM," and a black linen sheath dress with net top. More casual wear, such as Bermuda shorts and gabardine and wool slacks, form part of her everyday wardrobe, which she likes to purchase at Jax in Beverly Hills, where she shops and says hello to the salesgirls, Yuki and Korby.

A receipt dating from this period from Polly's 480 Park for a natural baby lama wool coat ($350) includes this note: "This Christian Dior coat ought to be very good for you both here and in California, the fabric is baby lama & is very beautiful light in weight & warm."

June: Ed Feingersh shoots "Day in the Life of Marilyn Monroe" for the July issue of *Redbook*.

Marilyn, escorted by Joe DiMaggio, attends a benefit for Sammy Davis Jr. at the Apollo Theatre in Harlem and receives a standing ovation.

Movie World's color illustration of Marilyn dressed for her "Heat Wave" number in *There's No Business Like Show Business* is accompanied by the headline "Earl Wilson says 'This is a *New* Marilyn.'"

Movieland shows a relaxed Marilyn, smiling broadly and lounging in a red armchair in a white dress similar to what she wore in *The Seven Year Itch*.

June 1: On her twenty-ninth birthday, Marilyn attends the premiere of *The Seven Year Itch* at the Loew's State Theatre in Times Square. Joe DiMaggio escorts her, and in one photograph seems actually to enjoy his role accompanying Marilyn, who is wearing a low-cut dress and long white gloves. He stays by her side while she signs autographs. The opening night audience includes Grace Kelly, Henry Fonda, Tyrone Power, Margaret Truman, Eddie Fisher, Judy Holliday, and Richard Rodgers.

Joe DiMaggio throws a surprise birthday party for Marilyn at Toots Shor's restaurant, but the couple quarrels, and she leaves with photographer Sam Shaw.

June 4: *Picture Week* puts Marilyn, riding an elephant, on its cover.

June 7: Marilyn attends a performance of *Damn Yankees* on Broadway.

June 11: Clifton Webb, who sees Marilyn during her intense period of playgoing, comments in *Picturegoer*, "She likes to talk about the theatre and the kind of thing that makes people tick. She is intense and completely straightforward. She reads all the time. She is in complete earnest towards her career."

June 12: Dave Garroway, host of the *Today Show*, interviews Marilyn and suggests that men must be afraid of her because she is such a national institution. "I don't know quite what you mean by that," she responds. Then she giggles and says, "I live here."

Garroway observes, "I heard you were smart, but I didn't know." Marilyn laughs and says, "I'm not. Don't let them fool you." In discussing her roles, she notes, "It's interesting that people if you happen to have blonde hair—naturally or not naturally . . . or if you're not out of shape in some way—you're absolutely dumb. You're considered dumb. I don't know why that is. It's a very limited view. It doesn't matter what the person looks like or what color hair they have or if they happen not to be out of shape. My time is to come as gravity catches up with all of us."

June 17: *The Seven Year Itch* is released.

June 27: Marilyn attends a performance of *Inherit the Wind* at the National Theatre on Broadway.

June 28: Dorothy Kilgallen publishes an article in the *New York Journal American* stating Lee Strasberg has replaced Milton Greene as Marilyn's mentor.

Summer: Marilyn spends weekends with the Strasbergs in their cottage on Fire Island. She also sees the Rostens in their country home on Long Island. She is photographed holding hands with Hedda Rosten.

Marilyn also manages to see Arthur Miller several times and has a brief meeting with Fred Karger, who observes that she seems dazed by alcohol and sedatives.

Marilyn swims in Richard Rodgers's pool in Weston, Connecticut, where Milton Greene and Rodgers are neighbors. She is shot in the pool wearing a life preserver, holding a glass as she half submerges herself in the pool, and in close-up, without makeup and with the water up to her neck.

Eve Arnold photographs Marilyn in a bathing suit reading James Joyce's *Ulysses* in Mount Sinai, Long Island.

Marilyn attends a photo shoot at Judy Holliday's apartment in the Dakota. Marilyn watches Holliday apply lipstick.

July: Marilyn purchases a bust of Queen Nefertiti for her Waldorf Astoria apartment.

John Wilcock interviews Marilyn for *Liberty*, a Canadian magazine, while she sits in a bar across from the Waldorf Astoria. She orders a Harvey's Bristol Sherry but spills it on her lap, then calmly cleans herself up as she continues the interview. On the magazine's cover she is pictured in a red dress, learning forward, face turned toward the camera with the caption "Marilyn Monroe: 'I'm no has-been!'"

A John Florea photograph of Marilyn in a black one-piece swimsuit, with a strap falling down to her left elbow, appears on the cover of *See*.

Redbook publishes a very tight close-up of Marilyn, with just a bit of the terry cloth robe from *The Seven Year Itch* visible around her neck. The caption reads, "The Marilyn Monroe You've Never Seen. An exclusive new kind of picture story on America's most provocative woman."

Screen Stars shows a smiling and cavorting Marilyn on its cover, with the caption "Let's Stop Pushing Marilyn Around!"

"My Love Affair with Marilyn," by Jim Henaghan, appears in *Motion Picture*. Henaghan writes, "I considered her [in 1951] a beautiful, naïve child who could never muster the guile to be a movie star, or to be photographed as anything more than just what she was. Then one day I was in the 20th Century-Fox commissary having lunch and she came in and sat at my table and ate with me. She was working in a picture and wearing something gray that seemed to fit well. When she finished eating she said, 'Let me get up first and you look at the back of my skirt and tell me if it fits tight enough.' It did. 'Now I'll walk away and turn,' she said, 'and you tell me if it fits tight enough from the side.' It did. And as we left the commissary side by side, I thought 'this animal is learning.' I was rather happy for her."

July 4: *Tempo*'s cover shows Marilyn in a one-piece red swimsuit, holding a "Beware of Danger July 4th" sign diagonally across her torso. Above the cover photograph is the headline "Marilyn's Big Problem."

July 5: The *Australian Magazine*'s cover carries Frank Powolny's shot of Marilyn sitting on a high platform, her legs dangling, as she clutches a red satiny robe that is falling to the floor as she holds the upper part in place with a hand strategically placed near her cleavage. She tilts her head upward and seems on the verge of puckering for a kiss.

July 22: In *Hemmets Veckotidning* (Sweden), Andre de Dienes publishes a photograph of Marilyn, her brown hair drawn back with a head scarf and squatting backward, her right hand and arm supporting her, while her legs are bent all the way back, so that her right barefoot heel touches the bottom of her derriere. Her right hand is raised high and thrust on the diagonal in a particularly dynamic, athletic pose.

July 24: *Epoca* (Italy) shows Marilyn photographed from the back. She is looking back at the camera, her hair and expression very much in *The Seven Year Itch* mode.

July 26: Marilyn signs with a new agency, Music Corporation of American (MCA).

August: Marilyn applies for a visa to visit the Soviet Union.

August 6: Marilyn spends a day in Bement, Illinois, the site of one of the Lincoln-Douglas debates. She gives a heartfelt speech, composed on the plane, and judges a beard-growing contest. She is photographed by Eve Arnold touring the Lincoln museum. In *The Unretouched Woman*, Arnold remembers that Marilyn's speech was "something about our late beloved President—she meant Lincoln, but it sounded as though Eisenhower had just died." Arnold shoots a series of photographs showing Marilyn combing her hair, putting on makeup, sleeping on the plane on the way to Bement, getting her hair dressed while seated in the plane, and descending the plane's stairs, umbrella in hand. While in Bement, Marilyn does local radio interviews and is photographed next to a bust of Lincoln.

August 7: Marilyn arrives in New York's LaGuardia airport at 2:00 a.m. from Bement via Chicago.

She is asked by a representative of the National Arts Foundation to agree to go to Moscow with a delegation of artists to begin cultural exchanges between East and West. She agrees to do so.

August 9: Marilyn's lawyer, Frank Delaney, writes to Frank H. Ferguson at Twentieth Century Fox. Delaney reiterates his position that Fox waited too long to exercise its option requiring Marilyn to do another picture. He also demands payment for several unpaid weeks of work.

August 17: *Variety* reports that Marilyn has been offered $200,000 for a twenty-five-day tour of Australia. She did not accept the offer.

August 19: The FBI files its first report on Marilyn, almost all of which is blanked out because the material relates to matters of national security.

Frank H. Ferguson in the legal department at Fox writes to Marilyn's lawyer, Frank Delaney, stating that under the provision of an "extension" in her contract, the studio is entitled to request that she make another movie. He stipulates the studio is agreeable to making good on unpaid paychecks Delaney mentioned in his August 9 letter to Ferguson.

September: *Cartoon Cuties* uses a publicity still of Marilyn from *Love Happy* on the magazine's cover.

Eiga no Tomo (Japan) shows Marilyn seated in a director's chair with her name on the back. She is dressed in a long silky dress and wears long jeweled earrings and a bracelet. She leans back, her body twisted in a swivel so that she looks at the camera while smiling, script in hand.

"Alone with a Million Lovers," by Norma Keller, appears in *Motion Picture*. Keller writes, "Acting is more than wiggling, and she knew it. During the filming of *The Seven Year Itch* in New York, it became the practice of producer Billy Wilder to shoot and reshoot scenes until he got exactly the right quality. A difficult dramatic scene was scheduled one morning. It was a scene where Marilyn had to explain to Tom Ewell what was troubling her. It was a scene without comedy or sex. It had to be serious and poignant. It required skillful and tender handling. No one seemed to know whether she could do it. The crew was prepared for a long, hard session of takes and rehearsals and then more takes. In twelve minutes the shooting was over. There were no retakes. The perfectionist Billy Wilder was astonished. Marilyn had acted the scene superbly—and in the first shooting. In the dressing room, Billy Wilder thanked her, and congratulated her. 'Don't seem so surprised,' she said. 'You give me a scene with real people in it, and I can act like a human being. I meant those lines I spoke. You know, Billy . . . that was the first time I ever felt really clean before a camera. And for this, I thank you!'"

"Marilyn in the House," by Helen Bolstad, appears in *Photoplay*. Amy Greene is quoted on Monroe as houseguest: "Marilyn is always reading and few people realize how much serious reading she does. And she loves to walk. She'd bundle up in some of Milton's outdoor clothes, call the dogs and tramp out through the woods. . . . Marilyn had never seen snow before, nor known cold weather. She, too, likes to drive. We'd take the convertible and with the top down, we'd go sailing along the highway. We both liked to feel the wind in our faces and the warmth of the heater on our legs. . . . I remember one day we were driving home from a friend's house. Marilyn looked up at the hillside and remarked that the trees were just dead, bare sticks. Then the next week, they began to turn green. To her, it seemed a miracle."

September 3–5: Marilyn spends the Labor Day weekend with the Rostens on Long Island.

Eve Arnold photographs Marilyn in a leopard-skin bathing suit, slithering through the grass; reading James Joyce's *Ulysses* in a striped one-piece bathing suit; and sitting on a children's playground merry-go-round.

September 10: Milton Greene photographs Marilyn in a "ballerina sitting."

September 25: The *American Weekly* puts a photograph of Marilyn on its cover. She is dressed in a black fur coat with matching black gloves, holding her hands together, almost in the manner of a prayer. The pose shows a meditative mood reflected in the headline: "'The Mystery of Marilyn Monroe,' by Maurice Zolotow."

September 29: Marilyn attends the Broadway premiere of *A View From The Bridge*. She meets Miller's parents, Isidore and Augusta, but carefully avoids running into Miller's wife.

September 30: Michael Chekhov dies, and Marilyn attends his funeral.

October: Marilyn tells columnist Earl Wilson that she is a fan of Goya.

Marilyn asks Elia Kazan to cast her in the title role in a Tennessee Williams film, *Baby Doll*, but he tells her she is too old to play the part of a twenty-year-old. In a notebook, she writes, "He said that I've become so deified as a sex symbol that the public would never accept me as a virgin and as a nineteen/twenty year old." She mentions that Tennessee Williams wants her to play the part in his film and has said, "I don't want anybody else."

October 5: Marilyn attends opening night of *The Diary of Anne Frank*, starring Susan Strasberg. Marilyn is photographed embracing Susan, signing autographs, and mingling among a crowd of partygoers that appears to be at Sardi's, a popular Broadway theater district restaurant.

October 6: Marilyn is quoted in *Mirror-News* (Hollywood), saying, "I love Keats . . . I'm reading G. B. Shaw little by little." She keeps a copy of *Leaves of Grass* beside her bed, and reads Whitman frequently.

October 11: Marilyn, accompanied by the Rostens, attends the recital of Russian pianist Emil Gilels at Carnegie Hall.

October 13: Marilyn attends the premiere of George Axelrod's *Will Success Spoil Rock Hunter?*, a play about a Hollywood dumb blonde, staring Jayne Mansfield in a role obviously modeled on Marilyn.

October 17: Miller's wife, Mary, throws him out of their Brooklyn house when she learns of his affair with Marilyn. He moves into the Chelsea Hotel.

October 19: In a photo in *Visto*, Marilyn thrusts her face forward, her eyes cast upward in a questing posture, and seems just as erotic in a simple blue-and-white striped top with a plunging neckline as in her more glamorous photographs. The composition represents Milton Greene's efforts to make her allure more complex and sophisticated.

October 31: A court decree makes the divorce from DiMaggio final.

Lee Strasberg convinces Marilyn to overcome her doubts about herself and prepare a scene from *Anna Christie* for the Actors Studio.

Inez Melson resigns as Marilyn's business manager, saying Marilyn's finances have become too complicated.

November: Irving Stein takes over the legal work for Marilyn Monroe Productions when Marilyn, for unexplained reasons, concludes that Frank Delaney is not representing her interests well.

Mid-November: "Marilyn, all dressed in mink, and Arthur [Miller], in his usual dark blue shirt, arrived together at the opening of Maxfield's new ice cream parlor," wrote Tichi Wilkerson and Marcia Borie in *The Hollywood Reporter: The Golden Years*.

Fox accedes to most of Marilyn's demands for a seven-year contract, which includes a $100,000 bonus for *The Seven Year Itch*, the right to make four movies with her own production company, and the right to appear in as many as six television and radio programs while also doing some recordings.

November 17: Marilyn attends the "1955 Thanksgiving March for Muscular Dystrophy Drive." She is photographed seated next to a young boy in a wheelchair. In another shot, she kisses the boy on his cheek.

November 18: Marilyn appears on a very French cover for *Cine Revue*. The shot, by Frank Powolny, has her leaning forward, with her right hand touching her cleavage, as she tilts her head back and projects the classic half-open, half-closed eyes and mouth, the very epitome of the screen siren. The cover's caption promises revelations about the secrets of love.

November 25: *Cinema* (Italy) displays on its cover Frank Powolny's publicity shot for *The Seven Year Itch*. Marilyn has most of her body blocked by a sofa, except for her head and her crossed legs jutting out over the furniture arm.

December: *Cinelandia* (Brazil) publishes Sam Shaw's photographs of Marilyn in a terry cloth robe. She stands, placing her hands suggestively on her lower body, while a close-up has her looking back at the camera with a rather sly coquettish look.

Milton Greene shoots three images of Marilyn in sweater girl fashions for the cover of *Movieland*.

Marilyn sees Marlon Brando several times and is photographed in intimate close-ups with him, and as his consort in a shot that features the actor dressed in formal clothes, cape, and walking stick. Marilyn seems to purr as she takes his arm.

December 12: Marilyn and Jayne Mansfield are photographed together at the opening of *The Rose Tattoo*.

Marlon Brando escorts Marilyn to dinner at the Sheraton Astor Hotel, after which they attend the opening night of *The Rose Tattoo*. She is photographed wearing a white fur stole, accompanied by Brando in a tuxedo. Later at the Sheraton Astor Hotel, she is photographed seated with the Strasbergs and the Rostens, meeting Jayne Mansfield, and talking with Arthur Miller.

December 24: Marilyn invites twenty-five guests for beef stew and a holiday party at her New York apartment. Among those attending are the Strasbergs. Lee she nicknames "Great White Father." His wife, Paula, Marilyn calls "Black Bart," because she perpetually wears black. Arthur Miller is "Arturo," Norman Rosten "Claude" (she sees a resemblance to the actor, Claude Rains), Marlon Brando "Carlo," and Sam Shaw "Sam Spade." She refers to herself as "Zelda Zonk."

Christmas: Marilyn takes James Haspiel, one of her devoted fans, on a shopping trip to Saks Fifth Avenue. She disguises herself with a silk kerchief and dark glasses, and wears no makeup. But she is still recognized by store salesmen and several customers.

December 29: The Fox board of directors meets to consider the new contract with Marilyn Monroe Productions. Spyros Skouras pushes the deal through, in spite of some opposition.

December 31: Fox offers a new contract: four movies over seven years, director approval, and freedom to work outside her Fox contract. Marilyn signs and sips champagne to celebrate.

Marilyn celebrates New Year's Eve with the Greenes in Connecticut.

1956

Pete Martin publishes "Will Acting Spoil Marilyn Monroe?"

Photographer Seymour Wally shoots Marilyn with her basset hound, Hugo.

Marilyn is photographed in London with poet Edith Sitwell.

Richard Avedon shoots publicity pictures for *The Prince and the Showgirl*, including one shot of Marilyn in feathers on a sofa.

Entre Nous (France) publishes a classic cheesecake photograph of Marilyn lying on grass, blowing on a dandelion gone to seed that she holds in her left hand, while the fingers of her right hand touch her hair.

Marilyn is nominated as "Best Foreign Actress" for a British academy award for her performance in *The Seven Year Itch*.

Marilyn writes to Bruno Bernard about the House Committee on Un-American Activities, referring to a "witch hunt. . . . They and the Hays Bureau should be buried alive. Those hypocrites who probably read dirty books and put them under their pillows at night."

January: Arthur Miller begins discussing a divorce from his wife, Mary Slattery, while discussing marriage with Marilyn. Miller takes Marilyn on walks through the streets of Brooklyn Heights and tells her about his childhood. At the same time, the FBI is investigating him.

Marilyn establishes her residency in New York, using the address of press agent Lois Weber (124 East 60th Street), as she prepares to have her name legally changed to Marilyn Monroe.

January 4: The *New York Morning Telegraph* headline blares, "Battle with Studio Won by Marilyn. Actress Wins All Demands." She is to receive a $100,000 flat fee per film, plus $500 for expenses.

January 16: *Time* publishes "Winner," an account of how Marilyn got the best of Fox in contract negotiations.

January 26: The Women's Division of the Federation of Jewish Philanthropies of New York presents Marilyn with a citation, "In recognition of her unique ability to bring pleasure to millions of Americans through her abundant talents, her glowing personality, her open heart and her generous spirit. . . . In gratitude for her co-operation in helping to make this day a success and thereby bringing hope and comfort to thousands of men, women, and children who look to us for help."

January 30: *Time* publishes "Who Would Resist?" which declares, "The bitter battle was over. Marilyn Monroe, a five-foot five and a half inch blonde weighing 118 alluringly distributed pounds, had brought to its knees mighty Twentieth Century Fox."

Redbook publishes "Marilyn Monroe's Marriage."

Cecil Beaton photographs Marilyn on a bed draped with a Japanese wall hanging. Diana Vreeland interprets the pose as a portrayal of Marilyn as a "geisha. She was born to pleasure, spent her whole life giving it."

February: Marilyn appears on the cover of *Picture Digest* in front of a fireplace roaring with flames. The accompanying headlines read, "Sex on Celluloid" and "Meet the Human Torch."

Cecil Beaton's photograph of Monroe appears in *Harper's Bazaar*.

February 5: Laurence Olivier, his agent Cecil Tennant, and playwright Terence Rattigan arrive in New York to discuss with Marilyn a film of *The Sleeping Prince*, to be produced in London with Olivier and Marilyn in the starring roles.

February 7: After waiting for over an hour, Olivier meets Marilyn at her 2 Sutton Place apartment, and it is agreed that he will star in the film, as well as direct and co-produce it.

February 8: Marilyn does her "black sitting" session with Milton Greene. Marilyn poses in black hat and fishnet stockings, her face partially in shadow. She also appears in a shot where she lies down, her left leg extended in the air, as she covers part of her face with her hands. She also kneels, drink in hand, smiling. She props herself up with her arms and draws her knees into her body, with half her face in the dark—a study in moody bifurcation. Greene's photographs will eventually punctuate the text of Norman Mailer's *Of Women and Their Elegance*.

In the evening Marilyn, wearing a white fur coat over a low-cut dress, long black gloves, and jeweled earrings that stretch all the way down her neck, attends the premiere of *Middle of the Night*, a Paddy Chayefsky play directed by Josh Logan.

February 9: In the company of Laurence Olivier, Marilyn calls a press conference in the Terrace Room of the Plaza Hotel to announce their joint project, *The Sleeping Prince* (later titled *The Prince and the Showgirl*). Publicity shows a smiling Marilyn, flanked by Olivier on her right and Rattigan on her left, gazing at her. In front of more than 150 reporters and photographers, one of the straps on her dress breaks, setting off a flurry of photography until a safety pin repairs the strap. One shot shows the dangling pin after it comes undone—twice.

February 12: Walter Winchell announces on his radio program that Marilyn has become the "sweetheart of the left intelligentsia which includes among its members, Communist militants."

February 17: With Maureen Stapleton, Marilyn performs a scene from *Anna Christie* at the Actors Studio to a round of applause, but she doubts she has given a good performance. Afterwards she suffers from laryngitis.

February 18: Marilyn draws up her first will. She bequeaths $100,000 to Arthur Miller, $25,000 to Lee and Paula Strasberg, $20,000 to Dr. Margaret Hohenberg, $10,000 to Xenia Chekhov (Michael Chekhov's widow), $10,000 to the Actors Studio, and $10,000 to Patricia Rosten, daughter of Norman and Hedda Rosten. Marilyn also allots $25,000 for the care of her mother.

February 19: Marilyn and Olivier attend a performance of *The Diary of Anne Frank* and are photographed speaking with Susan Strasberg.

Marilyn does a number of poses with flowers for Cecil Beaton, who positions her in bed, in an armchair, and on a sofa, as well as against a curtain Jackson Pollock could have designed. She wraps her arms around herself, bringing her left hand up over her right shoulder and her right hand atop her left shoulder, creating an almost serpentine Laocoön effect.

February 20: *Time* publishes "Co-Stars," about the Monroe-Olivier matchup.

February 22: Marilyn is photographed giving an interview to Elsa Maxwell, gossip columnist and professional hostess, at the Ambassador Hotel.

Cecil Beaton photographs Marilyn in front of a Japanese wall hanging.

February 23: Marilyn applies to legally change her name to Marilyn Monroe.

February 25: Marilyn returns to Hollywood to star in *Bus Stop*. Hundreds of reporters meet her at the airport, and she conducts a press conference. She is photographed in a dark business suit, wearing a tie and dark gloves, seated next to Milton Greene. She seems more at ease, more comfortable in Greene's company, than in the press conference with Olivier.

Monroe stays in West Los Angeles at a nine-room house at 595 North Beverly Glen Boulevard, rented by Greene. The location puts her close to both UCLA and the Fox studios.

February 27: Pre-production work begins on *Bus Stop*.

February 29: Marilyn, accompanied by her lawyer, Irving Stein, finally appears in court, and Judge Griffin fines her fifty-six dollars for three traffic violations: driving without a license, driving too slowly, and driving after her license had expired. He tells her, "Laws are made for all of us, rich or poor, without race or creed or whether your name happens to be Miss Monroe or not, and this kind of acting won't win you an Oscar."

March: Marilyn and James Cagney are photographed together in Beverly Hills at a *Look* party.

The *National Police Gazette* shows Marilyn in a *Seven Year Itch* pose, leaning forward to make her breasts more visible in a low-cut white dress. Next to her photograph is the headline "Suppressed Facts of Marilyn Monroe's Secret Life!"

Photographer Gene Lester photographs Marilyn in a chair, wearing long black gloves, with Milton Greene sitting on the floor beside her. She also poses lying on the floor in her elegant dark gown, nestling her face into a pillow. She changes into a flaming red gown for another Marilyn on the floor shot—this time arching her back and raising her legs in front of a fireplace, and in another resting her head on a white fur in a sinuous pose reminiscent of her famous calendar shot—although this time she is fully clothed.

Gordon Parks shoots a different Marilyn, dressed in a black leotard top and slacks, standing, her back to the camera, while her head turns back toward the viewer.

March 1: Jack Warner holds a press conference to welcome Marilyn into the Warner Bros. "family," while announcing that the company will distribute *The Prince and the Showgirl*. Marilyn receives the key (complete with logo) to the studio. Marilyn, Warner, and Greene (in a jolly mood), are photographed several times. Director Billy Wilder shows up to congratulate Marilyn.

March 3: *Le Ore* (Italy) features a 1952 photograph of Marilyn in a black, lacy negligee, with the caption "Marilyn, La Bella Addormentata Di Laurence Olivier."

Filming of *Bus Stop* begins.

Irving Stein calls Natasha Lytess to announce her services are no longer needed and that she should not call Marilyn.

March 5: Lytess tries to call on Marilyn at home but is denied access.

March 12: Marilyn misses her plane to Phoenix by twenty minutes and arrives a few days later.

Marilyn legally changes her name to Marilyn Monroe, stating, "I'm an actress and as such, I consider that my family name is a handicap." She now uses the "pseudonym of Marilyn Monroe, a name become famous" that she would like to "make mine definitely."

March 15: Marilyn arrives to shoot *Bus Stop* in Phoenix. She is photographed wearing a black fur as she disembarks from the plane with Greene, camera in hand, beside her. Then she is photographed with her co-star, Don Murray, and her director, Josh Logan.

Milton Greene keeps tight control on the set, allowing few photographers to shoot Marilyn at work or journalists to interview her.

Arthur Miller writes to Saul Bellow, who is in Nevada, establishing the six-week residency to qualify for a divorce: "I am going out there around the end of the month to spend the fated six weeks and have no idea where to live. I have a problem, however, of slightly unusual proportions. From time to time there will be a visitor who is very dear to me, but who is unfortunately recognizable by approximately a hundred million people, give or take three or four. She has all sorts of wigs, can affect a limp, sunglasses, bulky coats, etc., but if it is possible, I want to find a place, perhaps a bungalow or something like, where there are not likely to be crowds looking in through the windows. Do you know of any such place?" Because of the *Bus Stop* shooting schedule, Marilyn is not able to visit Miller.

March 16: Late to the set, Marilyn feels humiliated when Logan drags her into a scene.

March 17: Running across the rodeo grounds during a shot, Marilyn loses a shoe. But she keeps going, realizing the scene is now more dramatic. She is upset when Logan seems about to shout "Cut!" But then, he allows the cameras to run as the spectators roar. Marilyn, watching his indecision, loses some respect for her director and becomes distrustful.

March 18: Marilyn and Greene have one of their first arguments over expenses charged to Marilyn Monroe Productions. He objects to funding Lee Strasberg's visit. Paula Strasberg is already on retainer as a drama coach at $1,500 a week.

March 22: Darryl Zanuck leaves Fox to become an independent producer.

March 26–30: Location shooting continues in the snows of Sun Valley, Idaho. Interiors are shot at the North Fork General Store.

Arthur Miller consults with attorney Joseph Rauh about his expectation that he will be called to testify before the House Committee on Un-American Activities. Miller worries that he will not be able to obtain a passport to accompany Marilyn to England to shoot her film with Olivier, and that he will not be able to attend the London premiere of his play, *A View From the Bridge*.

March 28: *Mascotte* (Italy) produces on its cover the "Golden Dreams" nude calendar shot (the pose in which she is upright), but paints over her bare breasts and bottom, simulating a blue two-piece swimsuit.

March 30: Marilyn is photographed on her way back to Hollywood. At a stop in Boise, Idaho, she is photographed wearing sunglasses and a straw sun hat and having a coffee.

April: The crew of the first atomic submarine, the *Nautilus*, hangs up a poster of Marilyn Monroe inside the ship to build morale.

April 5–9: Marilyn is hospitalized with acute bronchitis at St. Vincent Hospital in Los Angeles. She is exhausted and running a high fever.

April 24: Marilyn returns to the set of *Bus Stop*. Logan devises a method of shooting scenes without calling for cuts. This time-consuming, expensive way of filming nevertheless achieves a breakthrough for Marilyn, who simply resumes scenes after faltering without having to wait for camera cues. She sees in the rushes that Logan is staying with her and not interrupting her painstaking, fitful approach to her part.

Don Murray realizes that Marilyn's difficulty concentrating means that there will have to be multiple takes of scenes and says to himself, "Hey, Don, you've got to be your best on every take."

Marilyn seems delighted with rushes of her early scenes, in which she is called on—in the character of Cherie—to talk about her past in many more lines of text than was usual in a Marilyn Monroe movie.

Marilyn returns to stay with the Greenes on Beverly Glen Boulevard, but she also meets Arthur Miller in a room she rents at the Chateau Marmont.

May 1: Miller establishes residency in Reno in preparation for his divorce.

May 4: *Hayat* (Turkey) shows a casual Marilyn, sitting on a rock ledge and dangling her left leg in the water. She is dressed in a blouse open down to her cleavage and wearing striped slacks that she seemed to favor when relaxing.

May 12–13: Miller spends the weekend with Marilyn at the Chateau Marmont in Hollywood.

May 14: Marilyn makes the cover of *Time* and appears in "To Aristophanes and Back." Ezra Goodman, who researches the article for the magazine, concludes: "It may be, as has been psychiatrically observed about her, that she has such contempt for herself that she is really trying to make peace with the world, not by adjusting to reality, but by reconstructing herself and the world around her. . . . There is in her some sort of enigmatic, almost magical, quotient, which no one has really been able to define, that has gotten her where she is today in spite of a background that should normally have found her ending up a schizophrenic in a state mental hospital or an alcoholic in the gutter. Perhaps the quality that many people find attractive in her is her very insecurity, her unhappiness, her sleepwalking through life. But the riddle that is Marilyn Monroe has not been solved. It is doubtful whether a year of ambulance chasing, flagpole climbing, and flat footing would do the trick. That is probably one for the analyst's couch." *Time* does not print these remarks, but instead provides a rather banal and anodyne portrait.

May 18: Arthur Miller applies for a passport to attend the London premiere of *A View From the Bridge*. He submits an affidavit declaring he is not a Communist Party member.

May 21: Marilyn lashes out at Don Murray with the train of her costume. Refusing to apologize, a despondent Monroe calls Miller in Reno. He reassures her, but also collapses under the stress of learning that she seems to count on him alone. Nonetheless, he manages to talk her back into working. Years later, Don Murray gave a full explanation, saying Marilyn was angry because he had asked for another take of a scene that satisfied her: "Anyway, we did the scene over, and this time—after I ripped off the tail of her dress and she grabbed it back and told me off—instead of putting her head down and rushing at me, she lashed my face with the dress. I got a cut on the eyelid and Marilyn ran off, and although it didn't hurt much, I was really angry because it was very unprofessional. So, I followed her to bawl her out, and Josh Logan got in front of me, and made me laugh by telling me the story about the Roman general who won all the wars by avoiding the battles. At that point I forgot about the whole thing, and after that it was a non-incident. When Marilyn came back on the set she had totally calmed down and she was fine. She didn't apologize—and I didn't expect her to or want her to—but the next day she came to me and started talking about another scene we'd done, and everything was okay."

May 22: Marilyn attends Susan Strasberg's birthday party.

May 27: Marilyn announces to the press, "My real home now is New York."

May 29: Marilyn finishes shooting *Bus Stop*. She appears on a *Look* cover and inside in "New Marilyn."

Josh Logan takes Marilyn to dinner at the home of William Goetz, who is producing Logan's next movie, *Sayonara*.

May 31: Marilyn meets President Sukarno of Indonesia at a Hollywood cocktail party hosted by Josh Logan. Sukarno tells her she is a "very important person in Indonesia. Your pictures are the most popular of any that have ever played in my country. The entire Indonesian population is interested in my meeting you." He asks her if she is going to marry Arthur Miller. She shrugs and laughs. She is amused, telling Norman Rosten that Sukarno "kept looking down my dress, you'd think that with five wives he'd have enough."

June: *Film Life*'s cover shows a typical glamor shot of Marilyn, her right hand caressing her neck as she buries her face in her upraised left forearm. The headline reads: "Is Marilyn coming back too late?"

June 1: Marilyn turns thirty. Reporters surprise her with a birthday cake just as she is boarding an airplane. She is photographed blowing out one tall candle on the cake. They question her about Arthur Miller.

June 2: Marilyn flies from Los Angeles to New York and arrives at Idlewild Airport at 7:55 a.m. She is photographed in the back of a limousine, holding a birthday cake with one candle on it, which she is about to blow out.

Marilyn returns to her apartment at 2 Sutton Place South.

Arthur Miller writes from Nevada to Saul Bellow about press attention, now that his relationship with Marilyn is public knowledge: "All hell breaks loose. The phones all around never stop ringing. Television trucks—(as I live!)—drive up, cameras grinding, screams, yells—I say nothing, give them some pictures, retire into the cabin. They finally go away."

June 5: *Picture Week* transforms Marilyn into a redhead, showing her breasts just barely covered by what looks like a black fur stole.

June 8: The House Committee on Un-American Activities (HUAC) serves Miller with a subpoena to testify on June 14 in Washington, D.C. The committee agrees to delay the hearing until June 21, so that Miller can complete his Reno residency.

June 11: In a brief hearing before a judge, Miller is granted an uncontested divorce, charging his wife with "mental cruelty."

June 12: Reporters meets Miller at the airport in New York and ask him about Marilyn. He says very little, although he admits that a meeting with her "may happen one of these days."

June 15: Al Delgado, an agent at MCA (Music Corporation of America), which began representing Marilyn when she broke with Charles Feldman, writes to a colleague about the damage incurred at the Los Angeles home Greene had rented for Marilyn: "It's a very serious case, because we're talking about a luxurious house with expensive furniture, and the inventory is probably 40 pages long. When the owner will be back, I think that Milton will have some problems and he might be sued. . . . I'll do my best to refurbish a part of the furniture. I must admit that I don't really like this story, because the house was in perfect condition when they moved in." A settlement of the case occurred in the fall of 1956.

June 19: Marilyn calls her lawyer, Irving Stein, to say she wishes to modify her will and leave all her property to Arthur Miller. She apparently is concerned that Miller's divorce, alimony, and child support, and the cost of legal representation for his HUAC testimony, will bankrupt him.

June 20: Spyros Skouras, Fox's president, meets with Marilyn and Miller to advise the playwright to cooperate with HUAC. Miller refuses, and Marilyn admires his integrity and courage.

June 21: Miller testifies before HUAC and refuses to name those he met at Communist-supported meetings and events, although he explains his own participation in political activities.

June 22: A *New York Times* headline reads, "Arthur Miller Admits Helping Communist-Front Groups in '40's." The New York *Daily News* headlines, "Miller Admits Aiding Reds, Risks Contempt." Marilyn holds a meeting with the press. She holds on to Miller, who is at her side, expresses her support for him, and says she has never been happier. She shifts attention away from Miller's politics and to their plans to marry and honeymoon in England while she works on *The Sleeping Prince*. She is photographed leaning against him, and in other shots she looks triumphant.

June 23: Reporters stake out Marilyn's apartment, responding to rumors that she and Miller will marry that night.

June 24: Miller and Monroe drive to his home in Roxbury, Connecticut. Marilyn meets with Miller's parents, Isidore and Augusta, and with his children Jane (eleven) and Robert (nine).

June 25: Marilyn and Miller have dinner at his cousin Morton's in Roxbury and then pose for reporters.

June 26: Miller emerges from his Roxbury home to request that reporters grant the couple privacy. In return, he promises to hold a press conference to announce their plans. Agreeing to the bargain, the press returns to New York City.

Laurence Olivier responds to Josh Logan's letter explaining Marilyn's working methods on *Bus Stop*. Oliver writes that Logan's comments have been "carefully noted."

June 27: Morton Miller, Arthur's cousin, rushes Arthur's and Marilyn's blood to the state Bureau of Laboratories, as required by law.

June 29: On the way to an afternoon press conference with Marilyn and Miller, amidst a crush of reporters who chase after them, one journalist dies when her driver loses control of her car.

Marilyn and Miller are married in a civil ceremony in the Westchester County, New York, courthouse, with photographs taken of Marilyn and Miller toasting each other in front of shelves of law books. Present at the brief ceremony were Milton Greene, Lee and Paula Strasberg, John Moore (Marilyn's friend, decorator, and dress designer), and Miller's cousin Morton and his wife, Florence. Although Miller has ordered a Cartier ring, it is not ready, so he borrows his mother Augusta's wedding ring.

July: *Vogue* features Marilyn in "Portrait."

Guns puts Marilyn on its cover in one of her *River of No Return* costumes, squinting and leaning toward Arvo Ojala, who is showing her how to shoot a Colt single-action .45.

Lee Strasberg meets with Milton Greene and negotiates a salary of $25,000 a week for his wife Paula's services as a drama coach.

Hedda Rosten is hired at $200 a week as Marilyn's private secretary.

July 1: Marilyn and Miller marry in a Jewish ceremony. She signs a conversion certificate that is witnessed by Milton Greene, Arthur Miller, and Rabbi E. Goldberg, who presides over the wedding. Norman Norell designs Marilyn's veil and beige chiffon dress. Miller presents Marilyn with a gold ring inscribed, "A. to M., June 1956. Now is forever." Marilyn is photographed feeding Miller wedding cake with both her hands. There are twenty-five guests, including George Axelrod (screenwriter of *The Seven Year Itch*), Miller's children, his brother Kermit, sister Joan, the Strasbergs, Rostens, and Greenes. They dine on roast beef, thin slices of turkey, and champagne.

July 2: *Newsweek* publishes "Engagement Party."

Miller decides to sell his Roxbury, Connecticut, house. The *New York Herald Tribune* carries a classified ad for the "Love nest of the playwright and the movie star. 7 rooms, 3 bathrooms, pool, tennis court, garage for 2 cars, small studio. 2 hectares. $29,500 ($38,500 with 12 hectares more)."

July 2–9: Milton Greene photographs Marilyn during her costume fittings for *The Sleeping Prince*.

July 6: Arthur Miller is issued a temporary passport so that he can join his wife in England.

July 7: *Point De Vue Images Du Monde* shows a very French-looking Marilyn, shot in tight close-up by Ted Baron. Although the photograph was taken in 1954, it seems in sync with the "new Marilyn"—still sexy, but now with an aura of sophistication and intrigue, suggested by the horizontally striped turtleneck that covers her upper body.

Cecil Beaton's photograph of a smiling Marilyn luxuriating in a white fur is on the cover of *Settimo Giorno*.

July 9: Marilyn appears in the "People" section in *Time*.

July 10: HUAC votes to recommend that the House of Representatives cite Miller for contempt of Congress.

July 13: Marilyn's plane leaving Idylwild Airport for London is delayed by a mob of fans and reporters. Miller and Marilyn are photographed together, his white jacket matching her white coat. They seem relaxed, and kiss in public—although in one shot Miller clearly has his eye on the camera, not Marilyn. Marilyn blows kisses at the press just before she enters the TWA plane.

July 14: Marilyn's plane arrives in London at 10:40 a.m., an hour late. She is photographed in dark glasses, walking down the airline stairway with Miller right behind her. Olivier and his wife, Vivien Leigh, welcome Marilyn and Miller at the airport and pose for pictures, escorted by seventy policemen in front of something like 150 journalists. Marilyn fields questions in a brief interview at the airport bar, but refuses to speak into a microphone, calling it "too impersonal." An Austin Princess limousine, escorted by four policemen, takes Marilyn, Miller, Greene, and Arthur Jacobs (Marilyn's publicist) to Surrey, where a country home, Parkside, an hour from London, will be their base. It is a Georgian manor house belonging to Lord North, proprietor of the *Financial Times*. The house has five bedrooms, a five-hectare park, and a rose garden. Throughout their stay, Marilyn and Miller will have to cope with reporters at their gate.

Picture Post publishes a Milton Greene photograph of Marilyn, shot at the bottom of Laurel Canyon. Wearing a white blouse (only her upper body is showing), she crosses her arms in a winsome way.

July 15: Photographers shoot Marilyn and Miller walking together in the park, and later question her during a press conference in the Lancaster room of the London Savoy Hotel. It is an occasion for smiles all around—not just for Marilyn, but for Miller and Olivier, as well. She is presented with a bicycle, compliments of the *Daily Sketch*. Marilyn and Olivier are photographed in an intimate conversation.

Olivier arrives after noon to show Marilyn photographs of *The Prince and the Showgirl* set.

July 16: After another press conference at the Savoy, Marilyn heads for Claridge's for lunch.

Life publishes "Wedding Wine for Marilyn."

8:00 p.m. A crowd of students from Shoreditch Teacher's Training College heads toward Marilyn's residence, chanting, "We want Marilyn." Marilyn watches them, but is advised that for security reasons she should not make an appearance.

Elle's cover shows an ethereal-looking Marilyn, gazing upward. Milton Greene's photograph (taken in 1953) counters the usually available-looking Monroe by making her seem more elusive, justifying the headline, "Le Mystere De Marilyn Monroe."

July 17: Marilyn and Miller attend a Vivien Leigh performance in Noel Coward's *South Sea Bubble*. Crowds besiege the theater exits, hoping to see Marilyn. At 10:50 p.m., with a police escort, the couple leaves the theater through the front doors.

July 18: Miller and Marilyn depart at 2:00 a.m., after spending a few hours at Oliver's London home.

Rehearsals begin for *The Prince and the Showgirl* at Pinewood Studios. Jack Cardiff, the film's cinematographer, puts Marilyn at her ease.

Marilyn and Miller visit Shakespeare's birthplace cottage in Stratford-upon-Avon.

July 19: Marilyn is late for rehearsal, but the footage of her makeup tests is outstanding.

July 20: Hairdressers try various wigs on Marilyn, with Milton Greene by her side, whispering in her ear.

July 21: *Vie Nuove* (Italy) puts a smiling Marilyn and Arthur Miller on its cover.

July 21–22: Marilyn and Miller spend a quiet weekend trying to avoid the press. Nonetheless, they are photographed bicycling. Breaches of security—fans and journalists somehow gain entrance to the grounds of their residence—make it difficult to preserve any privacy.

Cinematographer Jack Cardiff visits them to discuss his work on *The Prince and the Showgirl*. He finds Marilyn warm and sociable.

July 23: Marilyn has a day off when the music for the film is previewed. Paula Strasberg, Hedda Rosten, Amy, and the Greene's son, Joshua, arrive.

July 24: Laurence Olivier is determined to ban Paula Strasberg from the set.

Playwright Terence Rattigan hosts a party for the Millers. Included among the one hundred guests are Alec Guinness, Dame Margot Fonteyn, John Gielgud, Tyrone Power, and Douglas Fairbanks Jr. Gossip columnist Louella Parsons is also present. The party begins at nine, but Marilyn and Miller do not arrive until 11:00 p.m. They dance cheek-to-cheek and do not leave until 4:00 a.m.

July 25: By a vote of 379 to 9, the House of Representatives cites Miller for contempt of Congress.

Marilyn and Miller spend the day mostly in their bedroom in the Parkside House residence.

Gladys writes to Marilyn, "I am very unhappy, daughter. I wish there was some way to join you in England where I am sure we would have a lovely time. May God be with you and may He find a way for us to be together again very soon. Love, Mother."

Australian Women's Weekly carries an image of Marilyn cradling a bird in her hands and throwing back her head, smiling broadly (so that her gum line is visible) as if in ecstasy. The headline reads, "Marilyn Monroe Wedding Day Pictures."

July 26: The day is spent working on lighting for the film.

July 27: Work continues on the Pinewood set, after making sure of the security (it is a closed set) and ensuring Marilyn's dressing room is in order.

July 28–29: Marilyn and Miller have the weekend off.

July 30: Marilyn and Paula Strasberg arrive nearly an hour late for rehearsal at Pinewood. A dismayed Olivier had not been informed that Marilyn would bring an acting coach. Dame Sybil Thorndike welcomes Marilyn warmly.

Marilyn appears in "Conquest" in *Time*.

July 31: Olivier upbraids Marilyn for showing up three-quarters of an hour late. She has trouble picking up on her cues. Marilyn seems upset, and Dame Sybil Thorndike encourages her. Marilyn seems to recover herself later in the afternoon.

August: *Screen Stories* features Marilyn on the cover, dressed as Cherie, with the headline, "Starring Marilyn Monroe . . . better than ever in her first come-back picture!"

Photoplay (English edition) employs a Frank Powolny photograph to present a transitional Marilyn—somewhere between the gold digger of *Gentlemen Prefer Blondes* and the more mature performer of *The Prince and the Showgirl*. She has something of Rose Loomis's predatory smile and allure, emphasized by her low-cut, black-and-red gown.

Marilyn attends several sessions with Anna Freud in London. Freud specializes in treating children and adults deprived of parental care as children. Freud invites Marilyn into the nursery where she treats children, and Marilyn enjoys playing and joking with the young patients. Freud later recorded a brief assessment: "Adult patient. Emotional instability, exaggerated impulsiveness, constant need for external approval, inability to be alone, tendency to depression in case of rejection, paranoid with schizophrenic elements."

August 1: Marilyn does not show up for rehearsal at Pinewood until noon.

August 2: Marilyn arrives on the set late but in a good mood. She is accompanied by Arthur Miller and Hedda Rosten, who return to Parkside House after touring the studio. Milton Greene and Paula Strasberg remain to vie for Marilyn's attention.

Gladys writes to Marilyn, "I have decided that the sooner I am able to leave here the better. I know I am a big topic of discussion here and it's not because of you, Marilyn. There seems to be a lot of interest in me, as well. Perhaps when I am released I will tell you about it though I doubt you would be interested in anything that has to do with me, your only Mother. Love, Gladys Baker Eley."

August 3: Rehearsals for *The Prince and the Showgirl* end, and at lunchtime cast and crew leave for the weekend.

Collier's publishes "That Old Monroe Magic."

August 6: The crew sets up the stage and lights in preparation for filming.

August 7: Filming of *The Prince and the Showgirl* begins. Marilyn arrives at 8:30 a.m. and begins her makeup session with Whitey Snyder. She does not emerge from her dressing room until 11:30 a.m. The first scene, with Dame Sybil Thorndike, is completed in eight takes. Marilyn's dress is so tightly molded to her body that she cannot sit down and instead relaxes herself by flicking her fingers—a tension-relieving practice advocated by the Strasbergs. Paula remains at Marilyn's ear, making it difficult for Olivier to establish a rapport with his co-star. Everyone is exhausted after a full day of shooting.

August 8: Marilyn arrives at 8:45 a.m. and seems quite happy, although the call to the set was for 6:45. Still, most of what has been planned for the day is accomplished, and Marilyn looks radiant in the rushes.

August 9: Marilyn works through the day, aided by Paula Strasberg's lavish compliments.

August 10: The filming has settled into a routine dictated by Marilyn's arrivals at 8:45. Dame Sybil smooths the way for her.

August 12: Marilyn goes for a bicycle ride. Olivier's managing director requests a full accounting of Marilyn's expenditures but receives no response.

August 13: Olivier, in full makeup, fumes as Marilyn fails to emerge from her dressing room. Privately, to Miller, she expresses her fury over Olivier's condescension.

August 14: When she has trouble learning her lines, Marilyn does not consult the script. Instead, she wanders off to consult with Paula and check her makeup. When Olivier gets angry, Sybil Thorndike steps in, explaining the strain Marilyn is under. Afterward, Marilyn works without stumbling over her dialogue. According to the third assistant director, Olivier says, "It's high time someone gave that silly girl a real telling off."

August 15: Marilyn arrives on the set early (at 7:30 a.m.) in a pleasant mood. By lunchtime, however, she seems confused.

August 16: Marilyn and Olivier remain at odds. Colin Clark describes her looking at Olivier as though he was "from another planet."

August 17: Marilyn performs well in a scene shot at 11:00 a.m., in which she is eating a late supper—doing take after take, as the chicken salad and caviar are replaced because of the hot lights. Olivier says she does not actually have to eat the food, just mime doing so, but she wants to experience not only the food, but also the champagne and seems not to be pleased when apple juice is substituted. Colin Clark notices that she likes the young boy playing Olivier's son and imagines that is because the boy is on her side in the script.

August 18: A more subdued Miller and Monroe attend another Terence Rattigan party. Miller is in a white dinner jacket, but Marilyn seems less well composed. Colin Clark provides an unflattering picture of Miller: "He struts around as if MM were his property. He seems to think his superior intelligence puts him on a higher plane, and treats her as if she is just an accessory." He seems to be the vain one, not Marilyn. Again, according to Clark, the "party never gelled."

August 20: Marilyn does not appear on the set until 11:00 a.m. It seems there is some estrangement between Miller and Monroe, which Clark sensed at Terence Rattigan's party. A frustrated Olivier finds it impossible to confer with Marilyn so long as she seems tied to Paula Strasberg.

August 21: Trouble with doors through which Marilyn is supposed to burst sends Olivier into a rage and Marilyn into laughter.

August 22: Vivien Leigh visits the set and compliments an astonished Marilyn. Then Leigh makes a quick exit. That afternoon Marilyn works harder than ever.

Marilyn becomes ill while shooting a scene. This may have been an attack of endometriosis.

August 24: Clark attributes part of Marilyn's difficulties to Rattigan's "idiotic script," which provides no motivation for her character.

Marilyn's cook and butler are fired for selling stories to the press.

Clark reports that Miller is deeply disenchanted and tells Olivier that Marilyn is "devouring me."

Miller announces that he is going home to see his children.

August 25: Marilyn appears to be in a sulky mood during a Saturday shopping trip. She seems disappointed that no one seems to recognize her. But then she is mobbed and becomes upset. Clark again provides a negative view of Miller: "AM had also had quite a fright, though nothing really shakes his air of smug complacency.

He is much more pleased with himself than MM is with herself, that's for sure."

August 27: Marilyn is too ill to show up for shooting at the studio.

Life publishes "Unveiling of the New Monroe."

August 28: Marilyn shows up at the studio at 8:30 a.m., but does not look well. Olivier finds a scene to do that only requires her to lie on the floor and say a few lines, which she does quite well. In the afternoon, she feels much better and more relaxed.

August 29: Marilyn arrives at the set in poor shape, accompanied by a tense Milton Greene and Paula Strasberg. Marilyn manages a love scene with Olivier, but then retires to her dressing room, and she appears in no more scenes.

Bus Stop is released.

August 30: Miller leaves for Paris and then New York for ten days. Clark believes this absence is why Marilyn was so out of sorts the previous day. He continues to find Miller unsympathetic: "I never saw him look tenderly at MM, only with what looks like a sort of boasting self-satisfaction."

August 31: Marilyn is ill again and cannot work. Olivier shoots five hundred extras representing the crowd in the film's coronation scenes.

Milton Greene calls a gynecologist, who confirms Marilyn's pregnancy when he examines her at Parkside House.

September 2: Colin Clark hears a rumor that Marilyn is pregnant.

September 3: Marilyn performs two wonderful dance scenes.

September 4: Marilyn again seems quite confident in a series of two-shots with Olivier. She has no problem with her dialogue. Later, she seems pleasant but distant, and even a simple line gives her trouble. And then, near the end of the day, she recovers her form and does a scene well, Clark comments.

Miller cuts short his trip to America and returns to England as soon as he learns Marilyn is pregnant. Olivier's managing director rejects charges for Marilyn's private hairdresser, her secretary, and one of her lawyers.

September 5: Marilyn does not arrive at Pinewood until noon and does not seem well. She has difficulty maintaining her composure.

September 6: The studio receives a message that Marilyn is not well and that a physician has been summoned to her Parkside House residence.

September 7: Marilyn does not work, but she attends a production of *The Caucasian Chalk Circle* at the Palace Theatre in London.

September 8: More rumors circulate about Marilyn's pregnancy and possible miscarriage.

September 9: Marilyn accompanies Miller to a preview performance of *A View From the Bridge* at the Comedy Theatre. Miller introduces the play, as Marilyn sits on stage with actor Anthony Quayle.

Marilyn becomes a member of the Watergate Theatre Club, a private establishment created to present plays banned by the Lord Chamberlain from public theaters. The first production of this organization is *A View From The Bridge*.

September 11: Colin Clark is sent to Marilyn's Parkside House residence to collect her, but all he gets from her is a look of "mute appeal."

September 12: Marilyn returns to the studio, but keeps Olivier and the cast waiting. Colin Clark is sent to fetch her. She appears, but seems unfocused. Little work gets done, and Marilyn retires to her dressing room. Clark is sent to inquire whether she will be working the next day. She asks him why he was at her house the previous day, thinking he was sent to spy on her. He assures her he is on her side when she inquires about his loyalties.

September 13: With Marilyn still not reporting for work, Olivier concentrates on exterior shots. Other than Clark (according to Clark himself), the only British member of Olivier's team Marilyn seems to trust is Jack Cardiff, the cinematographer. Miller is in Paris seeing an agent, and Clark supposes Marilyn is lonely.

September 14: Caught between Milton Greene and Olivier, Clark is told by the director not to call on Marilyn again, because she is manipulating him into abetting her dilatory behavior.

September 15: Marilyn seems to revel in getting Clark on her side, even though he tells her that he has been warned not to fraternize with her. But she insists on taking him on a Saturday outing, including a swim and then back to her Parkside House residence.

September 16: Milton Greene warns Clark that Marilyn has a romance with everyone who works for her, but she will break his heart. Marilyn has told Milton that she kissed Clark, but Clark insists he has not fallen in love with her, and that there is no affair. Clark believes the problem is that everyone wants her to be "Marilyn Monroe" and not herself. Greene suggests that Marilyn cannot be happy for very long and that she will be disappointed in Clark, as well.

September 17: Miller attends rehearsals for the British production of *A View From the Bridge*, leaving an annoyed Olivier to deal with Marilyn alone.

An ill Marilyn Monroe summons Clark to her Parkside House residence. He finds himself alone with her in the middle of the night as she drifts off into a drugged sleep. When she wakes, she tells him the story of her life, referring to a dark side that Miller cannot seem to handle or accept. She drifts off into a sound sleep in his arms.

September 18: Marilyn arrives at the studio almost on time. Olivier explodes in laughter at Clark's disheveled appearance, the result of his having spent the night with Marilyn without having time to change clothes or groom himself. Although it is assumed that Clark has bedded Marilyn, he denies it. Olivier says he does not care, since Marilyn has arrived to work. After a good workday, Olivier is pleased if mystified as to how Clark has achieved results with Marilyn. But by the evening her fears of failing return, as she confesses to Clark that she is suffering from cramps and expecting a baby. She is afraid to be left alone. A doctor is summoned but finds no serious problem.

September 19: Arthur Miller returns from his trip to see his children. Marilyn awaits him, telling Clark she wants to make a good home for her husband after the picture is finished. But at the studio, she seems irritated and finds fault with her dress, hair, and makeup.

September 20: Olivier directs Marilyn in an intricate scene dealing with her entrance into the embassy and into the grand duke's chambers. The work is done in twenty-nine takes. Marilyn has trouble remembering her lines or speaking them accurately.

September 21: Shooting goes better as Marilyn performs the scene in which she is escaping from the grand duke. She manages to do it all in four takes.

September 26: Marilyn delights in Dame Sybil Thorndike's arrival on the set. Marilyn is nearly on time and appears to be enjoying herself.

September 27: The day is spent filming reaction shots with Marilyn in the hall of the grand duke's embassy. To Clark, she seems less alert, and he wonders if perhaps she is drugged. He mentions Milton Greene's habit of making sure Marilyn has the pills (uppers and downers) she needs to calm down or feel more energetic.

September 28: Hedda Rosten calls the studio to say Marilyn is ill and cannot work.

A letter from ABC arrives, offering Marilyn a part in *The Brothers Karamazov*, but she declines because of the stress in her personal and professional lives.

October: On the cover of *Sir: A Magazine for Males*, Marilyn is shown in the classic gold lamé gown in a Frank Powolny photograph later featured on a U.S. postage stamp.

Marilyn meets with Edith Sitwell, and they discuss poets, including Dylan Thomas and Gerard Manley Hopkins. Marilyn has been reading these poets late at night when she cannot sleep. She quotes to Sitwell these lines from Hopkins: "I wake and feel the fell of dark, not day / What hours, O what black hours we have spent / This night." Sitwell remembered that Marilyn was "very quiet and had great natural dignity . . . and was extremely intelligent. She was also exceedingly sensitive. . . . In repose her face was at moments strangely, prophetically tragic, like the face of a beautiful ghost— a little spring-ghost, an innocent fertility-daemon, the vegetation spirit that was Ophelia."

In an encounter with British critic Tom Hutchinson, Marilyn discusses *The Trial*: "[I]t's like we all feel, this sense of guilt. I know they say it's the Jewish thing with Kafka—that's what Arthur says anyway—but it goes beyond that. It's about men and women. This sense that we have fallen or something."

Marilyn attends a charity event and contributes a yellow watercolor titled "Myself Exercising," which is purchased by Terence Rattigan. In the picture, Marilyn depicts herself in profile as a circular shape in motion, with long, dangling hair.

October 1: Marilyn is given two days off while other scenes are shot.

October 3: Marilyn sends word to Olivier that she cannot come into work. Olivier is even more upset when he learns that Lee Strasberg is on his way to Pinewood and refuses to see Marilyn's acting teacher.

October 4: Marilyn arrives on the set bright and cheerful. Susan Strasberg visits to watch Marilyn work.

October 8: Marilyn arrives on the set early and completes a long scene with Olivier before lunch. Clark suggests she is enjoying a situation in which she is, by turns, teasing and controlling.

October 9: Olivier seems rigid in the love scenes with Marilyn, and that also seems to lower her confidence. Susan Strasberg suggests that Marilyn seeks control and yet shies away from it.

October 10: Marilyn seems troubled and has difficulty remembering even the simplest lines.

October 11: Dame Sybil returns and lightens Marilyn's mood.

Marilyn accompanies Miller and Olivier and his wife to the opening of *A View From the Bridge*. Marilyn wears a skin-tight, blood red silk strapless gown that excites considerable attention.

October 12: An Associated Press article reports, "Marilyn Monroe's close-fitting dress turned the London opening of her husband's latest play into a near riot." Marilyn responds to press inquiries by saying the dress is her husband's favorite color. And Miller adds, "Why should someone like Marilyn pretend to be dressing like somebody's old aunt?"

Marilyn has difficulty working, presumably because of her outing the previous night. Clark notes that Miller does not seem upset about the papers' attention to his wife's "low-cut crimson dress. Evidently it brought the house down more than the play." Miller does not seem to "mind a bit. His ego is impregnable," Clark concludes.

October 15: During a relatively uneventful day shooting the coach's arrival at the coronation ceremony, Clark observes an excited Marilyn.

October 16: Marilyn has a day off.

October 17: Concern over Marilyn's absences and lateness are expressed in a letter from the managing director of Laurence Olivier Productions to Milton Greene, requesting an accounting of her expenditures. No reply is forthcoming.

Paula Strasberg and her daughter, Susan, depart for home.

Marilyn experiences a happy day on the set owing to good reviews for her performance in *Bus Stop*. She does well filming reaction shots, even though she does not have much more to do than listen intently on the telephone.

October 18: Filming in the studio, a mock-up of Westminster Abbey, Marilyn performs well in scenes with no dialogue.

October 19: More shooting in the mock-up of Westminster Abbey ensues, with close-ups on Marilyn watching a king being crowned and reacting like a showgirl would. The scene calls for her character, Elsie, to feel overwhelmed and tearful. When she does not produce tears, glycerin is offered to fake her reaction, but she refuses it and breaks into a rash. After a break, she returns to the set and produces a tear, which trickles down her cheek.

October 20–21: Marilyn has the weekend off.

October 22: Dr. Hohenberg, Marilyn's psychiatrist, arrives for a consultation. Marilyn does not return to the studio.

Picture Post features a tight close-up of a smiling Marilyn with the caption "Marilyn makes headlines again."

October 23: Marilyn arrives on the set eighty-five minutes late, and then keeps everyone waiting almost another three hours, but she performs well in the ballroom scene.

October 24–25: Marilyn approves of her rushes, but is in a "bad temper," according to Clark. She is curt with almost everyone: Milton Greene, Olivier, and even with her dresser and makeup man. Not even Arthur Miller is spared. But she continues working, shooting another part of the ballroom scene, dancing with Olivier and making it seem that her character is indeed falling in love with Olivier as the grand duke.

October 26: Marilyn returns to the set to film the end of the ballroom scene.

Marilyn creates a trust fund for her mother out of one hundred shares of stock in Marilyn Monroe Productions.

October 27: Marilyn meets Dame Edith Sitwell again.

October 29: Gordon Bond, Marilyn's hairdresser, prepares her to meet the queen at the Empire Theatre, Leicester Square. Marilyn meets both the queen and Princess Margaret. Marilyn makes a perfect curtsy and speaks to the queen for perhaps a minute. Marilyn says she is reluctant to leave England. Marilyn invites Princess Margaret to a performance of *A View From the Bridge*, which the princess attends later. Bridget Bardot, who is present at the same ceremony, calls Marilyn "charming, beautiful, vulnerable, fragile."

October 30: Marilyn arrives at 12:35 p.m. for a 10:30 a.m. call. To Clark, she seems drugged the day after meeting the queen and receiving good press for her appearance.

Marilyn appears on the *Look* cover and in "Olivier and Monroe."

October 31: Marilyn seems increasingly distant from cast and crew as she dashes back and forth, shaking her hands to relieve tension. Paula Strasberg returns to the set.

November 1: Tensions are relieved by the appearance of Gene Kelly, who helps entertain at a party.

November 2: The cast films a trying scene, with Marilyn fussing over her makeup and making her dresser nervous. They are filming her character's dressing room at the theater.

November 3–4: Marilyn has the weekend off.

November 5: Now that Marilyn has fallen out with Milton Greene, Olivier seems to rely more and more on Arthur Miller to ensure Marilyn's arrival on the set.

November 6–7: More shooting in Elsie Marina's dressing room.

November 8: Marilyn seems cheerful as the backstage scene with Elsie Marina meeting the grand duke is shot. But Paula Strasberg tells Colin Clark that Marilyn is feeling ill, and he alerts the crew that she probably will not appear for the next day's shooting.

November 9: As predicted, Marilyn does not show up for work.

November 10–11: Marilyn has the weekend off.

November 12: According to Clark, no one can get through to Marilyn as this point, as filming of the reception line scene, in which the grand duke is about to meet Elsie Marina for the first time, proceeds.

November 13: The reception line scene is nearly completed.

November 14–15: Marilyn's last big scene is filmed.

November 16: Marilyn does post-syncing, in which she watches herself on the screen and records her voice to match her lip movements.

Shooting of *The Prince and the Showgirl* concludes eleven days late. Marilyn apologizes for her tardiness, attributing her lateness to poor health.

November 17: Cast and crew attend a wrap party that Clark describes as rather unpleasant, with the Americans and the Brits each believing the other side did not do enough to make the production team jell.

November 18: Monroe and Miller make their last public appearance in England, attending a writers' event at the Royal Court Theatre about British drama. She causes quite a stir, although she remains quiet.

Radio Cinema Television (France) publishes a close-up of a film still from *The Seven Year Itch*, the moment when Marilyn looks suggestively at Tom Ewell and closes one eye, as if winking at the idea of what two adults can do every night.

November 19: Retakes of scenes with Marilyn and Olivier are shot. According to Clark, Marilyn behaves like a "drugged prisoner of war." Marilyn leaves the studio "quickly and furtively," not even saying goodbye to her personal dresser or hairdresser.

Newsweek publishes "For Art's Sake."

November 20: At Pinewood, the *Prince and the Showgirl* staff is presented with gifts from Marilyn, although she does not make an appearance herself. They all follow the lead of a crewmember who pitches his gift into the refuse bin. Clark observes the scene and feels it is indicative of the staff's anger at Marilyn for being so aloof and causing so many delays in production.

Marilyn attends a press conference at 6:15 p.m. She is on time, but the press is unsympathetic, criticizing her messy hair and ridiculing her comments about reading authors such as Dickens. She tells reporters she is reluctant to leave England and praises Olivier. But Miller, Paula Strasberg, and Milton Greene—all New York Jews—were not much better at fathoming a California girl, Clark concludes.

For public relations purposes, the Oliviers accompany the Millers to the airport.

November 26: Colin Clark writes to a friend, announcing that filming of *The Prince and the Showgirl* is over after twenty weeks of work. He concludes that Olivier never did learn how to read Marilyn's tender and tough sides.

December: Cecil Beaton's photograph of Marilyn with short blonde hair in a pose reminiscent of a young Shirley MacLaine is on the cover of *Eigo no Tomo* (Japan).

December 4: Marilyn is a "star usherette" for a showing of *Baby Doll*, a benefit for the Actors Studio. She had coveted the starring role, but Kazan had told her that she was too old to play the twenty-year-old character.

December 18: Marilyn attends the premiere of Elia Kazan's *Baby Doll*, starring Caroll Baker, and afterward goes to the Waldorf Astoria for an evening of dancing with Arthur Miller.

Marilyn appears on a radio show broadcast from the Waldorf Astoria. She is photographed with the curl on her forehead to the left, apparently the only time she wore her hair this way.

1957

Marilyn donates her earnings from the world premiere of *The Prince and the Showgirl* to the Milk Fund for Babies.

Marilyn and Arthur Miller move into an apartment at 444 East 57th Street. They are joined by Hugo, their basset hound, and Butch, a parakeet. Their walls and curtains are white. She is photographed in a black dress with a huge white bow in front of a white baby grand piano. She is also photographed taking Hugo for a walk. Miller has his own room in which to write, but he also rents a room at the Chelsea Hotel.

The couple meets with Frank Lloyd Wright to discuss a design for their Roxbury, Connecticut, home. Later, Miller convinces his wife that Wright's plans are too expensive and impractical to implement.

January: *Coronet* publishes "Waif to Woman."

Vue features Marilyn in a sultry pose in a red dress with the headline "History's Hottest Siren."

True Romance recycles a 1951 photograph for its cover, showing Marilyn in a red sweater learning against a tree and smiling.

January 1: Marilyn receives the "Award of Achievement" from the *Motion Picture Herald* for being among the top ten moneymaking stars of 1956.

January 3: Marilyn and Arthur Miller fly to Jamaica for a delayed honeymoon. They stay in Lady Pamela Bird's luxurious villa.

January 19: Marilyn and Arthur fly from Jamaica to New York.

January 27: Miller begins making notes for what would eventually become his play, *After the Fall*, featuring Maggie, a character modeled on Marilyn.

February 18: A federal grand jury indicts Arthur Miller on two counts of contempt of Congress. Each count could mean up to one year in prison and a $1,000 fine.

At Doctor's Hospital, Marilyn begins treatment to help her carry a child to term.

February 28: Marilyn is nominated for a Golden Globe award for her work on *Bus Stop* but does not attend the ceremony, at which Deborah Kerr wins for her performance in *The King and I*.

March: On Arthur Miller's advice, Marilyn changes psychoanalysts, choosing on the advice of Anna Freud Dr. Marianne Kris, who sees her patient five times a week in a Central Park West office. Like Anna Freud, Kris is a child psychiatrist.

March 1: Miller appears before judge Charles F. McLaughlin in Washington, D.C., and pleads not guilty to charges of contempt of Congress.

March 22: Rumors say Marilyn has been turned down for a part in *The Brothers Karamazov* and that she is pregnant. She issues a statement: "I have nothing to say at this time. I am sure that everyone will agree that some things are private matters."

Spring: *Man to Man* publishes a picture of Marilyn in her *Seven Year Itch* terry cloth robe with the caption "When M. M. Was

Raped." The story refers to an incident when she was molested as a young child that Marilyn recounts in *My Story*.

April: *Movieland* shows a tight close-up of Marilyn on its cover, with a beauty mark conspicuous on her lower left cheek. Her lips are parted slightly, and her eyelids, just slightly drooping, suggest an unusual meditative mood. The article inside is about her participation in a benefit showing of *Baby Doll* for the Actors Studio.

April 1: Marilyn sees the first edited version of *The Prince and the Showgirl*. She finds the pacing of the film slow and the coronation sequence tedious. "American audiences are not as moved by stained glass windows as the British are, and we threaten them with boredom," she writes. She is disappointed, blames Milton Greene for tampering with the film, and resists his demand to be credited as executive producer.

April 10: Marilyn meets with representatives of the Free Milk Fund and Radio City Music Hall about the premiere of *The Prince and the Showgirl*.

April 11: Marilyn issues a statement saying she was not aware that Milton Greene was to receive credit as executive producer of *The Prince and the Showgirl*. He is, in effect, charged with mismanaging Marilyn Monroe Productions.

April 12: Monroe and Miller attend the annual April in Paris Ball, a fundraiser for French charities, at the Waldorf Astoria in New York City. She is photographed dancing with Arthur Miller and kissing him. She is also photographed with Elsa Maxwell and other attendees.

April 16: Marilyn announces the dismissal of attorney Irving Stein and accountant Joseph Carr, who are replaced on the board of Marilyn Monroe Productions by Robert H. Montgomery Jr. (Miller's lawyer), George Kupchik (Miller's brother-in-law), and George Levine (Miller's friend).

April 22: Marilyn's secretary, May Reis, arranges nine interviews and photo sessions for *Look*, *Wee*, *Redbook*, *Esquire*, and *The Mirror*, an appointment with gossip columnist Earl Wilson, publicity for *The Prince and the Showgirl*, and a Manhattan cocktail party.

April 29: *Time* features Marilyn in "Executive Sweet."

May: Robert Slatzer publishes in *Confidential* his account of an affair with Marilyn that occurred in 1952 when she was dating Joe DiMaggio. According to John Gilmore's *Inside Marilyn Monroe*, she was "mortified. She couldn't understand why someone she never knew was saying such things about her. She was advised to ignore such 'trash' and it would go away. 'Marilyn,' she was told, 'Forget it! Let the studio handle it.' No one handled it."

May 6: Richard Avedon photographs Marilyn, her torso covered in feathers (her sexual plumage) and wearing high heels, her left leg bent and brought up to her body so that the leg projects outward horizontally. Her right arm stretches out diagonally and clutches a fan, and her head is tilted right with her eyes half closed and her mouth wide open, suggesting the dynamism of her erotic allure. Another Avedon shot shows her in a spangled dress. She wraps herself in a silver fur stole that seems almost to waft out of the frame in her extended right arm, while her left hand touches her shoulder

The Prince and the Showgirl with Laurence Olivier

and she projects one of those dreamy poses with half-closed eyes—although this time with a closed mouth that suggests a little more mystery and not quite so much availability.

May 12: At Ebbets Field in Brooklyn, Marilyn makes the ceremonial first kick at a soccer match between the United States and Israel. She is photographed standing in an open field and with her tongue out as she prepares to kick the ball. She hits it hard and sprains two of her toes. But she stays to the end of the game and presents a trophy to the winning team.

May 13–14: Marilyn accompanies Miller to Washington, D.C., where he goes on trial for contempt of Congress. She stays with his attorney, Joseph Rauh, and Rauh's wife.

May 14: Miller's trial begins.

May 23: Marilyn speaks to reporters on the phone and meets others in the Rauh living room. She tells them she fully supports her husband and has spent her time reading books in the Rauh library. "A wife's place is with her husband," she declares.

May 24: Marilyn and Miller leave the Rauhs' home and travel by train back to New York City.

May 31: Miller is convicted on two counts of contempt of Congress and is fined $500 and given a one-month suspended jail sentence. He immediately appeals the verdict.

June: Miller and Monroe settle in Amagansett, Long Island, about two hours by car from New York City. They rent a house on Story Hill Farm. Miller writes, the couple stroll the beach, and Marilyn reads and makes visits to the Rostens nearby, where she is photographed walking hand-in-hand with Hedda and Patricia (the Rostens' daughter).

June 1: Marilyn turns thirty-one.

June 3: *Life* publishes "Unlikely Pair Make Great Match."

June 12: Sam Shaw shoots a crowd looking through a store window, while Marilyn holds and examines what looks like a strap for a handbag. He photographs Miller (without glasses) in an intimate pose with Marilyn, who seems about to kiss him, with one of the city bridges in the background. Other shots show Marilyn eating outdoors and reading a newspaper (the couple next to her seem not to notice).

June 13: Monroe and Miller attend the premiere of *The Prince and the Showgirl* at Radio City Music Hall. Marilyn sees a pregnant Amy Greene. Jack Warner, who distributed the film, is also there. A party at the Waldorf Astoria follows the screening.

June 17: *Newsweek* publishes "Talk with a Showgirl."

June 24: Inez Melson, Marilyn's former business manager, writes to Arthur Miller, "Marilyn knows that my feeling for her is that of a mother for a darling child. To me, she is not a famous personality but just someone for whom I developed a real fondness from the first day of our meeting. . . . I appreciated your letter so much for I know that you are a busy man and have much on your mind. I earnestly pray that your trouble [HUAC] will resolve itself not only because I do not think anything will be gained by subjecting you to such an indignity but I cannot bear to have another sorrow come into Marilyn's life. She needs so much love and affection and I am certain she has found it in her marriage to you."

July 2: Marilyn attends the inauguration of the Time-Life Building in Manhattan. She is supposed to arrive at 11:00 a.m., but does not appear until 1:20 p.m. Her host, Laurence S. Rockefeller, leaves, saying, "I've never waited that long for anyone." Marilyn explains that she is hung over owing to too much champagne the night before.

The same day, Marilyn is given a tour of the *New York Times*. A machinist demonstrates how a linotype-typesetting machine works, and she kisses the top of his bald head.

Marilyn is photographed returning home in a helicopter. Arthur Miller comments in *Timebends*, "What a frightening power she had! The event seems like the intrusion of a gross iron hand in to the vulnerable flesh of our existence and yet at the same time signified her triumph, proof of the immense public importance she had won."

Summer: At Amagansett, Sam Shaw photographs Marilyn in a summer dress, sitting at home; dressed casually talking on the phone; and out of doors lifting her arms and a leg as though in a ballet duet with the tree that she is leaping toward. She emerges soaked and radiant from the ocean in a black-and-white shot. A color photograph shows Miller about to cast his fishing rod. In other shots, Marilyn has her back to the camera as if walking away from its attention.

Marilyn visits White's Pharmacy and spends time at the makeup counter trying out various products.

A twelve-year-old girl knocks on the Millers' front door, and Marilyn, in dark sunglasses and a bathrobe, comes out to talk, until Miller tells her to come inside. "Okay, Papa," Marilyn responds.

Miller's children, Bobby and Jane, visit on weekends. Marilyn's moods vary. Susan Strasberg remembers Marilyn quoting from a reference to Goethe in *The Diary of Anne Frank*: "I'm either in the heights of elation or the depths of despair."

July 3: *The Prince and the Showgirl* is released.

July 16: *Picture Week* publishes a low-angle cover shot of Marilyn, her head tilted up, wearing one of those gossamer fantasy costumes that are part of Tom Ewell's daydream in *The Seven Year Itch*.

July 19: The judge reduces Miller's conviction to one count of contempt, suspends the one-year jail sentence, and fines him $500.

July 30: Goldfarb Flowers & Gifts bills Mr. Arthur Miller of 444 East 57th Street twelve dollars for three-dozen Lady Bountiful Roses, and two dollars for one bunch of baby's breath (probably to celebrate Marilyn's pregnancy).

August 1: Marilyn collapses in the garden outside her Amagansett cottage. She is rushed to the hospital, where an ectopic pregnancy is diagnosed. She had been about five weeks pregnant.

August 2: Miller issues a statement to the press: "Marilyn wants as many children as she can get. I feel the same way."

August 2–9: Marilyn recuperates in the hospital, telling a visiting James Haspiel that the fetus had been a male.

August 9: Marilyn drafts a long, two-page, single-spaced typewritten letter to "Bobby," Arthur Miller's son. She updates him about Hugo, her basset hound, who "has been up to all kinds of mischief." A donkey kicked Hugo in the nose, but ice packs took down the swelling, and there was no permanent damage. Hugo has brought home a woman's shoe and a child's toy, a stuffed dog. They are thinking of changing his name to Klepto. Hugo loves smelling the flowers, but misses Bobby and his sister, Janie. She tells the boy how much his father misses him, and she want Bobby to tell her what Janie would like for her birthday. She wants to know if Bobby has continued his horseback riding and if there is anything he needs. She ends the letter "Kiss Janie for me, if you see her. We are so lonesome for you both."

August 10: Marilyn leaves the hospital. She smiles and says, "I'm feeling wonderful. I definitely still plan to have a large family. I'm going to rest, rest, and more rest." She is dressed all in white, with Miller, also in a white suit, beside her.

August 12: Cecil Tennant, managing director of Laurence Olivier Productions, sends a final letter to Milton Greene, asking for a complete account of Monroe's expenditures on *The Prince and the Showgirl*.

August 22: Marilyn writes to Bobby as though Hugo is sending the letter. Hugo complains he is lonesome and apologizes for chewing up one of Bobby's baseballs, mistaking it for a tennis ball. But Daddy and Marilyn say they will get Bobby a new one. Hugo also confesses that he "jumped up high and knocked down the badminton set and chewed on the net. 'I am sorry I did this Bob, but what is a dog going to do?'" Hugo has stopped chasing the donkey because it kicked him in the nose. On the other hand, Hugo did chase away a rabbit that was going for the flowers. And Hugo claims to be a good watchdog. "The trouble is, I think, I miss you and Jane so much that if there is nothing to do here I tend to get into mischief. But Daddy and Marilyn don't mind too much. They always forgive me and pat me on the head." Maybe at camp Bobby can make a toy for Hugo. "Love from your friend and ankle-chewer. P.S. I really mean lots of love and slurpy kisses O X O X O X O X O X O X O X O X I know Daddy and Marilyn send their love too."

Marilyn writes a separate letter, just as long, from Hugo to Janie, telling her how much he misses her but is happy that she is having a good time at camp. He has been chasing anything that moves and has found a good hairbrush to chew on. He enjoys watching Marilyn put on the sprinkler where the birds gather. When about twenty show up, he enjoys rushing into the middle of them and scattering the group. "Also Janie I must confess (and I am not telling anybody but you) I have been sleeping on your bed. It's because it is *your* bed." He thinks Daddy and Marilyn are getting suspicious because of the mysterious prints on the bed. "The meals in this house are pretty good. I can't kick about that." He closes with "love and slurpy kisses." In a postscript, he complains about the ticks and fleas he has picked up.

Marilyn later writes a letter in all capitals to Bobby and Janie from Sugar Feeny, the cat, saying "THERE IS NEVER A DULL MOMENT IN THIS SHACK."

September 5: John Florea's ultra-sultry photograph of Marilyn makes the cover of *Cine-Revelation*.

September 17: Mary Bass of *Ladies' Home Journal* sends Marilyn a recipe for bouillabaisse and beef burgundy, enough to serve sixteen people. "Both freeze beautifully," Bass writes. In fact, Marilyn later makes the bouillabaisse, impressing her friend, the poet Norman Rosten, with her delicious meal.

End of September: Fox approaches Marilyn about appearing in a remake of *The Blue Angel*, the film that made Marlene Dietrich a star. But Marilyn makes no commitment.

October: Lena Pepitone is hired as Marilyn's maid.

Marilyn is photographed in a headscarf and sunglasses, waving from the front seat of a convertible, with the pipe-smoking Miller in the driver's seat. They are also photographed playing with Hugo down on the ground and laughing. They alternate between the city and Miller's Roxbury home and farm, where they live near Richard Widmark, Marilyn's co-star in *Don't Bother to Knock*.

October 1: *Look* publishes "Marilyn's New Life."

October 2: Marilyn attends a business meeting at Fox with Lew Schreiber, Zanuck's second-in-command. They discuss the possibility of her starring in *The Blue Angel*. Marilyn seems agreeable.

October 5: *Weekend* (Australia) uses a 1952 photograph (one Andy Warhol chose to silk screen in his multiple Marilyns) with the curious headline, "Marilyn Monroe's Husband Has Six Wives."

October 10: Only Marilyn's open-mouthed smile and her head (tilted upward slightly) are visible on the cover of *Cinemonde* (France).

October 13: Arthur Miller writes to Norman Rosten about Marilyn's spectacular work on *The Prince and the Showgirl*.

November: *Bild Journalen* (Sweden) puts on its cover a shot by Jack Cardiff (cinematographer of *The Prince and the Showgirl*) of a smiling Marilyn with windblown hair.

November 16: Another Jack Cardiff shot of an elegant Marilyn appears on the cover of *Neue Illustrierte* (Germany).

November 18: Marilyn and Miller attend the premiere of *Conversation Piece*, starring Miller's sister Joan Copeland. Afterwards, they attend a reception at the Barbizon Plaza Hotel. Marilyn is photographed with Copeland and with Miller's father, Isidore.

December: The cover of *Filmland* features Marilyn in one of the fantasy costumes from *The Seven Year Itch*, with the caption "Marilyn Monroe: I'm Still Learning About Love."

December 4: Marilyn replies to Mary Bass of *Ladies' Home Journal*, thanking her for recipes and apologizing for the delay in responding: "[W]e have been very busy and going and getting two places in order, in the country and in the city. Right now we are in the middle of knocking down walls in the apartment and all that sort of thing." She thanks Bass for the "wonderful afternoons we spent in your patio. In fact, Arthur and I have decided that a patio is a 'must' in our new home."

December 5: Inez Melson, Marilyn's former business manager, replies to Marilyn's letter: "You are such a dear and you know how dear you are to me." She thinks of Marilyn as a daughter and is all too happy to do "little things for your mother." Melson describes the sanitarium where Gladys lives and works on a big loom, making a rug. Gladys seems to be improving, serving coffee at the sanitarium bazaar and staying all afternoon in the garden. Melson shops to provide Gladys with clothes. Various receipts from the Rockhaven Sanitarium show that Melson took charge of the bills connected with Gladys's stay there.

Christmas: Marilyn gives Arthur the latest edition of the *Encyclopedia Britannica*. Susan Strasberg receives a Chagall drawing, and Lee Strasberg receives several books and records (he is a collector). Marilyn present Paula Strasberg with a string of pearls with a diamond clasp, originally a gift the Japanese emperor gave Marilyn during her honeymoon with Joe DiMaggio. Susan's brother, John, just turned eighteen, is given Marilyn's Thunderbird.

December 30: Fox considers making *The Misfits*.

1958

Marilyn is nominated as "Best Foreign Actress" for a British Academy Award for *The Prince and the Showgirl*.

Harvard Lampoon publishes "The Thank You Award: To Marilyn Monroe who in a sweeping public service has made no movies this year."

January: Marilyn attends a dinner party given by Gloria Vanderbilt for Isak Dinesen, author of *Out of Africa*, a book that impressed her.

January 2: Lew Wasserman of MCA, representing Marilyn, meets with Fox executives to explain that she will perform in *The Blue Angel* only if Spencer Tracy is her co-star.

January 3: Spencer Tracy's agent reports the actor is ready to sign a contract for *The Blue Angel*, so long as his name is above Marilyn's in the title credits. MCA responds that she is indisposed but apparently willing to accede to Tracy's stipulation. Negotiations begin with George Cukor, one of Marilyn's approved directors and a friend of Tracy's, to shoot the film.

January 4: Marilyn, with closed eyes and parted lips, seems lost in a sensuous sleep, garbed in a sparkling blue dress and swathed in a blue fur stole, in a Richard Avedon shot that appears on the cover of *Settimo Giorno* (Italy).

January 9: Marilyn cancels a meeting with her agents to discuss Spencer Tracy's request for top billing on *The Blue Angel*.

January 13: Marilyn tells her agents she will not do *The Blue Angel*, noting that Fox had begun to work on the picture after the deadline in her contract specifying start of production for a new film.

January 15: Marilyn's lawyer sends a letter to Fox stating it has failed to honor its obligation to put her in a picture in 1957. She was now owed $100,000 for a picture she did not make, and she now owes Fox two pictures, not three. Fox points out that shooting of *The Blue Angel* was postponed at Marilyn's request.

January 24: Stella Yusko writes to Arthur Miller asking if he and Marilyn might be interested in adopting a "healthy and beautiful baby, and the mother feels that you people would really make a good happy home for her, which she cannot do because of her other problems."

January 27: Marilyn accompanies Miller to receive a gold medal for drama from the National Institute of Arts and Letters.

January 28: Marilyn attends a March of Dimes fashion show at the Waldorf Astoria, held to benefit children with polio. She is photoraphed with several children, smiling and talking with them, as well as posing for the camera.

January 29: A young fan writes to Marilyn thanking her for "love and kisses. You have made me very happy." He tells her about a "horrid arithmetic exercise" and asks if she was good at school. "My mother sends her love, and my sisters! I take the liberty of sending you also love and kisses. Yours, Anthony." The letter contains his drawing of a motion picture camera, a slate, and a figure in a director's chair looking at a script.

January 31: Empire Office Furniture Company bills Marilyn $87.55 for a gray file cabinet, with three legal drawers and one vault.

February: Marilyn and Miller attend a Metropolitan Opera production of Verdi's *Macbeth*.

February 3: Profile Symmetry Salon, 52 West 57th Street, New York, New York, bills Marilyn Monroe for treatments and cosmetics.

March: Marilyn and Miller attend a Metropolitan Opera production of Alban Berg's *Wozzeck*.

Laurence Olivier visits the Actors Studio, but Marilyn avoids seeing him by staying in a back room.

In Roxbury, Marilyn falls on the stairs, spraining an ankle and cutting her right hand on a whisky glass she is holding when it breaks.

March 1: Profile Symmetry Salon, 444 West 57th St., bills "Marilyn Miller" for cosmetics.

March 17: Billy Wilder sends Marilyn a two-page treatment of *Some Like It Hot*.

Spring: At the Actors Studio, Marilyn performs as Blanche Dubois in a scene from *A Streetcar Named Desire*. Marilyn also plays Curley's attention-craving wife in Steinbeck's *Of Mice and Men*. The beautiful but bored woman is killed by Lennie (Ralph Roberts), a slow-witted giant of a man. Truman Capote watches Marilyn play Holly Golightly in scenes adapted from his novel *Breakfast at Tiffany's*. He wants her to play the character in the film version and is outraged when the studio selects Audrey Hepburn.

April 3: Marilyn and Miller meet with Lew Wasserman of MCA and his assistant, Mort Viner, to discuss how to handle Twentieth Century Fox, since United Artists would be distributing *Some Like*

It Hot. The group is also waiting to hear if Frank Sinatra will join the production (he was suggested for the part Tony Curtis would play). A memo states, "She [Marilyn] still doesn't like Curtis but Wasserman doesn't know anybody else."

British journalist Donald Zec sends a telegram to Marilyn saying he is on his way to New York and would like to call "FOR THAT CUPPA TEA." Marilyn writes on the telegram, "By all means I am a woman of her word" and gives him her telephone number.

April 15: Fox agrees to excuse Marilyn from her obligation to do *The Blue Angel*, and Marilyn accedes to the studio's claim that she owes them three, not two, pictures. Fox also agrees to pay her $100,000, even though she has not done another film for them.

April 21: Marilyn signs an amendment to her Fox contract, giving her the $100,000 for a picture she did not make, but still obligating her to do three pictures for Fox.

April 25: Billy Wilder sends a telegram to Marilyn expressing his delight that she will appear in *Some Like It Hot*. She is to receive her usual $100,000 fee, plus 10 percent of the profits. She is photographed signing a contract with the film's producer, Walter Mirisch.

April 28: Marilyn and Miller meet with Kermit Bloomgarden, a producer of Miller's plays. The threesome is photographed around a piano, with Miller at the keyboard.

April 29: Marilyn's agents tell her that Fox has agreed that she can make *Some Like It Hot*.

May 21: Marilyn is photographed at an event honoring Arthur Miller with the gold medal of the National Institute of Arts and Letters. She becomes the center of attention and the target of autograph seekers. Miller is photographed smiling at the attention his wife receives.

May 22: Italy's *Settimo Giorno*'s cover features Jack Cardiff's photograph (it looks like a painting) taken in 1956 during his work on *The Prince and the Showgirl*. This is an unusual shot of Marilyn in a bonnet-like hat. Her bust vanishes in a hazy bluish mist that brings out her blue eyes and demurely flirtatious expression.

Life photographs document Broadway producer Kermit Bloomgarden's visit to the Miller apartment. They shoot Miller at the piano, with Marilyn hugging him, and Marilyn at Miller's feet in the living room. Bloomgarden is interested in producing an early version of *After the Fall* that Miller was working on.

May 27: Richard Avedon photographs Marilyn as Theda Bara in a sumptuously composed layout, with oriental carpets and drapery. She lies on a bed covered with a tiger skin and silken fabrics. She is wearing very dark eye shadow, a jeweled headdress, and an ornate, snake-like brassiere with an elaborately jeweled waistband. She frames her face with her braceleted arms above her head.

June: Richard Avedon photographs Marilyn standing and leaning backward to the right, her head tilted backward, her mouth open, and her eyes closed. It looks like she is snapping her fingers, perhaps listening to music in an ecstatic moment.

June 1: Marilyn turns thirty-two.

June 18: Marilyn receives an invoice for photographs taken by Carl Pentz showing her in various hats: large and floppy, straw, furry, floppy, and wide-brimmed.

June 26: Mary Leatherbee at *Life* sends Marilyn a telegram: "THE PICTURES ARE STUPENDOUS. WE HAVE BEEN CRYING WITH JOY ALL DAY. THANK YOU THANK YOU."

June 28: *The Goddess*, Paddy Chayefsky's negative portrayal of a Marilyn Monroe-like character, is released.

July: Arthur Miller works on the play that will eventually become *After the Fall*. Kermit Bloomgarden announces a premiere for December 18.

July 5–6: In Roxbury, Arthur Miller confers with his friend and publisher, Frank Taylor, about producing *The Misfits* and securing John Huston as the director.

July 7: Miller accompanies his wife to the airport. They are photographed hand-in-hand as Marilyn boards the plane. She flies from New York to Los Angeles to meet with Billy Wilder about *Some Like It Hot*.

Marilyn is billed $154.50 by the Brooks Costume Company for her Theda Bara oriental costume, headdress, and armband.

July 8: Marilyn arrives in Hollywood to begin work on *Some Like It Hot*. Over two hundred reporters observe an actress who has been away from Hollywood for almost two years. She makes a radiant entrance, photographed as she walks down the plane's stairs, dressed in a white silk blouse, white skirt, white shoes, and white gloves that complement her platinum blonde hair.

At the Beverly Hills Hotel, accompanied by her secretary, May Reis, Marilyn appears at a press conference with Billy Wilder, Jack Lemmon, and Tony Curtis. In one photograph, Tony Curtis serves as waiter, holding a tray, as Wilder feeds Marilyn an hors d'oeuvre. In another, Marilyn smiles next to gossip columnist Louella Parsons.

July 9: Richard Avedon, doing the photo layout for *Life*, sends Monroe a telegram: "DEAREST MARILYN THE NEW PHOTOGRAPHS ARE NOT AS GOOD AS WE BOTH WOULD WANT THEM TO BE STOP WILL CONTACT YOU AS SOON AS I RETURN FROM EUROPE ABOUT SEPTEMBER 6TH AND COME TO HOLLYWOOD TO RE-SHOOT AT YOUR CONVENIENCE STOP OH BROTHER WE MISS YOU HERE LOVE DICK." The photographs were later reshot, even though Marilyn had received a telegram from *Life* expressing enthusiastic approval of the first sitting.

Marilyn and Louella Parsons attend a party given by composer Jimmy McHugh.

July 10: Marilyn attends the premiere of a play, *Gigi*, at the Paramount Theatre on Hollywood Boulevard. She is swathed in an elegant silk-like material that she bunches together with her long black gloves.

July 14: Pre-production work begins on *Some Like It Hot*.

Arthur Miller sends a description of *The Misfits* to John Huston: "The setting is the Nevada back country, concerns two cowboys, a bush pilot, a girl, and the last of the mustangs up in the mountains. . . . The script is an early draft. If you are interested I'd want to sit and talk over my notion of further developments and of course would like to hear yours." Miller mentions there is a starring role for Marilyn.

July 16: Marilyn writes to Arthur Miller's son, "Dear Bobby-bones," telling him about the making of *Some Like It Hot*. She is learning to play the ukulele and suggests a duet with Bobby playing the guitar. She feels lonely and is thinking of buying a bird. She has had to return a gift, a cocker spaniel, because he bites. "His name was 'Walter' and he was a golden-haired spaniel and beautiful but he seems just too 'schizo'—short for schizophrenic—you remember you explained what that meant." She wants to know about what sports he is playing, what books he is reading, and how his friends are doing. She reminds him to write to his father and includes some stamps "if you feel like writing. If not maybe you can trade them in for candy bars somewhere. Goodbye for now. I'll write again, leaving you with this thought: Hugo can only get brighter as he gets older—he might even get smart enough to go camping."

August 4: Shooting of *Some Like It Hot* begins. Marilyn arrives on the set with Paula Strasberg and her hairdresser, Agnes Flanagan. Whitey Snyder, as usual, does Marilyn's makeup.

August 7: While taking a ukulele lesson, Marilyn is called and told that the United States Court of Appeals for the District of Columbia has reversed Miller's conviction for contempt of Congress by a vote of 9 to 0.

August 8: Marilyn invites reporters to speak with her about Miller having won his appeal. She declares that she always expected her husband to be exonerated.

After watching the rushes of her appearance in *Some Like It Hot*, Marilyn suggests that her first entrance should be more dramatic.

Wilder and his co-writer, I. A. L. Diamond, come up with the blast of steam that shoots out at Marilyn as she walks down the train platform.

Sam Shaw and Sidney Skolsky visit Marilyn on the set.

August 11: Marilyn is on time and knows her lines for the scene shot at the Goldwyn studio.

August 12: Marilyn shoots her "Running Wild" song to a playback and has some trouble lip-syncing the lines.

Autumn: The cover of *Sunbathing Review* features an Andre de Dienes photograph taken in 1949 at Tobey Beach near New York City. In the close-up shot, Marilyn is seen smiling, her hands joined together almost in prayer, and touching the left side of her face.

September 1: Filming of *Some Like It Hot* is on hiatus for Labor Day.

September 2–3: Scenes inside the Pullman car are filmed.

September 11: Outdoor beach scenes are shot in Coronado, California. Marilyn stays in the Vista Mar Cottage at the hotel, located about two hours from Los Angeles.

Marilyn writes to the Rostens, likening the production of *Some Like It Hot* with going down with the ship. "We are going through the Straits of Dire. It's rough and choppy but why should I worry I have no phallic symbol to lose." In a postscript she alludes to a Yeats poem: "Love me for my yellow hair alone." Yeats wrote "only God, my dear / Could love you for yourself alone / And not your yellow hair."

September 12: Marilyn calls Miller to express her distress over *Some Like It Hot*. He leaves their home in Connecticut to join her in California.

September 13: Marilyn and Miller stay at the Hotel Bel-Air. Several photographs of him on the set and in the beach scenes document his growing involvement with the production.

September 14: Marilyn is hospitalized for exhaustion, possibly aggravated by a drug overdose.

September 15: Production is halted, and the producers consider replacing Marilyn. Ultimately, her contribution is deemed unique and irreplaceable.

September 16: George Cukor, on Marilyn's list of approved directors, accepts the assignment to work on her next picture.

September 18: Inez Melson, Monroe's former business manager, writes, "I did not try to reach you at the hospital since I felt that you were there for a rest as much as anything and certainly it isn't restful to have people telephoning." She tells Marilyn all about her parakeets, adding, "Your children are going to love the birds and have lots of fun with them."

In an undated letter, perhaps written during this period, Marilyn writes by hand, "Dear Inez, Thanks for your sweet letters to both of us. It's a wonderful thing to know I have a real friend & not only I thank you for your kindness but my husband does too. . . . There aren't words to express what you have done for my mother. I called my half sister yesterday and she will get in touch with you. She was so pleased to know that someone like you was looking after her. . . . How is your new bird? I'll see him sometime."

September 29: Shooting with Marilyn resumes, but she balks at showing up for the beach scene and does not arrive until 2:30 p.m. She has difficulty remembering even the simplest lines.

October 6: Shooting shifts to interior scenes of the hotel. Marilyn shows up at 10:00 a.m., an hour late, and begins to find fault with her makeup. She does well in one long uninterrupted scene, but then begins to blow her lines during a shorter set-up in a hotel corridor.

October 7: Preparations for shooting in a hotel room are halted after Marilyn reports she is not feeling well. She shows up after 1:00 p.m., running a slight fever, and manages to do one hallway scene.

October 8: Marilyn stays in her hotel bed with a temperature of 102 degrees.

October 9: Marilyn returns to shoot a two-minute bathroom scene that takes all day to shoot.

October 10: Cast and crew wait several hours for Marilyn to arrive and perform in the ballroom scene, where she sings "I'm Through with Love." Marilyn shows up at 5:00 p.m and works until 11:00 p.m. getting the crucial scene done.

October 11: During an off-day party, Billy Wilder is struck with back pain. He is carried to his bedroom for an anti-inflammatory shot.

October 13: On call for 11:30 a.m., Marilyn arrives at 3:30 p.m. and goes to her dressing room. At 6:05 p.m., Wilder, tired of waiting, leaves. When Marilyn finally arrives at 6:15, nearly everyone has left the set.

October 15: Marilyn has a day off.

October 16: When Marilyn does not show up by noon, Wilder has a production assistant call her hotel room. She is not there, and no shooting is done that day.

Fairfax Drug Company, 601 South Fairfax Avenue, Los Angeles, California, bills Mrs. A. Miller $4.42 for two prescriptions.

October 17: Marilyn shoots two ballroom scenes and has no trouble with her lines or with lip-syncing. But Tony Curtis senses something has changed. She seems especially radiant in the ballroom scene when Curtis, still in drag, kisses her.

October 18: Marilyn fails to show up on the set of *Some Like It Hot*. She is pregnant and tired.

Fairfax Drug Company, 601 South Fairfax Avenue, Los Angeles, California, bills Mrs. A. Miller $5.15 for one prescription and $4.94 for another.

October 19: The press, aware of rumors that Monroe is pregnant, begins phoning Tony Curtis and others for confirmation.

October 20: Marilyn arrives on time, but no longer calls the director "Billy." He is now "Mr. Wilder." She is carrying Thomas Paine's

Rights of Man, which she takes to her dressing room. At 11:30 a.m., a production assistant knocks on her door and says the cast and crew are waiting for her. She tells him to "drop dead." When he urges her to report to the set, she tells him to "fuck off." When she finally shows up, she does the famous "Where's the bourbon?" scene, which, according to Tony Curtis, took eighty-one takes.

October 21: Marilyn stays home sick, and so does Wilder, still suffering from a bad back.

Fairfax Drug Company, 601 South Fairfax Avenue, Los Angeles, California, bills Mrs. A. Miller $26.37 for two prescriptions.

October 27: Wilder works on completing all scenes with female band members.

Marilyn writes to Norman Rosten, "I haven't been writing anyone, let alone poems—it's so spooky here! Arthur looks well though weaker—from holding me up. . . . I need something to hold on to. . . ." She signs the letter "e. e. cummings."

October 28: Fairfax Drug Company, 601 South Fairfax Avenue, Los Angeles, California, bills Mrs. A. Miller $39.50 for two prescriptions.

November: The cover of *Screen* features a Richard Avendon photograph (taken in 1958) of a beaming Marilyn, wrapped in a fur stole over a shimmering black dress with a plunging neckline.

November 3: Tony Curtis is upset by all the snickering in the screening room during a viewing of rushes of the scene in which Sugar Kane seduces Curtis's playboy millionaire character. As he exits the room, a journalist asks him what it is like to kiss Marilyn Monroe. A disgusted Curtis responds, "It's like kissing Hitler."

November 4: On the cover of *Tempo* (Italy), Marilyn seems almost disenchanted or rueful in a shot of her in a glamorous gown and flashy earrings, with her left hand resting on her cheek, accentuating her meditative mood.

November 6: At this point, *Some Like It Hot* is twenty-nine days behind schedule. Billy Wilder does not invite Marilyn to his party and does not speak with her often.

November 10: Marilyn collapses on the set of *Some Like It Hot*. She is taken to her hotel room and later flies to New York for hospital tests. She is advised to stop drinking and taking drugs.

November 11: Motherhood Maternity Shops bills Arthur Miller, of 444 E. 57th Street, $5.18 for a bed jacket.

November 23: *Novella* (Italy) publishes a cover photograph (taken on March 31, 1955) of Marilyn in close-up, jeweled and smiling, during the Madison Square Garden charity event in which she rode an elephant.

November 26: Marilyn sends a telegram to Georges Auric of the French Cinema Academy, explaining that because she had been working hard and is now pregnant, she cannot attending the ceremony awarding her the Crystal Star for "The Best Foreign Actress" for her work in *The Prince and the Showgirl*.

December: Producer Kermit Bloomgarden postpones the premiere of *After the Fall* to February or March, since Miller has been unable to complete the play.

December 2: A Fox executive writes to Marilyn asking if she is pregnant. In that case, the studio wants to extend the period during which it is required to employ her in a picture.

December 14: Huston meets with Miller to discuss *The Misfits*. The director requests revisions.

December 16: Marilyn is admitted to the Manhattan Polyclinic Hospital. She is recovering from a miscarriage.

Joe Wolhandler, vice president of Rogers & Cowan, a public relations firm, writes to Marilyn to assure her that the kind of story about *Some Like It Hot* published in *Time* "WILL NOT APPEAR ANY MORE." The story contained negative comments about Marilyn from Tony Curtis, Jack Lemmon, and Billy Wilder. "WE ARE PREPARING BYLINE PIECES BY JACK LEMMON, TONY CURTIS, BILLY WILDER AND THE OTHERS, ALL ON A STRONG UP-BEAT APPROACH WHICH WILL BE BREAKING AROUND THE COUNTRY FROM HERE ON. . . . AS YOU KNOW, TIME MAGAZINE IS, OF ALL THE GHOULISH PRESS, IN A CLASS BY ITSELF FOR UNMITIGATED NAS-

TINESS AND INACCURACY. I DON'T BELIEVE THEY ARE
QUOTING WILDER AND CURTIS ACCURATELY. WE HAVE
ASKED FOR RETRACTION ALTHOUGH KNOWING THEM,
I DON'T KNOW IF WE WILL GET IT."

December 17: Marilyn's miscarriage is announced to the press.

Some Like It Hot is sneak-previewed at the Village Theatre in Westwood. Jack Lemmon watches "all the kids, their parents, whoever
. . . screaming with laughter. It was an absolute smash."

December 18: Arthur Miller's mother blames Billy Wilder for Marilyn's miscarriage. The press is told Wilder made her run upstairs fourteen times when the temperature was 104 degrees. Tony Curtis will
later write that the thermometer never went above eighty degrees.

December 20: Poet Louis Untermeyer, a friend of Arthur Miller's,
writes Marilyn, "It's grimly ironic that while the rest of the country
was enjoying the comedy of your impersonations in *Life*, you were
going through your personal tragedy [miscarriage]. We hope you are
not taking the irony too bitterly. . . . Arthur's tribute was a model of
good taste, artistic balance, and love. It must be an added comfort
to know that everyone loves you—especially now."

December 22: *Life* publishes Richard Avedon photographs of
Marilyn impersonating Jean Harlow, Theda Bara, Clara Bow, Marlene Dietrich, and Lillian Russell. Arthur Miller writes an accompanying laudatory text, "My Wife Marilyn."

December 24: Gladys writes to Marilyn, "Have I pushed you
away, dear daughter I would love a visit from you. The holidays are
so sad. So very sad. . . . I have tried to reach you so often but it is
very difficult. Please do me the favor of a telephone call or a return
letter. May God bless you."

1959

Marilyn is awarded the "Ducal, Actriz de Cine" (Chile).

January: Marilyn continues working with Lee Strasberg at the
Actors Studio. She reads several screenplays, but none looks right
for her.

Carl Sandburg visits her in her New York apartment.

She spends time at the Roxbury, Connecticut, house making improvements.

January 6: Norman Rosten writes to "Marilyn dear," responding to her evident disappointment in *Some Like It Hot*: "About the movie—don't jump! Look at it this way: it is a completely enjoyable film, full of fun and YOU. It is not a starring vehicle for you because the story is simply not set up that way . . . BUT . . . nothing could really destroy your wonderful quality that gives the film the one touch of 'seriousness' (humanity) it needs for any sort of balance. It will not hurt you one little bit, and let everyone be more watchful the next time." The note is signed "Philosopher Claude" (Marilyn liked to think Rosten resembled the actor Claude Rains).

January 19: Joe Wolhandler, vice-president of public relations firm Rogers & Cowan, writes Marilyn to tell her that the December 22, 1958, *Life* layout of her photographs sold more copies (6,300,000) than any other issue in the history of the magazine. More could have been sold, but no more copies were available.

January 20: Lew Schreiber at Fox, having received notice that Marilyn is ready to work, reviews her list of approved directors, since she cannot be required to work until the studio has a commitment from one of the sixteen directors on her list.

January 23: Joe Wolhandler of Rogers & Cowan, public relations, writes to tell Marilyn he has denied several rumors, including the report that she is—or is not—adopting a baby, and that she is entering a clinic in Houston, Texas. In a postscript, he adds, "I AM IN THE BUSINESS 20 YEARS AND I STILL DON'T KNOW HOW THESE THINGS HAPPEN."

January 28: *Some Like It Hot* is previewed at the Bay Theatre in Pacific Palisades. No one laughs, except Steve Allen and a few friends invited to the screening.

January 29: A preview in Westwood for a much hipper audience results in uproarious laughter.

February 5: Marilyn is photographed in a two-shot with Carson McCullers, kissing her at McCullers's home in Nyack, New York, and later with McCullers and Isak Dinesen, with the threesome seated and looking over a manuscript in Dinesen's hands. In another shot, Miller is at the table with Marilyn and McCullers. He toasts Dinesen. They dine on oysters, white grapes, champagne, and a soufflé.

Marilyn attends a screening of *Some Like It Hot* at Loews on Lexington Avenue in New York. The capacity audience laughs with approval. Arthur Miller loves the picture, but Marilyn is upset because she looks like a "fat pig." She is photographed in the audience putting her hands to her face.

February 10: The press quotes Wilder's vow never to do a film with Marilyn again.

Marilyn and Miller attend a performance of *Macbeth* at the New York Metropolitan Opera. She is photographed autographing one of the programs.

February 13: On its cover *Se Og Hor* (Denmark) features a shot of Karen Blixen (Isak Dinesen) and Marilyn (dressed in a fur stole and low-cut dress) smiling over a large manuscript.

February 15: *De Post* (Belgium) puts a very business-like Marilyn, dressed in a black suit, on its cover.

February 19: Fox approaches Elia Kazan about doing a film with Marilyn.

February 21: *Revue* (Germany) puts John Florea's photograph on its cover, showing a deeply tanned Marilyn wearing jeweled earrings and a bracelet, a jewel on the waistband of her elegantly-patterned light blue, silvery dress. With her closed mouth and hooded eyes, she seems mysteriously enticing.

February 26: At the French Film Institute in New York City, Marilyn receives the Crystal Star as "Best Foreign Actress" for her performance in *The Prince and the Showgirl*. At the party afterward, she is photographed holding and kissing a dachshund.

March: *Cosmopolitan* publishes "The New Marilyn Monroe," with a cover painting by Jon Whitcomb.

Journalist Evan Michaels follows Marilyn, dressed in a camel's hair polo coat, on her errands. The doorman in Marilyn's apartment building tells Michaels, "The first time I saw her she was coming from the grocer's with a big bag. And some little boy said, 'Marilyn, Marilyn, give me your autograph.' And do you know, she put her big package down and smiled and signed the little boy's notebook." A doorman on the evening shift tells Michaels, "She's the most sociable of anybody. She just loves kids. . . . She'll always say hello to a little kid on the street or in the elevator. And you should see the way she treats Mr. Miller's two children. Just like she was their mother. She's always buttoning up Robert's coat if it's a cold day, and she goes out shopping with Jane for pretty dresses and things." Michaels accompanies Marilyn to a cake shop on First Avenue. He interviews a woman at the counter, who tells him Marilyn loves poppy seed rolls and rye bread. She avoids chocolates, but purchases pasties, cookies, tarts, and cakes. At Gristedes, she buys unusual cheeses and prime cuts of meat. At Sutton Place Stationers, also on First Avenue, she borrows books from a rental library, usually accompanied by Miller, reports the store's owner, Jack Newman: "She's just like an everyday housewife who's crazy about her husband." Michaels observes her examining enameled pots and pans in Bloomingdale's. She watched a chef prepare French pastries and took the recipes home with her. When she overhears women praising a shop that carries the Polish sausages Miller likes, she cabs over to the address, only to find the shop is gone, replaced by a parking lot. "Oh," Marilyn says, "they're tearing down this whole city, and it makes me mad. Isn't it a shame to see everything go?"

March 4: Elia Kazan sends a telegram to Fox promising to arrive on April 1 to work with screenwriter Calder Willingham on a film starring Marilyn. Fox officially notifies Marilyn that she is assigned to *Time and Tide*, a film Kazan will direct. She is to appear for work on April 14.

March 8: Marilyn wins a Golden Globe award for "Best Actress in a Comedy" for *Some Like It Hot*.

Some Like It Hot with Jack Lemmon and Tony Curtis

March 17: Marilyn arrives in Chicago to publicize *Some Like It Hot*. She is photographed wearing a fur coat and walking down the plane's stairs. Photographs show her having a good time.

At the Ambassador Hotel, Marilyn meets novelist Saul Bellow, who escorts her to the Pump Room, where she signs the guest book, "Proud to be the guest of Chicago writer Saul Bellow." Bellow writes to his editor, Pascal Covici, "I have yet to see anything in Marilyn that isn't genuine. Surrounded by thousands, she conducts herself like a philosopher." Bellow recalled how a bodyguard left a bathroom door ajar, since he had been ordered not to let Marilyn out of his sight. Bellow reflected, "I always felt she had picked up some high-tension cable and couldn't release it. She couldn't rest, she found no repose in anything."

At a press conference, a reporter spills a drink all over the front of Marilyn's dress, but "she remained calm, showed no anger, didn't act like the great star she was," noted Mervin Block, another reporter.

March 29: The world premiere of *Some Like It Hot* is staged at Loew's State Theatre on Broadway. The laughter is so loud one audience member remembered his ears were still ringing the next day. Marilyn is interviewed in the lobby, and she reverts to her childhood stammer. Later, she attends a party in her honor at the Strasbergs.

Marilyn looks heavy in photographs and weighs perhaps 135 pounds, a high for her.

April 2: Richard Avedon photographs Marilyn looking straight ahead, eyes wide open and her mouth slightly open, apparently lost in thought as she holds one of her jeweled earrings. Altogether it is an elegant composition, far more subtle than her earlier cheesecake and glamour shots.

April 8: The Hollywood premiere of *Some Like It Hot* at Grauman's Chinese Theatre receives a poor review in the *Los Angeles Times*.

April 19: Marilyn appears on the cover of *Oggi* (Italy), smiling and wearing a modest dress and a three-strand pearl necklace.

April 20: *Life* publishes "Walk Like This Marilyn."

May 13: Marilyn wins the David Di Donatello Prize (equivalent to an Oscar) as "Best Foreign Actress" for *The Prince and the Showgirl*. She appears in a tight-fitting, sleeveless dress with a flesh-colored bodice embroidered with black scrolling foliage and beading, over which she wears a bolero jacket. A reporter asks her, "Do you have a couple of words in our language for the Italian viewers?" Marilyn confers with Anna Magnani, who has presented the award, and then says, "Sono commossa . . . grazi" (I am touched, thank you.) Another reporter asks, "How do you feel about this madness every time you come out and make a public appearance? It looks as if we're all going to die of suffocation in here. Does it bother you that you cause such turmoil?" Marilyn replies, "I'm honored."

May 20: Marilyn arrives late to attend the ceremony awarding Arthur Miller a gold medal for drama from the American Academy of Arts and Letters.

June: Miller sends a revision of *The Misfits* to John Huston. Later in the month, the director will meet with Miller to say the screenplay needs more work.

June 1: Fan James Haspiel watches Marilyn buying a birthday cake on her thirty-third birthday.

June 22: Marilyn enters Lenox Hill Hospital for gynecological surgery to treat her endometriosis. Dr. Oscar Steinberg tells her she will not be able to have children.

June 23: Marilyn undergoes surgery to open her fallopian tubes and remove scar tissue.

June 25: The lawyer for Marilyn Monroe Productions sends Fox a telegram demanding payment of the $100,000 the studio promised for the picture it did not make on time. Once again, Marilyn asserts that she owes the studio two pictures, not three.

June 26: Miller takes Marilyn to their New York apartment after her hospital stay. Judging from various reports, the couple's mood has darkened.

Summer: Marilyn installs dark wood beams and an additional room next to the kitchen in her Roxbury, Connecticut, home. She puts photographs of Miller and posters of his plays on the solarium walls. She shops in Roxbury and nearby Woodbury, going out several times a week. Susan Strasberg and her parents visit and notice Marilyn no longer gazes adoringly at Miller, and that he treats her coldly. During this period Marilyn writes in a journal, "There is no love here anymore." She seems to take no pleasure in her renovated home.

Producer Jerry Wald proposes the idea of Marilyn starring in *Let's Make Love*, to be directed by George Cukor and co-starring Gregory Peck.

July 4: Miller meets again with Frank Miller, a publishing executive who also worked at MGM, to discuss *The Misfits*.

July 6: *Lunes* (Uruguay) shows Marilyn dressed in a black lacy negligee and sitting up in bed next to a skeletal figure. His glasses are on the bed cover, and only his thin arm and part of a bony shoulder are showing. The balloon caption suggests a ravenous Marilyn has nearly devoured Miller and his writing.

July 14: Miller writes to John Huston about *The Misfits*, "I have been holding it for months, not knowing what to do with it. I'd only add that Marilyn is advisable for the girl."

August 3: The cover of *Woman's Day* features an unusual shot of Marilyn with her hair styled to the left. The photograph looks painted, with an idealized Marilyn dressed in white fur wearing long jeweled earrings. The caption reads, "Marilyn Monroe's Beauty Secrets."

August 10: Marilyn writes herself a check for $33,300, drawn on Marilyn Monroe Productions.

August 14: Marilyn writes herself a check for $1,763, drawn on Marilyn Monroe Productions.

August 15: Marilyn and Miller attend a performance of *Macbeth* at the Boston Arts Center Theatre.

August 26: Fox capitulates to all of Monroe's demands, including paying her for two pictures she has not done.

September 1: Marilyn has her hair dressed (ten dollars) and tinted (twenty-five dollars) by Lilly Daché Beauty Salon of 78 East 56th Street, New York, New York, in her home.

Marilyn's dark mood lifts as she continues work at the Actors Studio.

Lester Markel of the *New York Times* interviews Marilyn.

September 2: Miller wires John Huston that the revised screenplay is almost finished.

September 16: Fox makes a deal with George Cukor, one of Marilyn's approved directors, to work on *The Billionaire*, later retitled *Let's Make Love*.

September 17: Fox sends Marilyn a letter stipulating that she is to report for pre-production on her next film on November 2.

Marilyn has her hair dressed (eight dollars) and tinted (twenty-five dollars), a manicure (ten dollars), waxing (thirty dollars), and a pedicure (ten dollars) at Lilly Daché Beauty Salon, 78 East 56th Street, New York, New York.

September 18: Fox agrees to Marilyn's work on *The Misfits*.

September 19: Marilyn, accompanied by George Cukor, meets Nikita Khrushchev during his visit to Hollywood. Coached by Natalie Wood, Marilyn speaks in Russian to the Soviet leader, expressing her wish for world peace and better relations between her country and his. She also extends greetings from her husband. "I am honored," Khrushchev replies. "Your husband is a great man. We think highly of him in my country."

Marilyn meets with Billy Wilder, and they seem to reconcile.

September 20: Marilyn meets with Jerry Wald and George Cukor about the production of *Let's Make Love*. Marilyn has not read the script yet and agrees to wait until revisions are made at Cukor's request. She does, however, demand that Jack Cole be hired to help her with the dance scenes, because he has served her so well on *Gentlemen Prefer Blondes* and *There's No Business Like Show Business*.

At the airport Marilyn is photographed in an elegant black dress and fur coat boarding a plane and looking radiant. She flies to New York to attend Yves Montand's Broadway concert, substituting for Miller, who is still hard at work on revisions of *The Misfits*. Montand had appeared in the French stage and film versions of Miller's *The Crucible*.

September 21: Marilyn has a shampoo (two dollars) and has her hair dressed (four dollars) at Lilly Daché Beauty Salon, 78 East 56th Street, New York, New York.

September 22: Marilyn attends Yves Montand's one-man show, which has been a great success. While Miller is at home still working in *The Misfits*, Marilyn goes out in the company of Montgomery Clift, who will co-star in the film with her.

September 24: Miller sends a second draft of *The Misfits* to John Huston.

Marilyn writes to Jon Whitcomb, who did a *Cosmopolitan* cover of her: "I would love to have the picture from you and I repeat 'at last to be a Whitcomb girl!'" She looks forward to meeting him and introducing him to Arthur Miller.

September 26: Huston wires Miller: "SCRIPT MAGNIFICENT."

Marilyn and Miller attend the premiere of Judy Garland's show at the Palace Theatre.

September 27: Marilyn and Miller attend an American Friends of the Hebrew University event at the Bellevue Stratford in Philadelphia.

September 29: Lester Markel escorts Marilyn on a tour of the *New York Times* headquarters. She watches the typesetters, visits the morgue (the archive of clippings and photographs), and causes quite a commotion. "The *Times* is such a friendly place," Marilyn tells Markel.

October 4: Sylvia Plath records in her journal: "Marilyn Monroe appeared to me last night in a dream as a kind of fairy godmother. An occasion of 'chatting' with audience much as the occasion with Eliot will turn out, I suppose. I spoke, almost in tears, of how much she and Arthur Miller meant to us, although they could, of course, not know us at all. She gave me an expert manicure. I had not washed my hair, and asked her about hairdressers, saying no matter where I went, they always imposed a horrid cut on me. She invited me to visit during the Christmas holidays, promising a new, flowering life."

October 5: Miller writes to Huston: "Not since 'Salesman' have I felt such eagerness to see something of mine performed. Marilyn asks to be remembered to you, as always; she is slowly getting into tiptop for the great day."

October 14: Jack Cole, Marilyn's favorite choreographer, who worked with her on *Gentlemen Prefer Blondes*, *River of No Return*, *There's No Business Like Show Business*, and *Some Like It Hot*, arrives in New York City at the Dance Players Rehearsal Hall to work on Marilyn's new film. He leaves in anger when she fails to show up.

October 19: After several days of working very little with Marilyn, Cole is doubtful she will be ready for even one musical number by November 3.

October 24: Cukor arrives in New York to select some location shots and to consult with Marilyn. He learns that she is unhappy with the script, and Miller is hired to do two weeks of rewrites for $15,000.

October 31: Huston wires Miller to say Clark Gable has agreed to appear in *The Misfits*.

November 1: Pollock-Bailey Pharmacists, 401 East 56th Street, New York City, bills Mrs. Arthur Miller $220.58 for Amytal and other drugs and cosmetics.

November 2: Marilyn, photographed wrapped in furs, and Miller depart New York for Los Angeles

November 9: Marilyn reports to the Fox lot. Philippe Halsman photographs her.

Life publishes "Marilyn, Part of a Jumping Picture Gallery," photographs by Halsman. "In a burst of energy the subject overcomes gravity," Halsman wrote. "He cannot control all his muscles. The mask falls." Marilyn jumps with her fists closed and knees bent, "like a little girl," the photographer observes.

November 12: After showing up late the previous three days, Marilyn doesn't return to the *Let's Make Love* set after noon.

November 13: Miller hands in his *Let's Make Love* rewrites, which are immediately sent to Gregory Peck, who has been selected as her co-star. But Fox lets him go when he objects to how much Marilyn's part has been built up and his diminished.

November 15: Marilyn does costume fittings for *Let's Make Love*, dressed in a white strapless gown, which she raises with her right hand in a wing-like spread. Other shots show her in the black leotard and large sweater that figure in several scenes in the movie, and in a long checkered black-and-white coat.

November 17: Photos of Marilyn in a low-cut black dress and matching high heels, kicking up her right leg, twirling a wrap, turning right and left in profile—all publicity shots by Earl Gustie for *Some Like It Hot*—appear on the cover of *Chicago Tribune Magazine*.

November 20: Marilyn does more costume fittings for *Let's Make Love*.

December 4: Miller offers the role of Perce in *The Misfits* to Montgomery Clift, who accepts, completing a cast that includes Clark Gable and Eli Wallach.

A publicity still shot by Richard Avedon for *Some Like It Hot*, showing Marilyn in a powder blue dress, appears on the cover of *Platea* (Argentina).

John Huston arrives in Los Angeles. He approves the casting for *The Misfits*, but wants to make cuts in the screenplay.

Richard D. Zanuck (son of producer Darryl Zanuck) writes to Marilyn, offering her the role of Temple Drake in a film adaptation of William Faulkner's *Requiem for a Nun*.

December 8: Marilyn writes herself a check for $7,052, drawn on Marilyn Monroe Productions.

December 15: Marilyn does makeup and wardrobe tests.

December 17: The tests show a surprisingly dull Marilyn in unflattering hair, makeup, and clothing.

December 18: Marilyn calls in sick and does not appear at the studio. Miller is asked to do more revisions of *Let's Make Love*.

December 19: Eliza Kazan writes to Arthur Miller with a mixed review of a *Misfits* draft: "The last big sequence (Mustangs) can be a masterpiece. And it's perfect for Huston. I thought you went on and on about what it all meant though. I'd have liked it better without nearly so much thematic finger pointing. And I thought the very end unresolved. Perhaps it all suffers from not quite pointing to any definite ending. And to tell it all, I thought the girl a little too—well too a lot of things, too right, too often, too pure, too aware. But, on the whole, damned good. I hope you work on it more before you start the shooting."

December 21: Marilyn calls in sick.

December 22: Marilyn calls in sick.

December 23: Marilyn calls in sick.

Miller begins a second set of revisions for *Let's Make Love* for an additional $5,000, with a due date of January 4.

December 24: Marilyn calls in sick.

December 25: Yves Montand and Simone Signoret send Marilyn a hand drawn "Happy Christmas!!" card, showing stick figures representing all three of them.

1960

Maurice Zolotow publishes *Marilyn Monroe*.

John Myers paints Marilyn as a "modern Mona Lisa."

Marilyn, a registered Democrat, is selected as an alternate delegate to the national convention, representing Roxbury, Connecticut.

January: On Dr. Kris's recommendation, during the filming of *Let's Make Love* Marilyn meets psychiatrist Ralph Greenson for the first time. She consults with him about her difficulties with Paula Strasberg.

January 6: Marilyn leaves the Fox lot after only a half hour of rehearsal.

January 8: Marilyn's agent calls Fox to say she will be ready to work in ten days, with a January 18 start date.

Marilyn writes a check to herself for $5,000 drawn on Marilyn Monroe Productions.

Miller begins a third set of rewrites for *Let's Make Love* for a fee of $7,500.

January 11: John Huston informs Frank Taylor, now serving as producer of *The Misfits*, that he is making cuts in the screenplay.

January 12: Marilyn writes herself a check for $10,000, drawn on Marilyn Monroe Productions.

January 15: Fox holds a press party for Yves Montand, who has been cast (at Arthur Miller's suggestion) to replace Gregory Peck in *Let's Make Love*. Marilyn seems in better health and ready to work. Group photographs are taken of Miller, Simone Signoret (Montand's wife), Montand, Marilyn, and Frankie Vaughan, a popular British singer, and Milton Berle, who also appears in *Let's Make Love*. Marilyn is photographed with producer Buddy Adler, gossip columnist Dorothy Kilgallen, and director George Cukor. Marilyn and Miller join Montand and Signoret for dinner. The couples occupy adjoining bungalows in the Beverly Hills Hotel.

January 17: A terrified Montand, who does not know much English, works on his lines with his wife, the actress Simone Signoret.

Marilyn suddenly informs the studio that she will not be coming in the next day.

January 18: Filming of *Let's Make Love* resumes.

Stern (Germany) shows Marilyn, all in black, during a number from *Let's Make Love*.

January 22: Dr. Marianne Kris calls her colleague Dr. Ralph Greenson, asking him to attend to Marilyn, who is having anxiety attacks. Greenson is well known because of patients such as Frank Sinatra, Peter Lorre, and Vivien Leigh. The psychiatrist begins work with Marilyn, visiting her in her bungalow, in an effort to reduce her reliance on drugs, advising her to rely for prescriptions only on him and an internist, Dr. Hyman Engelberg.

January 25: Marilyn is filmed singing "My Heart Belongs to Daddy." It is a production number in which she is surrounded by a group of adoring men, who ferry her across the stage in a routine reminiscent of *Gentlemen Prefer Blondes*—except that it is less raucous and more casual. Marilyn, wearing a large loose-fitting sweater and tights, is lofted onto the shoulders of her retinue. The result is mere imitation of her earlier performances. This is not her best work. She is dealing with inferior material, and she knows it.

January 26: Marilyn arrives on the set on time at 7:00 a.m., but then departs abruptly in full makeup two hours later. Producer Buddy Adler looks at the rushes and is shocked. Marilyn looks overweight, and he dislikes her chalky white makeup, similar to what she used in *Bus Stop*.

January 29: Marilyn does her first scene with Montand. They work well together after he confesses that, like her, he is scared to go in front of the cameras.

Miller flies to New York to work on *The Misfits*.

February 4: Miller returns to Los Angeles, finding Marilyn hard at work.

Jack Cole, Marilyn's choreographer on *Let's Make Love*, sends her a telegram: "THE UNIVERSE SPARKLES WITH MIRACLES BUT NONE AMONG THEM SHINES LIKE YOU REMEMBER THAT WHEN YOU GO TO SLEEP TONIGHT. TOMORROW WILL BE FUN THERE IS NO OTHER WAY ALL MY LOVE JACK COLE."

February 9: Marilyn is awarded a star on the Hollywood Walk of Fame.

February 10: After several days of steady work, Marilyn calls in sick just after Miller leaves for Ireland to consult with John Huston about *The Misfits*.

February 11: Marilyn shows up for work, but is sent home because she seems unable to proceed.

February 13: Marilyn and Yves Montand appear on the cover of *Paris Match*.

February 14: Marilyn and Miller send Steffi Sidney (Sidney Skolsky's daughter) a wedding present: a sterling silver cigarette box with the inscription "For this wonderful day—affectionately, Marilyn and Arthur."

Epoca (Italy) shows Marilyn in a white halter-top in a photo taken during a party for *Let's Make Love*.

February 17: Simone Signoret spends the night telling Marilyn about film work in France, and Marilyn behaves like "a kid who's delaying the moment for lights out," Signoret recalls in a memoir.

February 18: Marilyn stays home without notifying the studio. When she doesn't answer his knock at her residence, Montand slips a note under her door: "Don't leave me to work for hours on end on a scene you've already decided not to do the next day. I'm not your enemy, I'm your pal. And capricious little girls have never amused me." Monroe calls Miller in Ireland, and he in turn calls the Montands, asking them to return to her door. Ashamed, she begs their forgiveness, admits her fault, and promises not to do it again.

February 21: Marilyn arrives on the set at 10:30 a.m. Academy Award nominations have just been announced, but her performance in *Some Like It Hot* has not been acknowledged. Nevertheless, Marilyn happily congratulates Simone Signoret on her nomination for *Room at the Top*.

February 25: Marilyn completes a solid week of work, but the film is now ten days behind schedule.

Raf's Record Bar, 193 South Beverly Drive, bills Miss Marilyn Monroe $2.98 for a Frank Sinatra-Count Basie LP, and $3.98 each for two albums, *Swinging Lovers* and *Swing Affair*, both by Sinatra.

February 26: Marilyn's agent notifies Lew Schreiber that she is upset about working with actress Mara Lynn, whose hair color has to be changed so that it is not blonde. But the rushes show Lynn's hair is red. Biographer Barbara Leaming thinks the red hair triggered Monroe's memories of her mother.

February 27: Arthur Miller returns from Ireland.

March 7: The last day of shooting *Let's Make Love* occurs on the day the Screen Actors Guild calls a strike. Marilyn keeps asking director George Cukor to do more takes of a theater scene. "Just one more, George. I think I can do it better," she says to the director, according to Gene Allen, the film's art director. Cukor finally tells the cameraman not to put additional film in the camera and then he allows Marilyn to continue doing takes. "Cukor did everything he could to appease her and make her feel wanted, because he really saw a lot in her," Allen recalled for Richard Buskin.

March 8: In New York, Marilyn receives a Golden Globe award for her performance in *Some Like It Hot*. The ceremony takes place in the Coconut Grove in the Ambassador Hotel, with Glenn Ford presenting the honor. Marilyn, dressed in a strapless gown and covered in white fur, is photographed clasping the gold trophy to her chest and smiling with her eyes closed.

March 10: Martindale's Book Stores (Los Angeles) bills Marilyn Monroe Miller $28.86 for three volumes of the life and works of Sigmund Freud.

March 12: A wistful Marilyn appears on the cover of *L'Europeo* (Italy).

March 26: Facing the camera, with her arms swinging to the left, Marilyn, in a black dress, seems to be illustrating the German tagline in *Revue*: "Eine Party mit Marilyn."

March 29: Marilyn writes to Lester Markel at the *New York Times*. She likes the Sunday piece on playwright Sean O'Casey. She provides her assessment of various contenders for the presidency, including Rockefeller, Humphrey, Nixon, Stevenson, William O. Douglas, and Kennedy. She considers Rockefeller "more liberal than many of the Democrats," and declares that Stevenson "might have made it if he had been able to talk to people instead of professors." Nixon has no soul. Douglas is ideal, but his divorce is an impediment. She is disappointed with the *Times*'s coverage of Castro and feels the United States should support and develop democracy. She includes some political slogans: "Nix on Nixon," "Over the hump with Humphrey (?)," "Stymied with Symington," "Back to Boston by Xmas—Kennedy."

April 4: At the Academy Awards, *Some Like It Hot* receives only one award, for costume design. *Ben Hur* wins eleven awards.

April 8: Simone Signoret leaves for France after winning an Academy Award, expecting that her husband would join her in a month after completion of *Let's Make Love*.

April 10: Marilyn, looking especially bright-eyed and expectant in a still from *Let's Make Love*, is on the cover of *L'Europeo* (Italy).

April 11: Marilyn and Miller fly from New York to Los Angeles. She has gained weight and seems depressed, brightening only when the cameras roll.

April 12: Marilyn appears for rehearsal on the Fox lot. She is photographed with producer Buddy Adler.

April 13: Shooting resumes on *Let's Make Love*, but goes slowly with Marilyn rarely working for more than four hours at a stretch.

Jack Cardiff, Marilyn's cinematographer on *The Prince and the Showgirl*, visits her on the set.

April 14: Marilyn pays thirty dollars to have her hair done at the Elizabeth Arden Salon in the Beverly Hills Hotel.

April 15: Miller returns to New York to work on *The Misfits*, and shortly afterwards Monroe's affair with Montand begins. Her work on the film improves.

Ben Lyon, who signed Marilyn to her first contract, writes to her on Twentieth Century Fox stationery: "Dear Marilyn—It was very sweet of you to send Jack Daniels over to me. I met him sometime back. He is a smooth character. Somehow he hit me on the back of my head about midnight and I was a sight for sore eyeballs for a couple of days. This time I am going to watch him. . . . Being here is a privilege they tell me. Sometimes I wonder."

April 16: Marilyn and Montand are photographed together during Josephine Baker's show at the Hollywood Hartford Theatre.

April 17: Schwab's Pharmacy, Hollywood and Beverly Hills, bills Mrs. Marilyn Miller $11.42 for two prescriptions.

April 30: Miller writes to Cukor, thanking him for treating Marilyn so well.

Early May: Miller evidently learns of Marilyn's affair with Montand, but remains quiet about it. Producer Cheryl Crawford accompanies Marilyn and Montand to a party at David Selznick's, where, it seems, it was apparent to all that Marilyn and Montand were lovers.

May 3: Dorothy Jeakins, who had done Marilyn's costumes for *Niagara* and *Let's Make Love*, writes Marilyn, resigning her position on *The Misfits*: "I am sorry I have displeased you. I feel quite defeated—like a misfit, in fact. But I must, above everything, continue to work (and live) in terms of my own honest pride, and good taste."

Marilyn writes herself a check for $4,800, drawn on Marilyn Monroe Productions.

May 6: Marilyn writes a check for $1,423.20, drawn on Marilyn Monroe Productions, to the Beverly Hills Hotel.

May 12: Schwab's Pharmacy, Hollywood and Beverly Hills, bills Marilyn Monroe Miller in Beverly Hills Hotel Bungalow 16, $40.95 for six Fleet enemas, five hairsprays, one Arrid, and assorted cosmetics.

May 14: Marilyn writes a check to herself for $2,500, drawn on Marilyn Monroe Productions.

May 16: Lucille Ryman writes to complain that Marilyn does not answer her calls, and supposes Marilyn's secretary is to blame: "I refuse to believe the girl I used to know, who could reach me by phone any hour of the day or night—no matter how slight the problem, has so quickly forgotten." *McCall's* wants Ryman to tell her "personal story of the Marilyn Monroe I knew." Before proceeding, Ryman wants to discuss the matter with Marilyn. No reply from Marilyn is extant.

May 20: Marilyn Monroe writes herself a check for $10,000, drawn on Marilyn Monroe Productions.

May 26: Schwab's Pharmacy, Hollywood and Beverly Hills, bills Mrs. Arthur Miller $25.75 for four prescriptions.

May 27: Marilyn writes a check to herself for $2,500, drawn on Marilyn Monroe Productions.

June 1: Cast and crew of *Let's Make Love* celebrate Marilyn's thirty-fourth birthday. She is photographed cutting her cake, as Cukor, Montand, and Frankie Vaughan—all of them smiling—watch her. She is also photographed sharing her cake with some children on the set.

In the evening, Rupert Allan gives a dinner in her honor at his home in Beverly Hills. She spends part of the evening talking about the theater with Tennessee Williams. Clifford Odets stays until four in the morning, reading palms.

Norman Rosten, Marilyn's short poet-friend (especially in comparison to Arthur Miller), sends her a birthday card picturing a couple embracing and bearing his own caption: "If you were only shorter!" In the card he refers to her as an old Gemini. As Lois Banner notes in *MM—Personal*, Gemini was Marilyn's birth sign, which "supposedly produces individuals split in personality between rationality and emotionality, boldness and shyness." Rosten includes a poem with the lines, "To be born isn't easy, / And to keep going can drive a soul crazy— / But let's us keep to it / Breathing will do it . . . A kiss I do send / All the way from this end, / (Hope it comes when it's raining / Or when you're complaining)."

June 2: Harry Brand, director of publicity at Fox, writes to Marilyn, thanking her for visiting a dying Joe Schenck and cheering him up.

June 10: Cukor films the last musical number, the film's title song, for *Let's Make Love*.

Journalen (Sweden) shows a tight close-up of Marilyn looking especially wholesome and Sandra Dee-like.

June 13: Marilyn writes a check to herself for $5,000, drawn on Marilyn Monroe Productions.

Mid-June: Production of *Let's Make Love* ends, twenty-eight days behind schedule—in part due to the actors' and writers' strikes, and, in part, to Marilyn's dilatory behavior. Wilfrid Hyde-White, a cast member, kisses Marilyn and says, "Thank you my dear for the longest and most remunerative contract I've ever had."

Columnists are now writing about the Marilyn-Montand affair.

June 16: Marilyn and Montand shoot their last scene together.

June 17: A letter from Paul, Weiss, Rifkin, Wharton & Garrison (probably written by John F. Wharton) suggests that an article in *Motion Picture* by Hedda Hopper is libelous, according to Sam Silverman, a libel expert in Wharton's firm. "I shall only say that bringing a libel suit might result in giving Miss Hopper a greater opportunity to display her venom. That doesn't mean that we wouldn't bring the suit if you wish us to." Marilyn did not wish to.

June 20: John Huston meets with Miller in New York for four days of meetings.

Marilyn performs in her last sequence for *Let's Make Love*.

June 21: Marilyn appears at the studio with laryngitis and so is unable to dub her musical scenes.

Marilyn and Montand attend the premiere of Billy Wilder's *The Apartment*, and then go to a party to celebrate the film at Romanoff's.

June 22: Marilyn does not show up for work and cannot be reached by phone.

June 24: Marilyn appears at the studio to watch her scenes with Montand.

John Huston leaves New York to look at locations in Nevada for *The Misfits*.

June 26: Marilyn flies to New York. She hires a limousine and awaits the arrival of Montand's plane. They drink champagne, as he explains he is returning to his wife.

June 29: Marilyn writes a check to herself for $400.27, drawn on Marilyn Monroe Productions.

June 30: Marilyn does costume fittings for *The Misfits*.

July 1: Fox assigns Marilyn her next film, *Goodbye, Charlie*. But the studio is not able to sign a director on Monroe's approved list, and she does not do the picture.

July 4: Canfield Corner Pharmacy, North Woodbury, Connecticut, bills Marilyn Miller $4.50 for two prescriptions (one is for Seconal).

July 5: *Look* publishes "Monroe Meets Montand."

July 8: Marilyn invites James Haspiel and a group of fans called the "Monroe Six" to the Fox studios on 54th Street to watch her costume, hair, and makeup tests for *The Misfits*. She even poses for Haspiel's color home movie.

July 11: Marilyn is supposed to do dubbing for *Let's Make Love* in New York, but Miller reports to her agents that she is not feeling well.

July 12: John Kennedy gives a speech in the Los Angeles Coliseum at the end of the Democratic Convention. With Sammy Davis Jr., Marilyn attends a dinner for Kennedy at Peter Lawford's Santa Monica beach house.

July 13: Marilyn returns to New York to do makeup tests, and has her hair styled by George Masters for her role in *The Misfits*.

July 16: Cukor refuses to fly from Los Angeles to New York and come in on a Saturday to direct Marilyn's dubbing.

Ralph Roberts gives Marilyn a massage as part of her preparation for returning to Los Angeles.

July 17: Marilyn flies to Los Angeles to do the dubbing on *Let's Make Love*, while Miller flies to Nevada to work with Huston on *The Misfits*.

July 18: The Erno Laszlo Institute for Scientific Cosmetology bills Mrs. Marilyn Monroe Miller, Reno, Nevada, $418.35 for several products, including Normalife Shake, Controlling Lotion, and various creams.

Marilyn has sessions with both Dr. Greenson and Dr. Engelberg.

July 20: Marilyn travels to Reno, Nevada, for shooting of *The Misfits*. She wears a white silk blouse and white skirt and a blonde wig. James Haspiel observes that she has "bags under the eyes and a period stain across the back of her skirt. I didn't want to see her like that, and I turned away." She is exhausted and suffering abdominal pain. In his memoir, *Timebends*, Miller admits that it was now "impossible" for him to deny that if "there was a key for Marilyn's despair, I didn't own it."

Marilyn is photographed riding through Reno in an open Thunderbird convertible.

July 21: Shooting begins on *The Misfits*.

Late July: The first week of filming goes well. Marilyn receives a $300,000 flat fee, plus 10 percent of the profits.

Both Paula Strasberg and Ralph Roberts (who plays an ambulance driver in the film) are there to assist Marilyn. Both are shown in a shot with Roberts massaging Marilyn's shoulders and Paula, wearing her signature dark clothing and hat, holding a script in her hand and talking with Marilyn. May Reis, Marilyn's secretary, is also present, as well as her hairstylist, Agnes Flanagan, and her makeup man, Whitey Snyder, who is shot with his arms around Marilyn (who seems to lean back in exhaustion). Other photographs show Marilyn talking to her stand-in, Evelyn Moriarty—who got to know Marilyn well, if briefly—her dresser, Sherlee Strahm, and her driver, Rudy Kautzky.

Marilyn and Arthur Miller stay in Reno at the Mapes Hotel in room 614. Photographs of the smiling couple belie their estrangement—although a photograph taken of Marilyn conferring with Paula Strasberg while Miller sits, unattended, in a director's chair, is indicative of the strain now put on him as husband and screenwriter.

July 24: Frank Taylor, the film's producer, and his wife, Nan, hold a party for cast and crew, including Marilyn and Miller.

July 25: Norman Rosten, Marilyn's poet-friend, sends Marilyn Monroe Miller at the Mapes Hotel a postcard of a Notre Dame Cathedral gargoyle, with hands under his jaws in a pose reminiscent of Rodin's *The Thinker*. Rosten writes on the card, "What does it all *mean*—? N/"

July 27: Cast and crew travel to Stix Ranch in Quail Canyon, a forty-five-minute drive from Reno.

July 30: Marilyn calls in sick.

July 31: Emmeline Snively writes to Marilyn: "I am so happy to hear that you are back in California making a picture. We have been following your steady progress over the years, and our students at Blue Book Models regard your success and constant development as an inspiration. I would like to see you if that could possibly be arranged."

August 1: Marilyn calls in sick.

August 2: Marilyn shows up for work but seems upset.

August 3: Rupert Allan, Marilyn's press agent, writes to James Roosevelt, explaining that Marilyn cannot record a brief greeting for the NBC-TV program October 7 on behalf of the Eleanor Roosevelt Institute for Cancer Research: "Miss Monroe deeply appreciates your interest in her being a part of this program but, much as she admired your worthy cause and your mother, she reluctantly must decline." Allan explains that she is working six days a week in the desert heat without any rest after having completed *Let's Make Love*.

August 5: Marilyn and Miller have a very public quarrel mentioned in the newspapers. They are "invited to attend a double *surprise* party for Mrs. Clark Gable and Mr. John Huston in the Table Room on the mezzanine of the Mapes Hotel Friday, August 5th at 7:00 p.m. There will be cocktails, a buffet and a special cabaret entertainment." Marilyn is photographed during an intimate moment with Gable.

August 6: John Bryson writes to Marilyn about his pictures of her, Yves Montand, and Arthur Miller for *Life*. He hopes she likes the pictures, which show "how intensely hard you work. I am very happy, however, to report that we close with a larger than full page of the picture of Arthur swabbing your back after a hard day's rehearsal. I think the little girl look in this is the best picture I ever took of you."

August 8: *Time* publishes "Marilyn and the Mustangs."

August 9: John Bryson writes to Marilyn again about his photographs of her on the set of *The Misfits*. He thinks the color proof "looks *great*."

August 13: Marilyn is photographed with Frank Sinatra at the Cal-Neva Lodge in Lake Tahoe, where he is singing. She appears along with Miller and several actors from *The Misfits*.

August 15: *Life* publishes "Marilyn's Movie Lover: With Account by David Zeitlin."

August 16: John Huston runs up huge gambling debts that cannot be covered by the production company United Artists, a development that threatens to shut down the production if Huston is not able to pay the casino what he owes them.

August 20: On a Saturday, Marilyn flies to Hollywood to purchase a dress for the premiere of *Let's Make Love* in Reno.

August 21: Marilyn flies back to Reno, but the premiere is canceled due to a devastating fire that causes power outages.

August 22: Marilyn resumes work on *The Misfits*.

August 23: Marilyn poses for several Magnum photographers assigned to cover *The Misfits*. Inge Morath (who will later become Miller's wife) photographs a heavy-looking Marilyn staring out of a hotel window, while Miller, smoking a cigarette, watches her from the shadows—a fitting expression of their estrangement. Henri Cartier-Bresson shoots Marilyn in hat and veil in a scene she plays as Roslyn Taber, recently divorced. Eve Arnold photographs Marilyn outdoors in pigtails, by turns happy and wistful. Elliot Erwitt's compositions are formal, with Marilyn the centerpiece in a pyramid of men, with Miller in cowboy hat at the apex and Huston just be-

The Misfits with Eli Wallach and Thelma Ritter

low him, while Gable flanks Marilyn on her left, and Montgomery Clift, Eli Wallach, and producer Frank Taylor are on her right. Bruce Davidson's Marilyn is pigtailed and pondering, sitting next to Arthur Miller, who is almost in a crouch. Cornel Capa concentrates on color two-shots of Gable and Marilyn, and Ernst Haas presents Miller in a director's chair, staring out into the desert, with Marilyn sitting just below the heavy cinema equipment.

August 24: *Let's Make Love* is released.

August 24–26: Marilyn works with the cast on rodeo scenes that demand several takes.

August 25: Max Youngstein, a United Artists producer, informs Huston that he has spent all the money available for the movie. Huston obtains $25,000 as an advance on *Freud*, the next movie he is going to direct.

August 26: Marilyn and Gable are filmed in a station wagon as he delivers a speech: "Honey, we all got to go sometime, reason or no reason. Dyin's as natural as livin'; who's afraid to die is too afraid to live, far as I've ever seen. So there's nothing to do but forget it, that's all. Seems to me."

August 28: Marilyn meets with Dr. Greenson and Dr. Engelberg, who advise her to rest for a week to detoxify.

August 29: Marilyn is admitted to Westside Hospital in Los Angeles, suffering from extreme exhaustion—giving Huston an opportunity to raise more money to cover his debts.

Producer Frank Taylor writes a letter to Clark Gable, announcing his intention to replace Marilyn.

Ralph Roberts goes to Marilyn's bedside, along with Paula and Susan Strasberg.

Arthur Miller arrives a little later, and is reportedly angry because Marilyn's hospitalization has been used to deflect attention from Huston's money worries.

August 29–September 4: During her hospital stay, Marilyn is visited by Marlon Brando, Frank Sinatra, and Joe DiMaggio. She tells DiMaggio that she is going to divorce Miller.

August 30: Hedda Hopper interviews Yves Montand.

August 31: Dr. Ralph Greenson submits a $1,250 bill to Marilyn "for professional services."

September 1: Montand's interview with Hedda Hopper is published, making Marilyn seem naïve about an affair that could not last.

Fecko Revyn (Sweden) puts on its cover a film still of Marilyn dancing in her sweater and tights in *Let's Make Love*.

September 5: Smiling in photographs with Miller at her side, Marilyn returns to the set of *The Misfits*, declaring, "I'm looking forward to getting back to work. I'm feeling much better. I guess I was just worn out." The two take separate suites at the Holiday Hotel in Reno.

September 6: Marilyn resumes work on *The Misfits*.

September 8: *Let's Make Love* is released to generally bad reviews.

September 12: Marilyn is unable to work.

Newsweek publishes "Who's a Misfit?"

Earl Wilson breaks the story that Marilyn and Miller will divorce.

September 13: Marilyn is unable to work.

September 19: Marilyn is unable to work.

September 21: Marilyn and Arthur Miller leave the Mapes Hotel.

September 23: Marilyn and Montgomery Clift shoot a long scene together. Huston is so impressed he offers her the female lead in his next film, *Freud*. She is to play Cecily, a psychoanalytic patient treated by Clift, who will play Freud.

September 30: Marilyn and Montand, sitting in director's chairs, appear on the cover of *Münchner Illustrierte* (Germany).

October 10: A melancholy Marilyn, dressed in black in a still from *Let's Make Love*, appears on the cover of *de Post* (Belgium).

Marilyn organizes a party for makeup man Frank LaRue, who is also Montgomery Clift's companion. The event takes place at Edith Palmer's Country Inn Restaurant near Dayton, Nevada. Clark Gable drives her there in his Mercedes.

October 11: Marilyn's renunciation of the mustang hunt is filmed. She is photographed in a long shot screaming at the cowboys, "Butchers! Killers! Murderers! You liars. All of you liars! You're only happy when you can see something die! Why don't you kill yourself and be happy? You and your God's country. Freedom! I pity you. You're three dear, sweet dead men. Butchers! Murderers! I pity you! You're three dead men!" Marilyn dislikes the histrionic, indeed hysterical, performance she is compelled to give. Miller objects to the long shot. Huston defends it as a cry from the wilderness.

Inge Morath takes still photographs of the scene, providing the close-up Huston eschewed. Marilyn is shown as the very epitome of dissent: fists clenched and her body jutting forward, legs far apart, appearing in more control of her emotions than the filmed scene suggests.

October 16: Marilyn and Montgomery Clift have dinner at the North Beach restaurant in San Francisco.

October 17: *The Misfits* company holds a joint birthday party for Arthur Miller and Montgomery Clift at the Christmas Tree Inn. Marilyn attends.

October 18: Location shooting for *The Misfits* ends. Marilyn and Miller depart for the Beverly Hills Hotel to finish studio shots for the film. She resumes her sessions with Dr. Greenson.

October 24–November 4: *The Misfits* company moves to stage 2 at Paramount studios.

October 29: Eve Arnold shoots a private session, including semi-nudes, with Marilyn at the Paramount photo studio, assisted by makeup artist Whitey Snyder and hair stylist Agnes Flanagan.

October 30: William Zinsser reviews Maurice Zolotow's biography of Marilyn, saying she has been honored with a long and serious book.

October 31: *Newsweek* publishes "Constellation is Born."

November 4: Huston shoots the film's happy ending with Marilyn and Gable.

Marilyn tells Huston she cannot appear in *Freud* because Anna Freud does not want the picture made.

November 5: Marilyn learns Clark Gable has suffered a massive heart attack.

November 6: *Piccolo* (Holland) shows the Marilyn of *Let's Make Love*—sexy, but almost in a wholesome Doris Day way.

November 7: Miller leaves *The Misfits* set, flies to New York, and stays in the Adams Hotel on East 86th Street. He tells his parents the marriage to Marilyn is over. Marilyn returns to their New York apartment.

November 8: On this election day, Marilyn does not return to her Roxbury, Connecticut, home, where she is registered to vote.

November 10: John F. Wharton, Arthur Miller's attorney, writes to Marilyn, stating "legal ethics do not permit me to continue as your lawyer, but nothing prevents me, nor ever will prevent me, from being your friend." She chooses Aaron Frosch to replace Wharton.

November 11: Marilyn flies to New York and gives Earl Wilson an exclusive. He reports: "The marriage of Marilyn Monroe and Arthur Miller is over, and there will be a friendly divorce." Marilyn lives at her apartment at 444 East 57th Street, attended by May Reis and Pat Newcomb.

Miller checks into the Adams Hotel on East 86th Street. Reis, who had been Miller's secretary before Marilyn employed her, now helps Miller sort out his papers in the 57th Street apartment. He takes various items, including a treasured photograph of Marilyn, and they agree he will keep Hugo, their basset hound, in Roxbury, and Marilyn will keep the apartment.

November 12: A *New York Post* headline blares, "Miller Walks out on Marilyn." Marilyn is photographed in a limousine, wearing a dark coat and headscarf. Other shots show her walking in dark sunglasses, with her left hand going to her throat in a protective gesture.

November 16: At 4:00 a.m., a reporter calls Marilyn to tell her Clark Gable has died. She calls her friend and masseur, Ralph Roberts, to speak about her grief and goes into a depression.

November 19: Art Buchwald, a *Washington Post* columnist, publishes "Let's Be Firm on Monroe Doctrine": "Who will be the next ambassador to Monroe? This is one of the many problems

President-Elect Kennedy will have to work on in January. Obviously you can't leave Monroe adrift. There are too many greedy people eyeing her, and now that Ambassador Miller has left she could flounder around without any direction."

November 21: *Life* publishes "End of Famous Marriage."

Newsweek publishes "Out of the Fishbowl."

Time publishes "Popsie and Poopsie."

November 23: Arthur Miller resigns as a director of Marilyn Monroe Productions.

November 26: A decidedly downcast-looking Marilyn appears on the cover of *Jours de France* with the headline "Marilyn: Un Cas De Conscience Pour Yves Montand."

November 27: Yves Montand embraces Marilyn (publicity still by John Bryson) on the cover of *Settimo Giorno* (Italy).

November 28: An emergency meeting is held in the law offices of Weissberger and Frosch to discuss the resignations of Miller and other advisors to Marilyn Monroe Productions.

December: *Cosmopolitan* publishes "Marilyn Monroe: The Sex Symbol vs. The Good Wife," by Jon Whitcomb.

Marilyn resumes daily psychoanalytic sessions with Dr. Marianne Kris.

December 7: Marilyn, dressed in black and holding up her left arm and hand in a white-gloved commanding gesture, appears on the cover of the *Australian Women's Weekly* with the headline "What next for Marilyn?"

December 11: For a *Family Weekly* profile, Marilyn repeats her desire to have a child: "I realize it takes more though to raise a child in show business, but it doesn't need to work out badly."

December 13: Marilyn informs Fox that she will not appear in *Goodbye, Charlie*.

Le Ore (Italy) puts a John Florea photograph on its cover showing Marilyn on her knees, stooping over to pick up a pile of paper money.

December 17: *Stern* (Germany) publishes a John Florea photograph showing Marilyn as Lorelei Lee examining a diamond necklace.

December 22: Marilyn sends a handwritten note to Inez Melson, her former business manager: "Dear Inez, Happy Holiday to you and Pat [Inez's husband]—I'll be in touch again soon, Love, Marilyn."

December 25: Marilyn spends a quiet Christmas with her publicist, Patricia Newcomb, and then with Joe DiMaggio, who sends her a basket of poinsettias.

December 31: Marilyn dines on spaghetti with sweet Italian sausages.

1961

Marilyn writes to Kay Gable, "I am thinking about you and I send my love to you and the children. I'll be in touch. Love, Marilyn"

January 7: Marilyn and Joe DiMaggio go to dinner and a Broadway show.

January 14: Marilyn draws up a new will, removing Arthur Miller as her beneficiary and substituting Lee Strasberg, with bequests to Marianne Kris, a small trust for her mother, and gifts to Michael Chekhov's widow and Patricia Rosten.

January 15: Marilyn and Joe eat dinner at the Le Pavilion restaurant, and then attend the closing night performance of *The Hostage* at the Eugene O'Neill Theatre.

January 17: Marilyn and Joe are photographed laughing over pages of Maurice Zolotow's biography of her and are later photographed at Le Pavilion.

January 18: In the *Lowell Sun*, a DiMaggio friend is quoted saying Joe will remarry Marilyn, but her publicist John Springer insists the couple are just friends.

January 20: Monroe divorces Miller in Juarez, Mexico, on the day JFK takes the oath of office.

January 21: Marilyn returns to New York and visits Lee Strasberg.

January 31: Marilyn attends a preview of *The Misfits*, accompanied by Montgomery Clift and Lee Strasberg. Arthur Miller also attends with his two children, but does not meet Marilyn. She is photographed in a dark dress and fur stole, wearing a bouffant hairdo.

Look publishes "Gable's Last Movie: Prelude to Tragedy."

W. Somerset Maugham writes Marilyn, "Thank you for your charming telegram of good wishes on my birthday. It was extremely kind of you to think of me; I was touched and much pleased. I am so glad to hear that you are going to play Sadie in the T.V. production of 'Rain.' I am sure you will be splendid. I wish you the best of luck. Yours very sincerely, W. Somerset Maugham."

February: *Coronet* publishes "Mosaic of Marilyn."

February 1: *The Misfits* receives mixed reviews. In treatment with Dr. Kris, Marilyn divulges her suicidal thoughts. Kris suggests that Marilyn should be hospitalized.

February 4: *Today* (England) shows a smiling Arthur Miller with Marilyn in the polka dress she wears in *The Misfits*. The headline reads, "Monroe and Miller: The Full Facts."

February 5: Following her psychiatrist's advice, a depressed Marilyn checks into the Payne Whitney Psychiatric Clinic and is upset when she is treated as a mentally ill patient who might do harm to herself.

Epoca (Italy) features a 1955 photograph of Marilyn, dressed in a terry cloth robe, bending her head to her knee and extending her left leg, while her right is tucked under her derriere.

February 7: Marilyn writes to Lee and Paula Strasberg, "I'm locked up with these poor nutty people. I'm sure to end up a nut too if I stay in this nightmare. Please help me. This is the last place I should be." But since the Strasbergs are not Marilyn's family, they have no power to seek her release.

February 9: Marilyn's institutionalization is reported in the press. She is permitted a call to Joe DiMaggio.

February 10: With Joe DiMaggio's help, Marilyn is released from Payne Whitney. Ralph Roberts picks Marilyn up. She sits in the backseat with Dr. Kris, and Marilyn berates Kris for betraying her trust.

Marilyn is admitted to Columbia Presbyterian Medical Center for three weeks of recuperation.

Roberts remembers Dr. Kris saying, "I did a terrible thing, a terrible, terrible thing. Oh God, I didn't mean to, but I did."

Marilyn's friend, the photographer Sam Shaw, writes from Paris to Marilyn's 444 East 57th Street address, offering her a room at his home. "We would have called during the recent turmoil but didn't know where you were. . . . There are some great art shows at this moment in Paris. Come over. An especially big Goya show of his prints. Marvelous impressionist show etc. and a pip of a Kandinski [sic]."

February 11: Andre de Dienes sends Marilyn a telegram calling her "Turkey Foot," his nickname for her: "STOP FEELING SORRY FOR YOURSELF. GET OUT OF THE HOSPITAL. LET'S GO DRIVING AND HIKING THROUGH THE RED-WOODS, INCOGNITO, AND TAKE BEAUTIFUL PICTURES LIKE NOBODY COULD EVER TAKE. IT WILL CURE YOU OF ALL YOUR ILLS. CALL ME UP. LOVE."

Nan Taylor, the wife of Frank Taylor, producer of *The Misfits*, writes to Marilyn: "It seems to me again, as it did last summer, very sad that we who have been given so much by you cannot give you even what little we might in return. You have my admiration for your courage, my gratitude for the many delights of charm and beauty and humor your presence has meant, and my deep sorrow for your troubles. I believe in your strength, Marilyn, as I believe in the sun. If at any time I can help in any way, please let me, Love, Nan."

February 12: The Strasbergs and Joe DiMaggio visit Marilyn at Columbia Presbyterian.

February 21: *Cinemonde* (France) shows a heavier Marilyn (during the *Some Like It Hot* period) wearing a strapless back dress, with a v-shaped front that shows off her cleavage and long white gloves.

February 26: A somber Marilyn appears on the cover of *Family Weekly*.

February 27: Marlon Brando sends Marilyn an encouraging telegram, saying, in part, "[D]on't be afraid of being afraid. It can only help. Relax and enjoy it. I send you my thoughts and my warmest affections. Marlon."

March: *Esquire* publishes A. T. McIntyre's article, "Making *The Misfits* or Waiting for Monroe or Notes from Olympus."

March 1–2: Marilyn writes to her psychiatrist, Ralph Greenson, about her admission to the Payne Whitney clinic. "I'd have to be nuts to like it in here," she says.

March 5: Marilyn is released from Columbia Presbyterian, accompanied by seven guards and Pat Newcomb, who helps her make her way through the crowds of fans, reporters, and photographers. In photographs she looks well rested and does not appear to mind the attention. She waves happily from the back seat of a limousine and returns to her 57th Street apartment.

March 7: With May Reis, Marilyn in mourning clothes attends the funeral of Arthur Miller's mother, Augusta, who died of a heart attack. Marilyn offers Arthur Miller her condolences and consoles his father Isidore.

March 13: Marilyn attends a party at the Actors Studio, escorted by her publicist, John Springer.

March 17: Marilyn becomes angered when she discovers her attorney has not shown her clippings reporting Marilyn is to blame for Gable's death. She says, "I must know my own business, so I can protect myself. Keeping things from me is no protection."

End of March: Marilyn joins DiMaggio for a vacation in North Redington Beach, Florida. They are photographed strolling happily together in evening clothes and also at the beach, where DiMaggio does some fishing. They take separate rooms at the Tides Motor Inn. They also attend exhibition baseball games in Fort Lauderdale, and Marilyn visits her half-sister, Berniece, in Gainesville. She stays in touch with Isidore Miller by phone.

April: In *Cinelandia* (Brazil) Marilyn's cover pose seems mask-like because of her heavily made-up eyes and brows, very full red lips, and silver-grey hair. She gazes slightly upward with a wistful expression.

April 1: Kay Gable writes to Marilyn, asking her when she plans to visit Los Angeles, so that she can visit her new baby, John Clark. "Do let me know when you plan to return to California. I'll let you be the second nanny in charge."

April 2: Marilyn and Joe are photographed returning from their Florida vacation.

April 11: Marilyn and DiMaggio attend an opening day baseball game at Yankee Stadium. Marilyn is photographed watching the action.

April 20: Fox informs Marilyn it is having difficulty finding a director for her because none of the names on her approved list are available to shoot a picture with her.

April 23: Marilyn attends Judy Garland's concert at Carnegie Hall.

End of April: Marilyn returns to Hollywood, resuming her life there and her therapy sessions with Dr. Greenson. She stays in the Beverly Hills Hotel but eventually finds an apartment on Doheny Drive.

May: Ralph Greenson writes to a colleague, "Above all, I try to help her not to be so lonely, and therefore to escape into the drugs or get involved with very destructive people, who will engage in some sort of sado-masochistic relationship with her . . . . This is the kind of planning you do with an adolescent girl who needs guidance, friendliness, and firmness, and she seems to take it very well. . . . Of course this does not prevent her from canceling several hours to go to Palm Springs with Mr. F. S. [Frank Sinatra]. She is unfaithful to me as one is to a parent."

Photographer Eric Skipsey shoots several pictures of Marilyn with her dog, Maf (a gift from Frank Sinatra), at the Beverly Hills Hotel.

Marilyn meets Ray Charles and Ella Fitzgerald at the Los Angeles Crescendo Club.

May 4: Fox informs Marilyn's lawyer that Lee Strasberg is still under consideration to direct a project with her. But Strasberg refuses a first offer of $22,500 and then on May 8, another one of $50,000, considering both offers too low for a man of his reputation.

Fox gives Marilyn permission to do *Rain* in a television production directed by Strasberg.

May 18: *Hayat* (Turkey) exhibits three publicity stills from *Let's Make Love* on the magazine's cover.

June: Jack Cardiff, cinematographer on *The Prince and the Show-girl*, visits Marilyn at her Beverly Hills bungalow. She seems despondent over the reception of *The Misfits*, her divorce from Miller, and the death of Clark Gable. She says she feels abandoned, but she also seems comforted by Cardiff's visit.

June 1: On her thirty-fifth birthday, Marilyn begins full-time treatment with Dr. Greenson. She writes to him, "In this world of people I'm glad there is you. I have a feeling of hope though today I'm three five. Marilyn."

George Chasin, a Hollywood agent, and his wife, Eileen, send Marilyn a telegram: "DEAR MARILYN HAVE A WONDERFUL DAY AND BEST WISHES FOR MANY MORE HAPPY HEALTHY BIRTHDAYS LOVE."

Marilyn sees Andre de Dienes for the last time. When he tries to kiss her, she objects, saying she is "tired of all that." He sees tears in her eyes, feels ashamed, and says goodbye.

June 2: Marilyn's lawyer, Aaron Frosch, asks for the contract to be rewritten for *Rain*, a television production of W. Somerset Maugham's novel.

June 12: Marilyn attends the christening of Clark Gable's son in Encino, California. Louella Parsons, also present, will later report her conversation with Marilyn in the October *Modern Screen*. Asked about Frank Sinatra and other men she is seeing, Marilyn responds, "Oh, we're just old friends. He had always been nice to me." About Joe DiMaggio, she says, "I just like being with Joe. We have a real understanding—something we didn't share when we were married. . . . It is a fine thing to be able to call someone your—friend. That's what Joe and I are. Friends." She said she was not friends with Miller, but added, "Arthur is a brilliant man. A wonderful writer. Maybe it wasn't his fault that he was a much better writer than he was a husband. I am sure that his writing is the most important thing in his life." To Parsons, Marilyn looked comfortable. "For the first time in many years," Marilyn told her, "I am completely free to do exactly as I please. To come and go as I see fit—make my own decisions. And this new freedom has made me happier."

June 14: Marilyn is Frank Sinatra's guest in Las Vegas for Dean Martin's forty-fourth birthday. A memo from the Sands casino president to his publicity director states, "[U]nder no circumstances is any backstage photographer permitted to photograph Mr. Sinatra and Miss Marilyn Monroe together at the cocktail reception to follow the performance on 14 June. Any photographer who attempts to do so will be permanently barred from the hotel. Be advised that this is not only a Sands requirement, it is a requirement of Mr. Sinatra's and, as such, will be absolutely enforced." Another memo notes that Marilyn's privacy is to be strictly observed: "She will be registered in Mr. Sinatra's suite. Under no circumstances is she or Mr. Sinatra to be disturbed by telephone calls or visitors before 2 p.m."

Marilyn is photographed at a table, laughing and seated with Dean Martin and Elizabeth Taylor. They are watching Sinatra perform.

June 15: Marilyn flies from Los Angeles to New York, where she is scheduled to have gallbladder surgery.

Marilyn meets with Rod Serling to discuss a television adaptation of W. Somerset Maugham's *Rain*.

June 21: Marilyn consults with her attorney, Aaron Frosch, and Lee Strasberg about *Rain*.

June 23: Louella Parsons reports in her column that Richard Burton has been offered the part of Revered Davidson in *Rain*. Burton declines because of his commitment to the Broadway production of *Camelot* and concerns about Marilyn's tardiness.

June 27: NBC writes to Frosch canceling the deal to broadcast *Rain*.

June 28: Marilyn, in pain, is hospitalized for gallbladder surgery.

June 29: Marilyn's gallbladder is removed in a two-hour operation. Joe DiMaggio is with her during her recovery.

July: Marilyn, recovering from her surgery, welcomes a visit from her half-sister, Berniece Miracle. Berniece worries about Marilyn's heavy intake of pills.

July 1: A publicity still from *The Misfits*, a two-shot of Marilyn and Clark Gable, is accompanied by a headline questioning whether Marilyn was culpable in his death.

July 11: Marilyn is released from the hospital. Two hundred reporters, photographers, and fans are there to witness the occasion. She is photographed in a wheelchair, then walking with two attendants. She smiles as a microphone is thrust at her. She returns to her apartment on 57th Street. Pat Newcomb helps take care of her, and her hair is now fashioned by Kenneth Battelle, a famous hairdresser. Berniece Miracle also visits.

July 14: Marilyn sends a telegram to Dr. Greenson on his twenty-sixth wedding anniversary: "I hope all your roses are in bloom today including the blackest red ones. Happy, happy anniversary to you and Mrs. Greenson."

July 16: Hedda Hopper publishes "Can Marilyn Ever Be Happy?" in *Chicago Sunday Tribune Magazine*.

July 25: On this hot summer day, Marilyn sends a coal scuttle filled with beer to the reporters stationed outside her apartment building, attaching a note: "Dear fellas, I know it's been a long, hot vigil so have a beer on me. I swear I'm not leaving. I'm staying—single."

July 26: Producer Harold Mirsch discusses with Marilyn a film project, *The Naked Truth*. He writes to her, enclosing a gift of Chanel No. 5: "This perfume is just a little thought from Paris and I hope it finds you well on the road to recovery. Will call you one of these days. Love Harold."

End of July: Marilyn returns to the Roxbury house to pick up her possessions, including a bust of Carl Sandburg, some books, and other artwork. Arthur Miller is absent.

August 7: Aaron Frosch, Marilyn's attorney, writes to her about Lee Strasberg's meetings with a Fox executive regarding a re-make of *Of Human Bondage*. The studio has some interest, Frosch reports, if Marlon Brando wanted to do the film with her. Another leading man, Paul Scofield, has also been proposed, and José Ferrer is under consideration as director.

August 8: Marilyn flies back to Hollywood. She keeps her Manhattan apartment, but stays temporarily in Frank Sinatra's Los Angeles home. Photographs show her relaxing with Sinatra, sun bathing, and reading *Look*. Then she rents a room at the Chateau Marmont.

August 11: Marilyn and her dog Maf are photographed (see entry for August 23).

August 23: Fourteen-year-old Barbara Heinz, dying from incurable bone cancer, receives, as she requested, a photograph from Marilyn with her dog, Maf. The inscription reads, "From Marilyn Monroe to Barbara Heinz. With love."

August 24: On the cover of *Hayat* (Turkey), Marilyn is pictured on the set of *The Misfits*, siting in a director's chair wearing a two-piece bathing suit, with her hair in pigtails.

September 8: Marilyn begins calling Tom Clay, host of the KDAY program *Words and Music*, because his stories about childhood and marriage touch her. He hangs up on what he believes is a crank caller. But subsequently, she gives him her address and invites him to her apartment.

September 11: Clay arrives at Marilyn's apartment at 9:30 a.m. and is shocked to discover that his caller is indeed Marilyn Monroe, and that she wants to talk about her loneliness. When he asks how such a famous person can be lonely, she replies, "Have you ever been in a room and felt loneliness? Well, multiply that by 40 rooms, then you'll have some idea about how lonely I am."

September 13: Marilyn's interest in Clay wanes as soon as she begins dating Frank Sinatra. They are spotted together in the Crown Room at Romanoff's in Hollywood. Dorothy Kilgallen writes in her column, "Marilyn Monroe looked as if she could have danced all night with Frank Sinatra."

September 14: Marilyn drafts a typewritten note to United Artists Corporation, asking for a $25,000 loan at 4 percent per annum, to be repaid in full on or before January 5, 1962. She receives the loan as an advance against royalties from *Some Like It Hot*.

September 21: Marilyn's flight from Los Angeles to New York encounters mechanical problems and returns to Los Angeles. A shaken Marilyn writes DiMaggio, "Love you, I think, more than ever."

September 22: Marilyn takes another flight to New York and visits DiMaggio.

Late September: Marilyn meets with journalist W. J. Weatherby, who later publishes *Conversations with Marilyn*.

October: *Modern Screen* carries a report by Louella Parsons, "Marilyn Monroe's Life as a Divorcee," derived from a conversation the columnist had with Marilyn in Kay Gable's home during the christening of John Clark Gable.

October 4: Marilyn attends a dinner party at Peter Lawford's house in honor of Attorney General Robert F. Kennedy.

October 5: Patricia Newcomb safeguards Monroe's privacy, informing her agency that Monroe has a new apartment on Doheny Drive in Los Angeles. Few friends, except for Ralph Roberts, see Marilyn, because her psychiatrist, Ralph Greenson, has advised her to avoid seeing too many people.

October 6: The *Times Recorder* reports that Marilyn is "not easy to spot on the street," with her "horn-rimmed glasses, peasant skirt and blouse," chewing gum.

October 8: Marilyn narrates her 1954 Korea tour in a special that appears on NBC's *DuPont Show of the Week.*

October 16: Fox assigns Marilyn a role in *Something's Got to Give,* directed by George Cukor. She is to report for work on November 15.

October 26: Marilyn's attorney, Mickey Rudin, meets with Fox executives, emphasizing that they must treat his client's opinions with respect and not just honor their contract with her. He also questions their choice of Cukor, since Cukor had not yet signed a contract to do another film with Marilyn.

November 9: Rudin tells Fox executives that Marilyn has qualms about the script for her new film. They remind Rudin that she does not have script approval.

November 14: Rudin asks for a copy of the latest version of the screenplay.

November 15: Marilyn does not report for work, and the studio suspends her.

November 17: Marilyn's savings account is the City National Bank of Beverly Hills has a balance of $40,000.

Douglas Kirkland shoots a memorable photograph of Marilyn clutching a white pillow. He describes her as "ghost-like" and "floating in slow motion."

November 18: Marilyn dines with the Greensons. Her psychiatrist involves her in his family life as part of her therapy. But he also requires Marilyn to stop seeing Ralph Roberts and others who, in the psychiatrist's view, have made her too dependent. Greenson expects to alleviate her anxieties, stemming from her childhood, by exposing her to a happy family setting.

November 19: Marilyn visits the home of Peter and Pat Lawford, joining them in a three-hour luncheon with President Kennedy.

November 23: Marilyn spends Thanksgiving with a friend and neighbor, Gloria Lovell. One of Gloria's friends, identified only as Jo, describes her impression of Marilyn, who is "no more like she is on screen than anything. . . . Her voice is different, although she has that little high pitched note, it's most exaggerated in her pix. She is as tall as I but oh so slender, thin face, little bucket, small breasts wears size 12 . . . very sweet nice as can be, very down to earth." Marilyn arrives in a short black skirt, black pumps, and a silk jersey pullover sweater, and has her hair tied up in a white silk scarf. "She wore the most elegant, sheared white beaver coat I have ever seen," Jo reports.

November 26: George Cukor agrees to direct *Something's Got to Give* for $300,000, plus 10 percent of the net profits.

December: Ralph Greenson writes to Anna Freud, "I have resumed treating the patient who Marianne Kris saw for several years. She has become a borderline paranoid addict and is very sick. You can imagine how difficult it is treating a Hollywood actress, who has so many serious problems and is completely alone in the world, and yet at the same time is extremely famous. Psychoanalysis is still out of the question and I am improvising constantly, often surprised at where it's leading me. I have no other options. If I succeed, I'll certainly have learned something but this case is requiring me to expend an impossible amount of time and emotions."

Marilyn Monroe meets poet Carl Sandburg for the first time, and they develop an instant rapport. They are photographed together, with Sandburg holding his guitar.

December 5: Marilyn writes a note to Marlon Brando, suggesting they set up their own production company.

According to biographer Keith Badman, Marilyn meets President Kennedy at the Park Avenue apartment of socialite Fifi Fell. To Kennedy, Peter Lawford jokingly introduces Marilyn, dressed in a dark red wig and wearing dark glasses, and holding a legal pad and pen, as his secretary. Kennedy retires early and alone to prepare for a speech the next day.

December 17: A stunning photograph, taken in 1955, appears on the cover of *L'Europeo*, showing Marilyn in an elegant strapless black dress, with an embroidered sash surrounding her bust. Her hands rests casually on her thighs, and she rocks her head backward just a bit to the left, closing her eyes and almost cooing to the camera with her lips.

December 19: Marilyn writes to Lee Strasberg, saying she has not been able to function well without his coaching. She adds, "For years I have been struggling to find some emotional security with little success, for many different reasons. It is true that treatment with Dr. Greenson has had its ups and down, as you know. However, my overall progress is such that I have hope of finally establishing a piece of ground for myself to stand on, instead of the quicksand I have always been in. But Dr. Greenson agrees with you, that for me to live decently and productively, I must work!"

December 20–21: Having finally been sent the script for *Something's Got to Give*, Marilyn demands changes. She also requests the cameraman from *Some Like It Hot*, and asks to be consulted about casting and publicity.

December 23: Joe DiMaggio arrives in Los Angeles. He buys a Christmas tree, caviar, and champagne.

December 24: Marilyn and Joe DiMaggio spend Christmas Eve together, decorating a tree with Mexican ornaments.

December 25: Marilyn and Joe spend Christmas Day at Ralph Greenson's home.

December 31: Dr. Greenson's daughter, Joan, visits Marilyn at her Doheny Drive apartment and celebrates New Year's Eve with Marilyn and Joe DiMaggio.

1962

Marilyn employs Ray Tolman to construct kitchen cabinets, a breakfast table, and a set of black walnut benches for her new Brentwood home.

Cherie Redmond begins doing secretarial work for Marilyn.

January 1: Eunice Murray receives her first weekly sixty-dollar check for employment as Marilyn's housekeeper. Murray also serves as chauffeur, cook, and social secretary—and she also spots the property that Marilyn purchases as her first house.

January 2: Fox production chief Peter Levathes officially announces the production of *Something's Got to Give*.

January 3: Marilyn's New York Bowery Savings Bank book has a balance of $597.77.

January 8: Marilyn is upset when she reads the news about Frank Sinatra's engagement to Juliet Prowse.

Columnist Sheilah Graham publicizes Marilyn's concerns about the *Something's Got to Give* script.

January 12: Marilyn's $57,500 bid is accepted, and she purchases a home in Brentwood.

January 15: Columnist Bob Thomas publicizes Marilyn's doubts about the *Something's Got to Give* script.

January 16: Fox announces shooting of *Something's Got to Give* will not begin until March 15.

January 20: Marilyn meets with Fox producer Henry T. Weinstein.

Marilyn meets with the visiting Carl Sandburg, who demonstrates—holding books over their heads—a series of exercises intended to alleviate insomnia. Photographer Arnold Newman takes pictures of the meeting, during which Monroe tells the poet her troubles. "You are *not* what is wrong with America," he tells her. They sip champagne and talk about Abraham Lincoln. "He is so pleased to meet you. He wants to know about you and you want to know about him," Marilyn reports. Sandburg, for his part, says, "She was very good company and we did some mock playacting, some pretty good imitations." Marilyn sat at Sandburg's feet, squeezing his hand from time to time.

January 24: Marilyn agrees to do *Something's Got to Give*, providing that the script changes are acceptable to her.

Advice columnist Ann Landers writes Marilyn a note: "Just read where you are back in Hollywood. Since I haven't seen or heard from you in a so long a time—naturally wondering how you are. . . . If you make another film in Hollywood I hope I can be with you again."

January 27: Joe DiMaggio writes Marilyn a note on Hotel Lexington stationery: "A beautiful Saturday morning for New York, and no place to go, but to sit back on my desk and scribble you a note. Shouldn't that be proof enough where my thoughts are? . . . You sound great on the phone. Keep yourself well!"

January 29: A deposit of $5,750 ($5,000 of which is borrowed from Joe DiMaggio) is paid to secure the Brentwood home that Eunice Murray found. It is built like a Mexican hacienda. Dr. Greenson accompanies Marilyn on her first visit to the home. In need of repair, the house, with its red-tiled roof, stucco walls, cathedral ceilinged sitting room, small solarium, three bedrooms, and kidney-shaped pool, appeals to Marilyn. It is well-landscaped and only ten minutes from the Fox studios. Over the front entrance, on Mexican tiles, appears this legend: *Cursum Perficio* (My Journey Ends Here).

February 1: Marilyn attends a dinner party at Peter Lawford's for Robert and Ethel Kennedy. Marilyn comes prepared to ask Kennedy questions about civil rights.

February 2: Marilyn writes to Isidore Miller. She wants to see him in Florida and hopes he is doing well. She writes about meeting Robert Kennedy: "He seems rather mature and brilliant for his thirty-six years, but what I liked best about him, besides his Civil Rights program, is he's got such a wonderful sense of humor."

Noon: Marilyn writes to Arthur Miller's son, "Dear Bobbybones." She wants to give him a telephone, but apparently he is not allowed to have one. Learning that he wants to play pool at a Danish hotel, she asks, "Did I ever tell you that I can really play pool? I learned when I was about sixteen and it is something that you never forget. I don't understand why they don't let you into play pool. Do they think you are a delinquent of some kind just because you like the game?" Apparently, some Danish sailors monopolized the table. She urges Bobby to try "some odd hour early in the morning." If he keeps trying, "they might just say yes . . . just to shut you up." She says she is going to get the book he recommended, *Lord of the Flies*: "I would love to read something really terrifying." She tells him about buying her new house, describing its features, which include "a large playroom, plus lots of patios, and a big Mexican wall goes all around the place with big high Mexican gates. . . . It's got a nice garden . . . the swimming pool is so large it doesn't leave too much lawn to take care of." She wants him to come for a vacation. And she expresses her excitement about meeting the attorney general: "I asked him what his department was going to do about Civil Rights and some other issues. He is very intelligent and besides all that, he's got a terrific sense of humor. . . . [H]e wanted to meet me. So, I went to the dinner and I sat next to him, and he isn't a bad dancer either. But I was mostly impressed with how serious he is about Civil Rights. He answered all of my questions and then he said he would write me a letter and put it on paper. So, I'll send you a copy of the letter when I get it because there will be some interesting things in it because I really asked many questions." She mentions Kennedy's age, thirty-six, "which astounds me because I'm 35. It was a pleasant meeting, all in all." Marilyn also mentions not hearing from Janie since Christmas: "I guess we are all a little sloppy about writing. However, I think we all know what we mean to each other, don't we. At least I know I love you kids and I want to be your friend and stay in touch."

Dorothy Parker writes to playwright John Patrick, expressing her disappointment that Fox ("20th-Century Fucks") has shelved "The Good Soup," a screenplay she calls a "bawdy farce," that Parker and her husband, Alan Campbell, have written expressly for Marilyn. "Marilyn would have been a terrible problem," Parker writes, "though I am crazy about her. The studio is beginning to view her as Marat must have regarded the lethally-poised Charlotte Corday.

Of course, Marilyn can't help her behavior. She is always in terror. Not so different from you and me, only much prettier!"

February 2–6: Marilyn goes to New York to consult with Paula Strasberg about the script for *Something's Got to Give*. Marilyn continues to consult with Dr. Greenson over the phone and takes some calls from DiMaggio. She also meets with representatives of *Life* and *Look* about future interviews.

February 6: Photographer Willy Rizzo meets with Pat Newcomb about a photo shoot scheduled for February 8.

Milton Ebbins, a Sinatra friend and vice president of Peter Lawford's production company, drives Marilyn to and from a dinner in honor of John F. Kennedy at the home of Fifi Fell, widow of John Fell, an investment banker.

Marilyn accompanies the Strasbergs to a performance of *Macbeth* at the Old Vic Theatre in New York.

February 7: Several newspapers articles suggest Marilyn's popularity is waning.

February 8: Newcomb calls Rizzo to postpone the shoot. Marilyn was tired and planning to move into her new home soon, Newcomb explains. But another appointment is set for the next afternoon.

Marilyn's Brentwood home is purchased with a fifteen-year mortgage at 6.5 percent interest, with payments of $320 a month.

Marilyn arranges to have a new kitchen built for $1,393.46.

February 9: Marilyn arrives at 6:00 p.m. for the photo shoot with Rizzo and apologizes, pleading extreme fatigue. Another appointment is scheduled for the next day.

February 10: In a four-hour afternoon shoot, Rizzo captures Marilyn in close-up and in various positions on a lounger and at the edge of her Brentwood home pool. He later said she seemed "immensely sad . . . and that sadness was very visible in the pictures."

February 11: Actress Edith Evanson visits Marilyn's Brentwood home to work on the Swedish accent Marilyn is to use for her disguise as a maid in *Something's Got to Give*, an identity Marilyn's character adopts when returning home to her husband, who presumes she has died in an air crash. "Everything was dark, heavy and depressing. It had a creepy feeling about it but I thought nothing of it because she talked of her plans for decorating and especially landscaping," Evanson told biographer Keith Badman. Marilyn pleaded with the actress to join her on a flight that day to New York, but Evanson had family responsibilities.

February 12: Nunnally Johnson completes a new draft of *Something's Got to Give*. Marilyn later writes on the script, "We've got a dog here." She pencils in several suggestions and rejects some lines as "not funny."

February 12–17: Marilyn eats at Sardi's, shops at Saks and other stores, and visits the Actors Studio, Carnegie Hall, and Loew's State Theatre.

February 13: Marilyn attends the premiere of Franco Zeffirelli's production of *Romeo and Juliet* at Manhattan's City Center. She attends a party afterward organized by Lee Strasberg. Marilyn arrives home at her 57th Street apartment at 2:30 a.m.

February 14: Marilyn attends a performance of *Brecht on Brecht* at the Theatre de Lys in Greenwich Village.

February 17: Arthur Miller marries Inge Morath.

February 17–18: Marilyn visits Arthur Miller's father, Isidore, at the Sea Isle resort in Islamorada, Florida. She stays at the Fontainebleau Hotel in Miami.

February 18: Marilyn takes Isidore Miller to dinner at the Club Gigi in the Fontainebleau Hotel. They also see a cabaret show at the Minaret.

February 19: Marilyn visits Joe DiMaggio in Fort Lauderdale.

February 21: Joe DiMaggio escorts Marilyn to the airport for her flight from Miami to Mexico. She flies to Mexico with Pat Newcomb and her staff on a shopping expedition to furnish her new hacienda-style home on Helena Drive in Los Angeles.

Bob East photographs Marilyn climbing the steps to her Pan Am flight, carrying a makeup case. She is dressed in white slacks and wearing sunglasses. She turns to look at the camera and acknowledges it with an open-mouthed smile.

February 22: Pat Newcomb arranges a Mexico City press conference. Wearing a green Pucci dress and green mull (cotton) scarf, she provides a witty performance while sipping champagne.

February 22–23: In Mexico, Marilyn visits Frederick Vanderbilt Field, under FBI suspicion as a subversive.

February 23: Isidore Miller writes to Marilyn, "I can't tell you how much your trip to Florida meant to me. I don't ever remember having such a good time! The guests of the Sea Isle Hotel can't get over how beautiful you looked the night there."

February 24: Marilyn is the honored guest at the home of Mexican actor, writer, and director Emilio Fernández Romo and his wife, Colunga. Marilyn is introduced to José Bolaños, a well-dressed, twenty-six-year-old actor and screenwriter.

February 25: With Frederick Vanderbilt Field, Marilyn attends a reception for Princess Antonia De Braganza of Portugal at the home of Mexican actor Dennis Bourke. Some reports say she cancels at the last minute, angering Field.

February 26: A demure Marilyn, all in white, is photographed sitting on a sofa during her press conference at the Continental Hilton in Mexico City.

February 26–March 1: Marilyn shops and sees the sights.

March 1: Marilyn visits a food plant with Mexico's First Lady, Mrs. Eva Samano de Lopez Mateos. Then they tour an orphanage, and Marilyn writes a check for $10,000 to support the institution's programs for needy children.

Marilyn begins making her $320 per month house payments.

March 1–2: Marilyn spends her evenings with José Bolaños at the Garibaldi Plaza nightclub, which hosts a farewell party for her.

March 2: Marilyn returns to Los Angeles from her vacation in Mexico. She tells a *Fresno Bee* reporter, "I no longer consider Los Angeles my home. . . My home is in New York." She refuses to answer other questions about her relationship with DiMaggio and her next film.

March 3: Edith Evanson resumes works with Marilyn, who seems like two people: one a mature woman, and the other a little girl. Evanson teaches Marilyn to speak like Garbo.

Marilyn resumes her sessions with Dr. Greenson and receives some kind of injection from Dr. Engelberg.

March 5: Marilyn attends the Golden Globe Awards in Los Angeles. She appears to be drunk and gives a muffled acceptance speech, collecting her gold statuette as the World's Favorite Female Star. She is photographed holding hands with José Bolaños, whom she met in Mexico and dated when she returned to Los Angeles. The photograph shows her in a modestly cut spangled dress, heavily made up and with a big smile that makes her face look somewhat brittle. Other shots of her—with drink in hand, and with Bolaños—seem to support the accounts of her soporific state. Susan Strasberg, who was there, later wrote that Marilyn was "in one of her armored vapor clouds. . . . She mimicked her old Hollywood whispery voice in her thank-you speech. . . . Each time she caricatured herself, she chipped a piece out of her own dream."

March 6: Marilyn meets Fox production chief Peter Levathes and indicates listlessly that she is ready to work.

March 8: Marilyn's psychiatrist, Ralph Greenson, delays his planned trip abroad because of her mental instability.

March 8–9: With DiMaggio's help, Marilyn moves into her new home. Ralph Roberts calls and offers his help. Marilyn puts her poodle, Maf, in the guesthouse and uses an old beaver coat Arthur Miller had given her as a bed for the dog.

March 9: Willy Rizzo photographs Marilyn for *Paris Match*.

A cheerful Marilyn appears on the cover of *Woman's Day* with the headline "Marilyn Monroe: 'The New Man in My Life.'"

March 11: Marilyn arrives at Greenson's home and tells him she is going to Palm Springs. After memorizing Nunnally Johnson's script for *Something's Got to Give*, Marilyn learns it has been rewritten by George Cukor and Walter Bernstein. Marilyn is sent forty pages of modifications, but she refuses to play the part as rewritten.

March 13: Marilyn flies to New York to meet with Lee Strasberg.

March 15: Marilyn has new locks installed in her Brentwood home after her secretary, Cherie Redmond, reports that several do not work.

March 16: Marilyn appears on the cover of *Fotogramas* (Spain), gazing at the Golden Globe award presented to her by Rock Hudson.

March 24: Marilyn arises at 8 a.m., an unusually early hour for her, to prepare for her meeting with President Kennedy. Installation of a hot water heater delays her preparations, and she rushes to Ralph Greenson's to wash her hair. After an afternoon of hairstyling, Marilyn joins Peter Lawford on a flight to Palm Springs. She meets Kennedy for a late afternoon stroll and a dinner party. She spends the evening in President Kennedy's quarters at Bing Crosby's home in Palm Springs. Most biographers agree that this is Marilyn's one intimate encounter with Kennedy, which is also the testimony of her friend and masseur, Ralph Roberts: "Marilyn gave me the impression that it was not a major event for either of them. It happened once and that was that."

March 25: Marilyn presents the president with a Ronson Adonis chrome cigarette lighter engraved with his initials, and he invites her to his forthcoming birthday celebration.

Marilyn returns to her Brentwood home, where Joe DiMaggio is waiting for her.

March 26: Shooting of *Something's Got to Give*, scheduled for April 9, is delayed until April 23 so that more work can be done on the screenplay.

March 27: Marilyn and Joe are spotted purchasing rotisserie chickens.

March 29: Nunnally Johnson completes another draft of the *Something's Got to Give* script.

March 30: Marilyn approves of Johnson's script.

March 31: Joe spends the night at Marilyn's Brentwood home.

April 2: Marilyn purchases a stuffed toy tiger from the San Vincente pharmacy for $2.08.

April 6: Marilyn refuses to appear in a *Glamour* magazine layout featuring Milton Greene's work.

April 7: A left profile shot of Marilyn in sequined gown and silver grey hair appears on the cover of *Garbo* (Spain).

April 8: Marilyn makes a surprise visit to Pat Kennedy Lawford and obtains the direct phone number for John Kennedy at the White House.

April 9: Marilyn becomes a founding member of the Hollywood Museum, sending a check for $1,000.

April 10: Marilyn appears on time for six hours of costume tests for *Something's Got to Give*. She is irritated that Cukor is not there to meet her. She looks radiant, and Peter Levathes tells the press, "This will be the *best* Monroe picture ever. Marilyn is at the *peak* of her beauty and ability." But that evening, producer Henry Weinstein finds her sprawled across a bed and unconscious after an overdose of barbiturates. He calls Ralph Greenson, who revives her.

It is announced to the press that Marilyn will be part of the entertainment at the president's Madison Square Garden birthday party. Marilyn agrees to pay $1,440.33 for the cost of producing a dress decorated with hand-stitched rhinestones, beading, and mirrors.

April 11: Marilyn meets with Bern Stern to discuss a photo shoot for *Vogue*.

Marilyn receives a letter from Kenneth O'Donnell, Special Assistant to the President: "Many, many thanks for your acceptance of the invitation to appear at the President's Birthday Party in Madison Square Garden on May 19. Your appearance will guarantee a tremendous success for the affair and a fitting tribute to President Kennedy."

Marilyn is charged $624 for a large, stainless steel Hotpoint refrigerator.

April 12: *Venus at Large*, a comedy by Henry Denker featuring characters based on Marilyn and Arthur Miller, opens on Broadway and receives negative reviews.

Marilyn announces her intention to consult with Lee Strasberg before *Something's Got to Give* starts shooting.

April 13: Marilyn consults with Walter Bernstein, Cukor, and her producers about the script. She insists she needs to see Strasberg to "oil the machinery." Physician Lee Siegel arrives to give her a vitamin injection. It is decided that shooting will not begin until April 23.

Broadway composer Richard Adler calls to say he has written special lyrics for Marilyn's rendition of "Happy Birthday." She tells him that she will be wearing a "historical gown" for her appearance.

Marilyn flies to New York.

April 13–14: Marilyn meets with Lee Strasberg.

April 14: Marilyn meets for an interview with reporter W. J. Weatherby. He is surprised at how much she has aged.

Marilyn has dinner with Rupert Allan in New York.

Mid-April: Eunice Murray moves into Marilyn's home and settles in the guest room.

April 15: Marilyn phones producer Henry Weinstein.

April 16: An alarmed Weinstein tells screenwriter Walter Bernstein that Marilyn wants major changes in the script. She rejects one section as "sentimental schmaltz."

April 18: Before leaving New York City to return to Los Angeles, Marilyn meets with Paula Strasberg, and Strasberg agrees to come to California as Marilyn's drama coach at a salary of $3,000 per week.

April 19: Marilyn develops sinusitis after her trip to New York City.

Marilyn's chauffeur drives her to the Prescription Center on Wilshire Boulevard in Beverly Hills to pick up sedatives, including Nembutal.

Marilyn goes to bed at 11:00 p.m. with chills and a fever.

April 20: At 3:30 a.m. Friday morning, Marilyn calls producer Henry Weinstein, explaining that she cannot come into work on Monday.

April 21: Tests at Cedars of Lebanon Hospital confirm that Marilyn is suffering from a viral infection.

April 22: Marilyn's temperature is 101 degrees. Her doctor, Lee Siegel, drafts a memorandum to the studio suggesting production should be postponed for a month; otherwise, Marilyn is likely to collapse.

April 23: First official day of shooting for *Something's Got to Give*. Marilyn is out sick with a cold and sore throat.

April 24: Marilyn again reports in sick, refusing to come in to meet the Shah of Iran, since she does not know his position on Israel.

April 25: Marilyn stays home ill and has a stainless steel kitchen sink installed in her Brentwood home for $272.

April 26: Marilyn remains at home, still ill.

April 27: On the last day of the shooting week, Marilyn again fails to show up at the studio.

April 30: This is Marilyn's first day on the set of *Something's Got to Give*. She arrives twenty-five minutes early for her makeup call. She runs a temperature but works a full day, even though she is exhausted and her doctor advises her to stay home.

May: Timothy Leary claims to have introduced Marilyn to LSD sometime during this month.

May 1: Marilyn shows up for work with a temperature and is sent home because she is contagious and can't work with the children in her scenes by the swimming pool.

May 1–4: Marilyn remains at home recovering from her illness. She continues, however, to see Dr. Greenson. His daughter drives Marilyn to and from the Greenson residence.

May 4: Marilyn is upset by press coverage suggesting that she is feigning illness.

May 5: At 5:00 a.m., Marilyn awakes with chills and sheets drenched in perspiration. Her fever is again 101 degrees, and her vision is blurred.

Marilyn hires a bicycle at the cost of eighteen dollars a month, a rental from the Hans Ohrt Lightweight Bicycles store in Beverly Hills. But Marilyn never acts on her plans to ride this English-style bicycle to the studio.

Marilyn purchases Rodin's *The Embrace*, and Poucette's oil painting *The Bull*, from Edgardo Acosta, Modern Paintings, 441 North Bedford Drive, Beverly Hills, California. Norman Rosten, who was with her, remembered her comment on *The Embrace*: "He's hurting her but he wants to love her, too." The bull appears against a fierce red background and seems reflective of Monroe's rage over "romance gone awry," as Lois Banner puts it in *MM—Personal*.

May 6: On this Sunday evening, Marilyn informs the studio that she cannot come in the next day.

May 7: Marilyn performs well as a wife returning home several years after she has been presumed dead. She kneels down to speak with the children she has not seen for so long. Robert Christopher Morley, who played her son, recalled, "[S]he was very tender . . . and in the fantasy world of being on the set and shooting the movie it was very nice to have Marilyn be my mother." Alexandra Heilweil, who played Marilyn's daughter, recalled, "I remember looking up at her, and it was as if she drifted out of a mist . . . the model of femininity to me. I think it was the way she carried herself and the

Something's Got to Give

sweetness of her voice—totally feminine and totally elegant." Alexandra's mother added, "Marilyn was magnificent. You never really knew how sick she was. And I can tell you she was sick indeed."

May 8: Cukor shuts down production after Marilyn, with an obvious fever and chills, cannot control her shaking and rests on the set's patio furniture. She again has a temperature of 101 degrees. Dr. Siegel confirms she must return home to rest.

May 9: Marilyn does not report to work. Cukor concentrates on location work.

May 10: Dr. Greenson departs for his trip abroad, leaving Marilyn in the hands of an associate, Dr. Milton Wexler.

May 11: Marilyn does not report to work. The Fox studio chief informs Marilyn's lawyer, Mickey Rudin, that although the studio had agreed to her performing for President Kennedy's birthday celebration in New York City, he now has rescinded this permission because the film is so far behind schedule.

May 12–13: Marilyn spends the weekend with Paula Strasberg and Joe DiMaggio. Ralph Roberts also visits before leaving for New York.

May 14: Marilyn returns, along with her coach Paula Strasberg, to the set to work on *Something's Got to Give*. She is early, cheerful, and cooperative. She does take after take (up to fifty) because of difficulties with the spaniel in a scene with children. She works for nine hours in 94-degree heat generated by studio lights.

May 15–16: Marilyn arrives punctually and works through the customary starts and stops of production without complaint. She watches the rushes and realizes that she is "sensational"—to employ the word the film's editor, David Bretherton, uses when she asks him about her performance and appearance. But she angers Cukor, who learns of her criticisms of his shooting style.

Marilyn's lawyers are notified they will receive a letter from Fox stating that she will be in breach of her contract if she attends the birthday gala for President Kennedy.

May 17: Marilyn works for five hours at the studio and then helicopters to Los Angeles airport en route to New York City, saying to reporters, "I told the studio six weeks ago that I was going. I consider it an honor to appear before the President of the United States."

In the evening Marilyn meets with writer Richard Meryman, who explains that *Life* wants to do an in-depth feature article about her. They agree to an interview in her Brentwood home.

May 17–18: In her New York apartment, Marilyn practices singing "Happy Birthday" for the president.

May 18: Marilyn receives a hand-delivered note stating that she is in violation of her Fox contract. But she continues preparing for her performance the next night.

May 19: At 2:00 p.m., Marilyn arrives at Madison Square Garden for a brief rehearsal.

She departs to have her hair styled by Kenneth Battelle at a cost of $150. Then she returns to her New York apartment for a $125 makeup session with Marie Irvine. Finally, her maid, Hazel Washington, helps hook Marilyn into her Jean Louis gown, and she arrives at Madison Square Garden approximately three hours before she is to perform.

Introduced to an audience of fifteen thousand as the "late Marilyn Monroe" after she delays her entrance (all part of the carefully rehearsed show), Marilyn performs flawlessly as the last of twenty-three entertainers and is clearly the highlight of the evening. Columnist Dorothy Kilgallen describes Marilyn as "making love to the president of the United States."

Marilyn also attends a party at the home of Arthur Krim, president of United Artists. She is photographed in a group of Kennedy supporters watching Diahann Carroll sing. To her right is Maria Callas and Arthur Miller's father, Isidore. She is also photographed with both Robert and John Kennedy, as well as presidential advisor Arthur Schlesinger Jr. Schlesinger and Robert Kennedy playfully compete to dance with Marilyn.

Contrary to sensationalistic reports, Marilyn spends the rest of the evening in her New York apartment with her friend Ralph Roberts and James Haspiel, one of her devoted fans.

May 20: Marilyn flies back to Los Angeles. Some sources say she is now feeling let down after the high of performing in New York City at the gala.

May 21: Marilyn arrives at the studio, but after keeping Cukor waiting for an hour, she tells him she is too tired to do her close-ups.

May 22: Marilyn, reporting to work with a fever, declines to work with Dean Martin when she learns he has a cold. Cukor shoots other scenes with Marilyn and Cyd Charisse and the children.

After work, Marilyn has her driver stop at Jorensen's Food Store to order a case of 1953 Dom Perignon champagne for $173.22.

Marilyn is billed $302.65 for limousine service from May 17 to May 20.

May 23: Cukor shoots Marilyn's nude swimming scene from 9:00 a.m. to 4:00 p.m., with a twenty-minute break for lunch. She takes off her flesh-colored bathing suit and swims in the nude. Photographers take shots of her naked for about an hour.

May 24–26: Marilyn works steadily through three days of shooting, including a Saturday.

May 27: Marilyn agrees to shoot on Sunday, but then phones in sick with an ear infection.

May 28: Marilyn phones in sick.

May 29: Marilyn works with Dean Martin, but has trouble saying her lines.

May 28–29: Marilyn visits Dr. Milton Wexler on both days.

May 30: Shooting is on hiatus for Memorial Day. Marilyn stays home working on a watercolor of a red rose she wants to present to President Kennedy for his forty-fifth birthday.

May 31: Marilyn shoots scenes with Wally Cox, who is playing a shoe salesman. She makes thirty-eight takes of four camera set-ups (about two-and-a-half pages of the screenplay).

June: In a draft of an undated telegram to George Cukor, probably composed after Fox fired her from *Something's Got to Give*, Marilyn writes the director: "I WOULD HAVE CALLED BUT I DIDN'T KNOW HOW TO EXPLAIN TO YOU HOW I BLAME MYSELF BUT NEVER YOU. . . . MY NEXT WEEKEND OFF I

WILL DO ANY PAINTING AND CLEANING AND BRUSH-
ING YOU NEED AROUND THE HOUSE. I CAN ALSO DUST.
ALSO I AM SENDING YOU SOMETHING BUT IT'S LATE IN
LEAVING I BEG YOU TO UNDERSTAND. LOVE. AMANDA
MARILYN." Amanda is her character's name in *Let's Make Love*.

June 1: Marilyn turns thirty-six. She works a full day with Wally
Cox and Dean Martin. Fourteen printed takes show her in medium
and close-up shots.

On the set, Marilyn is presented with a seven-dollar, single-layer
frosted cake (purchased from a local supermarket). Pat Newcomb
arrives with champagne. Photographer George Barris photographs
the birthday party, with shots of Monroe cutting the cake and
drinking champagne with Dean Martin and Wally Cox. George
Cukor presents her with Mexican figurines. Photographs show her
leaving the studio in a limousine with Wally Cox.

Marilyn departs for Dodger Stadium for a charity baseball game (for
muscular dystrophy) and afterwards has dinner with Joe DiMaggio
Jr. at Chasen's. She has a second meal at La Scala and does not
return home until 12:30 a.m.

June 2: Marilyn visits her psychiatrist's home. Greenson is abroad.
His children see that she is depressed. According to biographer
Keith Badman, she is upset because she has not been invited to
a special dinner hosted by President and Mrs. Kennedy, although
Arthur Miller and the Strasbergs had been invited to the White
House for another dinner on May 11.

Dr. Milton Wexler, Greenson's colleague, visits Marilyn at home.
He confiscates a considerable collection of drugs. Pat Newcomb
gives her own tranquilizers to Marilyn.

June 3: Marilyn's housekeeper, Eunice Murray, observes an
agitated Marilyn writing out questions for her psychiatrist. Marilyn
tells Greenson's children that life isn't worth living.

Marilyn is treated for sinusitis at Cedars of Lebanon Hospital.

June 4: At 3:00 a.m., Marilyn awakes with a headache.

Fox is told that Marilyn will not be coming into work. She is exhausted. Cukor shoots scenes with Dean Martin and Cyd Charisse. Marilyn's lawyer, Mickey Rudin, summons Greenson, who returns from his European trip early.

June 5: Eunice Murray calls the studio to report Marilyn is ill, and Dr. Lee Siegel is dispatched to her home. He discovers that she is suffering from sinusitis and has a temperature of 102 degrees.

Marilyn's lawyer, Mickey Rudin, receives a letter stating Fox's intention to sue for breach of contract.

June 6: George Cukor leaks a story to Hedda Hopper that Fox is looking for an actress to replace Marilyn in *Something's Got to Give*. He says Marilyn can no longer deliver a good performance, implying she has mental problems. Film production has shut down.

Dr. Greenson returns to Los Angeles from his European trip.

June 7: Greenson finds Marilyn at home in a drug-induced stupor, but promises Fox that she will be ready for work on Monday, June 11. Pat Newcomb relays the same message to the studio.

Biographer Keith Badman reports that Greenson had become so unnerved by his involvement in Marilyn's troubles that he struck her, injuring her nose. Biographer Donald Spoto reports a similar event.

June 8: Marilyn calls the studio at 8:00 a.m. to say she is ready to work. But she does not show up and instead goes to the San Vicente Pharmacy and purchases a sleep shade and ice bag.

In the afternoon, during a massage, she tells Ralph Roberts, "I hear Cukor is trying to get me fired. I hear it's in the works."

At 3:00 p.m., the studio announces Marilyn is fired. Her attorney is informed at 3:45 p.m.

At 5:00 p.m. Dr. Greenson tells Marilyn she has been fired, and she is enraged.

Marilyn places a call to Robert Kennedy at the Justice Department, hoping that he can intervene and have her reinstated at Fox, which is producing a film based on his book *The Enemy Within*.

The studio files a $500,000 lawsuit against Marilyn at the very end of the day.

Marilyn writes a check to pay for the gown and the stiletto heels she wore at the Madison Square Garden birthday gala for President Kennedy.

Marilyn writes another check to Ralph Greenson for $350 for "professional services."

Fotogramas (Spain) features a radiant Marilyn in a still (costume shot) from *Something's Got to Give*.

June 9: Marilyn calls Robert Kennedy again and, according to some reports, expresses her anger that he has not been able to help her.

Marilyn calls Spyros Skouras, who as president of Fox had always backed her, but now he tells her he does not have the power to reinstate her at the studio.

Marilyn does not attend Dean Martin's party, given in her honor.

June 10: Joe DiMaggio makes an early morning visit to Marilyn's home. Energized, she travels to New York, sees Isidore Miller, and has a meeting with Darryl Zanuck.

June 11: Marilyn has lunch with Truman Capote and tells him about her meeting with Kennedy. She has a brief reunion with Emmeline Snively, who is working in the city.

Marilyn sends telegrams to cast and crew, saying she wants to work with them.

Fox suspends production of the film.

Marilyn calls Darryl Zanuck in Paris. She explains that she has been ill but is ready to work. He agrees to intercede on her behalf. Having seen the rushes from the film, he is impressed with her performance.

June 13: Marilyn flies home and sees her physician, Dr. Hyman Engelberg, who gives her tranquilizers and a shot for anemia.

Robert Kennedy calls and invites her to a party at the Lawfords'.

Marilyn sends a telegram to Robert and Ethel Kennedy, expressing her regret that she could not accept their "invitation honoring Pat and Peter Lawford. Unfortunately, I am involved in a freedom ride protesting the loss of the minority rights belonging to the few remaining earthbound stars. After all, all we demanded was our right to twinkle."

June 14: Columnist Walter Winchell calls Marilyn's home, inviting her to attend Eddie Fisher's act at the Coconut Grove. Pat Newcomb answers, saying that Marilyn is talking to no one and slams down the phone.

Dr. Greenson drives Marilyn to plastic surgeon Dr. Michael Gurdin. She has injured her nose and cheekbone in a shower accident, but no bones are broken.

June 15: Marilyn receives a telegram offering her the starring role in a new musical written by Anita Loos, the author of *Gentlemen Prefer Blondes*. The offer is not accepted.

June 16: Frank Sinatra calls and invites Marilyn to dinner at the Villa Capri. They discuss roles for her in two films owned by his production company.

June 18: A rejuvenated Marilyn resumes plans for designing and decorating her Mexican-style home, accepting the first shipment of furniture from Mexico.

June 18–19: Realizing its mistake in firing Marilyn, the studio begins to work on a way to reinstate her.

Joe DiMaggio returns from London and offers to help Marilyn sort out her troubles with Fox.

June 20: Marilyn makes two calls to the Rostens.

June 20–21: Joe DiMaggio visits Marilyn.

June 22: *Life* publishes "They Fired Marilyn: Her Dip Lives On," photographs of her nude swimming scene for *Something's Got to Give*.

June 23: Willy Rizzo's photographs of Marilyn appear in *Paris Match*.

Marilyn calls Robert Kennedy at the Justice Department, apparently to say that she will be able to attend the party at Peter Lawford's.

Peter Levathes, head of production at Fox, visits Marilyn at home to discuss resuming film work. A noncommittal Marilyn listens as Levathes tells her to replace key members of her staff. Another meeting is scheduled.

Marilyn has two sessions with Dr. Greenson.

June 23–25: Marilyn works on a photo shoot with Bert Stern, including semi-nudes and fashion shots, as well as several somber poses. "All those black dresses, dark clothing, dark backgrounds . . . the layout had an elegiac quality. It was strange and eerie," Stern recalled.

June 24: Louis Alatorre of the Patios-Block Walls Company installs a new Inca red floor tile and does other work on her patio.

George Barris arrives at Marilyn's home to discuss a photo shoot. They also agree to work on Marilyn's autobiography.

Robert Kennedy pays a visit to Marilyn's home. Mrs. Murray notes that he is dressed informally in "slacks and an open shirt."

June 25: Mickey Rudin warns Marilyn about expenditures for wardrobe, hairdressing, makeup, drugs, and the coaching services of Paula Strasberg—all of which threaten to exhaust the $13,000 remaining in her bank accounts.

Marilyn calls the Justice Department.

June 26: Marilyn attends a dinner party at the Lawfords' that includes Robert Kennedy.

June 27: At 4:30 p.m., Robert Kennedy visits Marilyn's home, and she gives him a tour.

At 6:00 p.m., Robert Kennedy leaves Marilyn's home.

June 28: Marilyn and her attorney, Mickey Rudin, meet with Peter Levathes at Fox. She is apparently willing to make some changes in her staff.

Marilyn sees José Bolaños for the last time.

June 29–July 1: Marilyn meets George Barris on a Santa Monica beach for their photo shoot.

June 30: Dr. Engelberg gives Marilyn an injection.

July 1: Dr. Engelberg gives Marilyn an injection.

July 1–August 4: Dr. Greenson sees Marilyn twenty-eight times, charging fifty dollars an hour.

July 2: Marilyn makes two brief calls to the Justice Department.

July 3: Dr. Engelberg gives Marilyn an injection.

July 4: Richard Meryman arrives to interview Marilyn for *Life*. She has prepared by asking for his questions beforehand. She gives him a tour of the house and tells him about her plans for the garden. She is upset only when he asks what it is like to crank up for a scene. She finds the question disrespectful, saying she is not a machine. Meryman apologizes but remains on guard.

Wally Cox, starring in *Something's Got To Give*, calls and interrupts the interview for thirty minutes.

July 6: Marilyn does a photo shoot with Allan Grant for *Life*. She seems fragile and sad, but also playful.

Marilyn calls Joe DiMaggio twice.

July 8: DiMaggio visits Marilyn. They eat a simple dinner and go bike riding. He also goes shopping with her at Saks, where she purchases a cashmere sweater, two evening dresses, and high heels.

July 9: Richard Meryman shows Marilyn a transcript of his interview with her. Allan Grant also takes photographs.

July 10: Dr. Engelberg gives Marilyn an injection.

July 11: Out shopping, Marilyn runs into Hollywood show business reporter David Lewin. She is relaxed but becomes angry when discussing the Hollywood star system and executives who treat stars like lunatics. The people make stars, Marilyn insists, not studios.

Pat Newcomb tries to cheer up Marilyn by mentioning the enormous press attention she is receiving.

Briggs Deli in Brentwood delivers $215.41 worth of deli items and liquor to Marilyn's Helena Drive home.

July 12: At 3:30 p.m., Marilyn attends another meeting at Fox. She is business-like, dressed in a conservative Norman Norell dress and wearing horn-rimmed glasses. A verbal agreement is reached, stipulating that she will be paid $500,000 for *Something's Got to Give* and another $500,000 for one more movie. The studio demands the removal of Paula Strasberg, Pat Newcomb, and Ralph Greenson from involvement in the making of her films. Marilyn is also required to abandon her hard-won right to approve directors and cameramen, and to look at daily rushes. She counters with a demand for script approval and another that Jean Negulesco (her director in *How to Marry a Millionaire*) replace Cukor on *Something's Got to Give*. Fox then demands that she issue an apology for holding up production. Both sides withdraw threats of legal action.

Dr. Engelberg gives Marilyn an injection.

July 13: Marilyn calls Elisabeth Courtney, fashion designer Jean-Louis's assistant, about fittings for a new evening dress that she wishes to wear for a September 8 party in Washington, D.C.

Dr. Engelberg gives Marilyn an injection.

July 14: Marilyn is sent the completed *Life* interview and makes very few deletions.

A buoyant Marilyn sends Dr. Greenson a telegram congratulating him on his wedding anniversary.

Marilyn calls a locksmith to fix the locks on her filing cabinets.

July 15: Marilyn meets in Palm Springs with Sidney Skolsky, who still has her in mind for his Jean Harlow movie. They return to Los Angeles at about 4:00 p.m.

July 16: Marilyn calls the Justice Department.

Dr. Engelberg gives Marilyn two injections.

July 17: The locks on Marilyn's cabinets are fixed for $71.55.

Marilyn makes two calls to the Justice Department.

Dr. Engelberg gives Marilyn an injection.

July 18: George Barris comes to Marilyn's home to show her the results of their photo shoot. She puts *x*'s through the photographs she rejects but seems pleased overall with the work.

July 19: Pat Newcomb sends Marilyn the *Redbook* interview as another positive story about her.

Marilyn takes out a three-month subscription to the *New York Times*.

Marilyn hosts a dinner party for the Greenson children.

July 20: Marilyn is again treated for endometriosis and sees Dr. Greenson.

July 21–22: Marilyn undergoes another gynecological procedure in Cedars of Lebanon Hospital. Joe DiMaggio drives her home.

July 23: Marilyn places a call to the Justice Department that lasts one minute.

Both Dr. Greenson and Dr. Engelberg make house calls, the latter to give Marilyn two injections for her anemia.

July 24: Marilyn has a session with Dr. Greenson.

July 25: Screenwriter Hal Kanter produces another draft of the *Something's Got to Give* script.

Marilyn visits Dean Martin at his home on Mountain Drive and tells him about the new script that she will show him when they see each other at Cal-Neva Lodge in a few days.

July 27: The new script for *Something's Got to Give* is delivered to Marilyn. Her anxiety level rises as she contemplates resuming film production. Dr. Engelberg visits, and Marilyn also sees Dr. Greenson twice, at her home and his. Engelberg prescribes both chloral hydrate and Nembutal and gives Marilyn an injection.

July 28: Ralph Roberts arrives to give Marilyn her regular Saturday massage.

Marilyn puts in calls to Joe DiMaggio and Isidore Miller.

July 28–29: Marilyn departs in a private plane provided by Frank Sinatra for her stay at the Cal-Neva Lodge in Nevada. The weekend there has been reported and interpreted in many different ways. In *The Ultimate Marilyn*, Ernest V. Cunningham summarizes and quotes from five different versions.

Marilyn spends the weekend at the Cal-Neva Lodge in Lake Tahoe. She stays with Frank Sinatra, Peter Lawford, and Lawford's wife, Pat. Marilyn is said to have been drinking heavily and also to be drugged and miserable. According to biographer Keith Badman, it may have been at dinner that Peter Lawford told Marilyn that Robert Kennedy could not continue to take her calls or see her again. What she feared most was abandonment, which is why she put in a call to Joe DiMaggio, who was staying nearby but who did not do much because of his falling-out with Sinatra.

July 30: Disgusted at Marilyn's behavior, Sinatra orders her to leave Cal-Neva, along with Peter Lawford. They are driven to the Reno airport, and Marilyn flies to Los Angeles, where she is met by Pat Newcomb and Eunice Murray.

Marilyn places another call to the Justice Department, but Kennedy's secretary tells her he is out of the office.

Marilyn also calls Norman Rosten and speaks with him for thirteen minutes.

Near the end of the day Marilyn has a session with Dr. Greenson.

Briggs Wines & Spirits delivers food and alcohol costing $43.31.

At 2:15 a.m., Marilyn calls Ralph Roberts for a massage. She describes her Sunday at Cal-Neva Lodge as a "nightmare."

July 31: Dr. Greenson prescribes forty chloral hydrate tablets.

Marilyn calls her New York housekeeper, Florence Thomas, and in an eleven-minute phone call tells her to get the apartment ready for the following week.

Marilyn is driven in the afternoon to see her publicist Arthur Jacobs.

Marilyn calls her friend Henry Rosenfeld, a clothing manufacturer known as the "Christian Dior of the Bronx," to speak about a forthcoming trip to New York City.

In the evening, Whitey Snyder and wardrobe assistant Marjorie Plecher visit Marilyn, who has invited them to her home to celebrate their engagement. "She never looked better—she was in great spirits," Plecher remembered.

August: Alan Levy's interview with Marilyn is published in *Redbook*.

August 1: A bill for $840 drawn up on this date by Dr. Margaret Hohenberg indicates that Marilyn had resumed consultations with her former psychiatrist—most likely by telephone.

Erskine Johnson's "Hollywood Today" column gives Marilyn an award as the year's most celebrated no-show.

Marilyn signs a new contract with Fox for $250,000 for *Something's Got to Give*.

Marilyn takes delivery of new wooden furniture gates for the front of her property and is billed $313.92. She also pays $29.38 for nails with special heads for her front door.

Marilyn's spirits are lifted as negotiations with Fox seem on the way to reinstating her as the star of *Something's Got to Give*. Fox calls to reiterate its $1 million offer. She gets her choice of director, Jean Negulesco, but she says she will have to think about the studio's demand that she jettison Paula Strasberg.

Marilyn calls her stand-in, Evelyn Moriarty, and they talk for forty-five minutes about resuming *Something's Got to Give*.

Columnist James Bacon visits Marilyn at home and finds her in good spirits.

After Bacon leaves, Marilyn places a call to dress designer Elizabeth Courtney, ordering a $1,600 dress for the world premiere of a new Irving Berlin musical, *Mr. President*, in Washington, D.C., on September 25.

Marilyn then calls Saks and places an order for a $382.62 Gucci dress.

At The Mart on Santa Monica Boulevard, Marilyn purchases a coffee table and a wall hanging that depicts Adam and Eve. Bill Alexander, the shop owner, impulsively asks Marilyn to marry him. She tells him she will think it over.

Marilyn purchases a Roman-style white chest-of-drawers at Pilgrims Furniture Store on Wilshire Boulevard.

At Frank's Nurseries & Flowers, she purchases several items, including tuberose plants, a Mexican lime tree, and a hanging begonia basket for a total of $93.08. Then she returns to purchase hummingbird feeders and stands, more begonias, sedums, and terra cotta pots for a total of $63.53.

As of this day Marilyn's City National Bank of Beverly Hills account is overdrawn by $4,208.34. Her savings accounts at the Excelsior and Bowery banks total $1,171.06 and $614.29, respectively. Her Irving Trust Company and First National City Bank checking accounts contain $2,334.65 and $84.67, respectively.

Returning home, Marilyn receives visits from Dr. Greenson and Dr. Engelberg, who bills her twenty-five dollars for an injection.

Gene Kelly calls to speak with Marilyn about starring in *I Love Louisa*. They agree to meet on August 5 to discuss the details. Kelly finds her in excellent spirits.

At 7:00 p.m. Marilyn watches President Kennedy's thirty-two-minute televised press conference.

Joe DiMaggio visits. Friends say he asks Marilyn to marry him again. To photographer George Barris, she declares she does not want to marry again.

August 2: Broadway composer Jule Styne calls in the morning to offer Marilyn the starring role in a musical version of *A Tree Grows in Brooklyn*.

Dorothy Kilgallen calls. According to biographer Keith Badman (relying on what he calls a "hastily prepared CIA document"), Marilyn tells Kilgallen details about her break with the Kennedys and her intention to calls a press conference to reveal details about assassination plots against Fidel Castro and other government secrets.

Marilyn visits Dr. Greenson's office.

Marilyn calls Marlon Brando and invites him to dinner at the Rome. He was unable to come and suggested she call the following week to set a date.

Makeup man Whitey Snyder and hairdresser Agnes Flanagan visit Marilyn at home. She seems happy, and they enjoy cocktails and champagne.

Marilyn calls Paula Strasberg and, apparently following Fox's directions, severs her connection with her coach.

A distressed Marilyn calls Dr. Greenson, who pays a house call. On Greenson's advice, she takes a drive in a limousine, visiting a friend, Dudley Murphy, in Malibu. She signs the Murphy's guest book, listing her residence as "*nowhere*." She is reported to have told a local television crew that she has a "little book" and is going to reveal what is in it.

Marilyn attends an evening party at Peter Lawford's.

August 3: Dorothy Kilgallen reports on Marilyn's Sunday at Cal-Neva: "In California, they're circulating a photograph of her that certainly isn't as bare as her famous calendar, but is very interesting. Marilyn's dress looks as if it was plastered to her skin and the skirt is hitched higher above the knees than any Paris designer would dare to promote in the fall showings."

Marilyn appears on the cover of *Life*, with an interview inside: "Marilyn Lets Her Hair Down About Being Famous."

For breakfast Marilyn eats a grapefruit.

Marilyn calls dress designer Jean Louis, making arrangements to meet with him on Monday, August 6.

Marilyn writes a check for the Gucci dress ordered two days earlier.

Monroe tells photographer George Barris about the promising negotiations with the studio.

Marilyn receives an injection from her internist, Dr. Engelberg, and a prescription for twenty-five Nembutal tablets.

The Vicente Pharmacy in Brentwood fills two prescriptions for Marilyn for Nembutal and Phenergan.

Marilyn invites Pat Newcomb to stay at her home to recuperate from bronchitis.

Photographer Larry Schiller arrives to discuss a photo shot for *Playboy*.

Marilyn goes over the outstanding bills with Eunice Murray: $25 owed to the Sherman Oaks Veterinary Clinic; $111.45 owed to Thompson Electric Company; $1,480.45 owed to her publicist, Arthur Jacobs; $124.10 due to cover Murray's expenses; $200 due for Murray's weekly salary; $52.59 owing to the Department of Water and Power; $406.69 due the Bel Air Sands Hotel for Paula Strasberg's visit; $29.38 owing for nail heads for Marilyn's front door; $180 due for Norman Jefferies's salary; $382 due on Saks Fifth Avenue's July statement; $262.65 owing to Peter A. Juley & Son for fan mail pictures; $196.07 due on the General Telephone Company's July 30 statement; $358 owing to Dr. Hyman Engelberg (July 26 statement); and $1,200 owing to Dr. Ralph Greenson (July 31 statement).

In the afternoon, Marilyn calls her friend Norman Rosten for a long rambling chat. She invites him to visit. "Let's all start to live before we get old," she tells him. She is pleased with her *Life* interview.

Director J. Lee Thompson calls Marilyn about appearing in his adventure film, *The Mound Builders*.

Marilyn speaks with workman making repairs to her home.

At 4:00 p.m., Marilyn is driven to a regularly scheduled session with Dr. Greenson.

After a brief stop at the San Vincente Pharmacy to pick up a prescription for Nembutal (written by Dr. Lee Siegel on July 25), Marilyn returns home to find Pat Newcomb in a bathing suit, sitting by the pool. Newcomb sees that Marilyn is in a good mood.

Mickey Rudin visits to discuss resuming work on *Something's Got to Give*. No decisions are made, but he leaves her in good spirits at 7:00 p.m.

Marilyn and Pat Newcomb eat some of the food delivered by Briggs Delicatessen and costing $49.07.

Marilyn eats dinner with Peter Lawford and Patricia Newcomb at La Scala in Beverly Hills. A little edgy and drunk, she fails to recognize designer Billy Travilla when he stops by her table to say hello, even though he has worked on important films with her, such as *Gentlemen Prefer Blondes* and *The Seven Year Itch*. She had written on a copy of her nude calendar pose, "Billy Dear, please dress me forever. I love you, Marilyn."

According to biographer Keith Badman, Marilyn almost overdoses after her return home, but is revived by Murray and Newcomb.

August 4: Marilyn awakes at 8:45 a.m. and drinks grapefruit juice in a somber mood.

9:00 a.m. Isidore Miller calls, but is told Marilyn is dressing and that she will return his call. In fact, Ralph Roberts is giving Marilyn her regular seventy-minute Saturday massage. She seems in wonderful shape to him and "not tense."

10:30 a.m. Marilyn is upset because J. Lee Thompson's plane has been delayed, and he won't be able to meet her at 5:00 p.m.

Photographer Lawrence Schiller arrives for a short visit, but finds Marilyn is in no mood to discuss a contract with *Playboy*. Nevertheless, she takes him on a tour of her house.

To one workman, Marilyn seems to be "looking tired, not well groomed and as though she might have been crying."

Pat Newcomb does not appear until noon, after a refreshing sleep that irritates Marilyn. Murray suggests that getting so much sleep in Marilyn's house was "like feasting in front of a starving person." Marilyn is still annoyed about the delayed meeting with Thompson.

2:00 p.m. Marilyn receives two calls from Ralph Roberts and one from Joe DiMaggio Jr.

Marilyn takes delivery of furniture and writes a check for $228.80.

Sometime during the afternoon, Marilyn begins to write to DiMaggio: "Dear Joe, If I can only succeed in making you happy, I will have succeeded in the biggest and most difficult thing there is— that is, to make one person completely happy. Your happiness means my happiness, and . . ." For whatever reason, she stops writing and folds the note into her address book.

4:00 p.m. Frank's Nursery delivers citrus trees and flowering plants, and Marilyn works for a few minutes in the garden with Eunice Murray.

4:30 p.m. Joe DiMaggio Jr. calls a second time.

Several reports about this crucial period put Robert Kennedy and Peter Lawford inside Marilyn's home, arguing with her about threats she made to hold a press conference about her relationship with the Kennedys, and about what she has documented in her diary. Events at this point are hard to pinpoint and verify, since Eunice Murray first denied and then confirmed Kennedy's visit, and associates of Robert Kennedy, as reported in Donald Spoto's biography, dispute he was anywhere near Marilyn's home. In *Marilyn & Me*, Lawrence Schiller reports visiting Marilyn's home and meeting Robert Kennedy.

5:15 p.m. Dr. Greenson arrives, responding to a call made at 4:30. He finds a distraught Marilyn and relies on Eunice Murray to look after her employer.

5:30–7:00 p.m. A still disturbed Marilyn consumes perhaps as many as a dozen Nembutal capsules, pricking them with a pin to speed their entry into her bloodstream.

6:00 p.m. Ralph Roberts calls a third time, but fails to reach Marilyn when Greenson answers the phone and says she is not at home.

7:00 p.m. Dr. Greenson leaves. Peter Lawford calls, later saying he was inviting Marilyn to a dinner party. Joe DiMaggio Jr. calls, announcing that he has broken his engagement—a good thing, Marilyn tells him, because she feels his intended is unsuitable.

7:45 p.m. Marilyn calls Dr. Greenson to say she is happy about news from Joe DiMaggio Jr., which has put her in a good mood. But she is concerned that Greenson has taken her Nembutal tablets. In fact, as Patricia Newcomb later admits, she took the drugs over concerns that Marilyn would once again overdose herself.

8:00 p.m. Marilyn spends the rest of the evening in her bedroom, taking choral hydrate since no more Nembutal is available. Whether deliberately or by accident, Marilyn had taken a lethal combination of drugs that within a few hours would cause respiratory failure and death. If she called for help, her voice was too fuzzy or indistinct for Eunice Murray—watching television in another room—to hear. Marilyn calls Ralph Roberts, but he is out.

Sometime before 8:30 p.m. Marilyn speaks on the phone with Peter Lawford, and she sounds like she is fading out. One of Lawford's agents calls Mickey Rudin, who rings Marilyn's home around 9:00 p.m., but is assured by Mrs. Murray that Marilyn is all right.

Between 8:00 and 9:00 p.m. Henry Rosenfeld, the dress manufacturer who had helped to bankroll Marilyn Monroe Productions, calls and hears a groggy Marilyn, a common occurrence in his experience.

August 5, 3:00 a.m. Mrs. Murray awakens and notices a light is on in Marilyn's bedroom. A telephone cord trails under the bedroom door. Murray phones Dr. Greenson, who tells her to pound on Marilyn's door, which is locked. Through a window, Murray sees Marilyn on her bed, "looking strange."

3:40 a.m. Dr. Greenson arrives and breaks into Marilyn's room (going through her window). The phone is in her hand, and rigor mortis has set in. Ten minutes later, Dr. Engelberg arrives and pronounces Marilyn dead.

4:25 a.m. Emergency services receives a call from Dr. Engelberg: "I'm Dr. Engelberg, Marilyn Monroe's physician. I'm at her residence. She's committed suicide."

Sergeant Jack Clemons arrives to observe Marilyn's body lying on her bed, next to a bed stand holding empty pill bottles.

4:30 a.m. The Arthur P. Jacobs Agency, Pat Newcomb's employer, is informed of Marilyn's death.

8:15 a.m. Deputy Coroner Charles Pace delivers Marilyn's body to the Los Angeles County Morgue.

August 6, 10:30 a.m. Coroner Thomas Noguchi conducts Marilyn's autopsy. The body shows no evidence of trauma. The organs seem normal and healthy. Her stomach is empty. He finds no residue of pills. He takes blood for alcohol and barbiturate analysis. The liver, kidney, stomach and its contents, urine, and intestines are saved for further toxicological study. A vaginal smear is also performed. Test results later reveal traces of barbiturates (4.5 mg percent), choral hydrate (8 mg percent), and pentobarbital (13 mg percent).

August 8: Crowds gather outside the gates of Westwood Memorial Park. At an open casket, DiMaggio bends down to kiss Marilyn's forehead, whispering, "I love you, I love you. I love you."

After the ceremony, at which Lee Strasberg reads the eulogy, crowds rush past two guards, trampling flowers and looking for souvenirs.

August 18: Theodore H. Curphey, Los Angeles County Coroner, releases his findings: "It is my conclusion that the death of Marilyn Monroe was caused by self-administered drugs, that the mode of death is 'probable suicide.'"

August 20: An FBI report relays Robert Kennedy's statement that "he was aware there had been several allegations concerning his possibly being involved with Marilyn Monroe. He said he had at least met Marilyn Monroe since she was a good friend of his sister, Pat Lawford, but these allegations had a way of growing beyond any semblance of the truth."

August 28: Marilyn's death certificate is issued.

Sources for Quotes

1914, January 17: ". . . divorces Lyle Arthur Graves." (Miracle)

1917, May 17: "Gladys marries . . . Baker" (Gilmore, Miracle); ". . . gives birth" (Gilmore)

1919, July 30: ". . . half-sister is born." (Miracle)

1920: "Gladys becomes a film cutter . . . becomes friends with . . . McKee." (Spoto, Gilmore)

1921, April 12: "James Dougherty . . . is born." (Buchthal)

1923, May 23: "Gladys meets Stanley Gifford" (Taraborrelli)

1926, March 20: "Della leaves behind . . . Gladys" (Gilmore)

1926, June 1: "Norma Jeane Mortensen is born" (Morgan)

1926, June 13: ". . . brings Norma Jeane to live with the Bolenders" (Gilmore, Taraborelli, Victor)

1926, August 25: "Gladys moves back to Hollywood" (Miracle)

1931, September 14: ". . . could have been taken for brother and sister." (Banner)

1932, Summer: ". . . forming a living cross." (Morgan)

1933, June 13: ". . . in the vicinity of the Hollywood Bowl . . . discovers the Franklin white piano" (Morgan)

1933, October 12: "Sidney Skolsky . . . arrives in Hollywood" (Riese)

1934: "Grace's aunt, Ana Lower, also takes care of Norma Jeane." (Gilmore, Miracle)

1935, September 13: "Grace McKee places Norma Jeane in the Los Angeles Orphans Home" (Morgan)

1935, December 5: ". . . Grace McKee writes to Mrs. Sula Dewey" (Morgan)

1939: "At Emerson Junior High School . . . makes friends with Bob Muir" (Morgan)

1943, September: ". . . move into an apartment on Catalina Island" (Morgan)

1946: ". . . showed a portfolio of her pictures to Ben Lyon" (Luijters)

1946, May: "Norma Jeane dates Bill Pursel" (Morgan)

1946, August 2: "Norma Jeane joins the Blue Book Modeling Agency" (Morgan)

1947, December: "Marilyn meets Joseph Schenck" (Luijters)

1948: "Joseph Schenck asks Harry Cohn . . . to consider signing Marilyn" (Luijters)

1948, March 10: "Marilyn meets Natasha Lytess . . . and Fred Karger" (Buskin, Victor)

1948, May 26: "With Mickey Rooney, Marilyn attends the premiere of *The Emperor Waltz*" (IMDb)

1948, Summer: "Marilyn is photographed with producer George Jessel . . ." (Morgan)

1948, September 3 or 4: ". . . afterwards confides to Pursel" (Morgan)

1948, September 21: "She meets photographer Tom Kelley" (Victor)

1948, December 31: "At a Hollywood party that includes important directors such as Otto Preminger . . . she meets William Morris' agent" (Victor, Luijters. See Bernard for a rare shot of Marilyn dancing with Johnny Hyde)

1950, May 17: ". . . Fox studio head Darryl Zanuck stops production." (Shaw and Rosten)

1950, August 13: "With Johnny Hyde, Marilyn attends a party. . . . She meets Kazan and Olivier" (Buskin, Leaming, Victor)

1951: ". . . held by player Gus Zernial" (Morgan)

1951, January: "They meet in her room . . . or at the house of his agent, Charles Feldman" (Shaw and Rosten)

1952: "Marilyn is photographed . . . with ventriloquist Edgar Bergen" (IMDb)

1952, March 8: "Marilyn is supposed to meet Joe DiMaggio for the first time . . ." (Morgan)

1953: "André de Dienes photographs Marilyn eating an ice cream sundae." (Marilyn Monroe and the Camera)

1953, January: "She studies voice with Phil Moore and Hal Schaefer." (Victor)

1953, March 6: "Marilyn is reported by biographer Anthony Summers to have affairs with Billy Travilla" (Clayton)

1953, April 13: "Jean Negulesco . . . is upset with Natasha Lytess" (Victor)

1953, April 14: "Charles Feldman . . . issues a memo" (Shaw and Rosten)

1953, May: "Charles Feldman, Joe DiMaggio, and Lloyd Wright . . . all advise her on renegotiating her Fox contract." (Shaw and Rosten)

1953, August 8: "Feldman meets with Darryl Zanuck. For the first time Zanuck sides with Marilyn" (Clayton, Shaw, and Rosten)

1953, September 10: "Marilyn rehearses for . . . the Jack Benny Show" (Clayton, Buskin)

1953, October: "Marilyn is photographed with columnist Walter Winchell" (IMDb)

1953, November 4: "Los Angeles premiere of *How To Marry a Millionaire* . . ." (Luijters)

1954, February 23: "Marilyn and Joe fly to Hawaii" (IMDb)

1954, March 5: "Marilyn flies . . . to Los Angeles . . . Joe flies to New York" (IMDb)

1954, June 18: "Marilyn meets with Spyros Skouras" (Clayton)

1954, August: "Marilyn meets Paula Strasberg" (Leaming, Victor)

1954, October 4: "At 2:45 p.m. Marilyn's attorney, Jerry Giesler . . . issue a statement to the press" (Wolfe)

1955, February 4: "Marilyn attends her first session at the Actors Studio. Elia Kazan introduces her to Lee Strasberg" (IMDb, Buchthal)

1955, March 9: ". . . fundraiser event for the Actors Studio . . ." (IMDb)

1955, Spring: "Marilyn . . . visits poet Norman Rosten and his wife Hedda" (Meyers)

1955, April 8: "Marilyn appears on Edward R. Murrow's television show" (Buskin, Meyers)

1956: "Marilyn is photographed . . . with poet Edith Sitwell." (Buchthal)

1956, February 9: ". . . attends the premiere of *Middle of the Night*" (Victor)

1956, February 25: "Marilyn . . . conducts a press conference" (IMDb)

1956, May 31: "Marilyn meets President Sukarno of Indonesia" (Victor)

1956, June 2: "She is photographed in the back of a limousine holding a birthday cake" (Clayton)

1957: "Marilyn and Arthur Miller move into an apartment" (Morgan)

1957, April 22: "Marilyn's secretary, May Reis, arranges nine interviews and photo sessions" (Victor)

1957, October: "They alternate between the city and Miller's Roxbury home and farm." (Victor)

1959, January: "Carl Sandburg visits her in her New York apartment." (Buchthal)

1959, February 5: "They dine on oysters, white grapes, champagne, and a soufflé." (Buchthal)

1959, September 16: "Fox makes a deal with George Cukor" (Leaming)

1959, September 20: "She does, however, demand that Jack Cole be hired" (Morgan)

1959, December 25: "Yves Montand and Simone Signoret send Marilyn a . . . card" (Wolfe)

1960, January: "Marilyn meets psychiatrist Ralph Greenson" (Summers)

1960, June 1: "Clifford Odets stays until four in the morning reading palms." (Victor)

1961, End of April: ". . . eventually finds an apartment on Doheny Drive" (Morgan)

1962, January 1: "Eunice Murray receives her first . . . check" (Luijters)

1962, February 6: ". . . drives Marilyn to and from a dinner in honor of John F. Kennedy" (IMDb)

1962, February 24: "She is introduced to José Bolaños" (Clayton, Wolfe)

1962, March 5: "Marilyn attends the Golden Globe Awards . . ." (IMDb)

1962, April 8: "Marilyn makes a surprise visit to Pat Kennedy Lawford" (Taraborelli)

1962, June 1: "Marilyn departs for Dodger Stadium for a charity baseball game" (IMDb)

1962, June 11: "Marilyn has lunch with Truman Capote" (Buchthal)

1962, June 13: "Marilyn sends a telegram to Robert and Ethel Kennedy expressing her regret . . ." (Taraborelli)

Annotated Filmography

1947

Dangerous Years: Marilyn appears among teenagers and delinquents.

1948

Scudda-Hoo! Scudda-Hay!: Marilyn appears in a few scenes that are cut from the film.

Ladies of the Chorus: Because Marilyn has a starring role, this forgettable film has not been forgotten. In it she shows that she can perform well in musicals. Unfortunately, no one seemed to be paying attention— not yet.

1949

Love Happy: With just a thirty-second walk-on, Marilyn captures not only Groucho Marx's attention, but also that of the film's producer, who sent her out on a publicity tour for the film.

A Ticket to Tomahawk: One of four dancehall girls, Marilyn does not have an opportunity to do much other than fit into the ensemble.

1950

All About Eve: Marilyn is a standout as Miss Caswell, entering on the arm
  of the suave and cynical Addison Dewitt, played with customary aplomb
  by George Sanders.
Right Cross: Marilyn is Dusky Ledoux, a feisty waitress.
The Asphalt Jungle: Marilyn's first big break occurred in this John Huston
  film noir, in which she plays the mistress of a corrupt lawyer. She shows
  remarkable range in what could have been a stereotypical role.
The Fireball: This film features Marilyn on roller skates.

1951

Home Town Story: Marilyn appears in a routine secretary role.
Let's Make It Legal: As the film critic for the *New York Times* pointed out
  at the time, Marilyn did not have much to do except serve, along with
  Robert Wagner, as talent the studio wanted to showcase.
Love Nest: Marilyn is ogled by Jack Paar.
As Young As You Feel: Once again, Marilyn plays a secretary.

1952

Don't Bother to Knock: Marilyn is sensational in a dramatic role, but this
  low budget film noir did not attract that much attention and did not do
  well at the box office. After this work, Darryl Zanuck and other executives at Fox felt it was safer to cast Marilyn in comedies that did big
  business.
Monkey Business: Marilyn is very funny as the secretary who does not
  know the difference between punctuation and being punctual.
We're Not Married: Marilyn plays a beauty contestant and does a good job
  with her minor role in this anthology film with several plotlines.
Clash by Night: Watch this picture to see Marilyn play a working class girl
  not so different from her actual self. She gets to wear jeans, as she did
  in her off-screen life.
O. Henry's Full House: Marilyn has just a brief but poignant scene with
  Charles Laughton.

1953

Niagara: This film constantly grows in reputation. In part this phenomenon is due to director Henry Hathaway's ingenious adaptation of film noir to color and CinemaScope, turning the usually dark haired femme fatale into a blonde temptress. Hathaway was one of the few directors who understood and respected Marilyn, and she reciprocated his admiration by giving a great performance.

Gentlemen Prefer Blondes: This musical revealed Marilyn's enormous gift for comedy, which Howard Hawks first spotted when he directed her in *Monkey Business*. Unfortunately, the very success of this picture doomed Marilyn, making it almost impossible for her to secure the dramatic roles she coveted.

How to Marry a Millionaire: This mildly amusing film capitalizes on the comic flair Marilyn showed in *Gentlemen Prefer Blondes*, but *Millionaire* does not do much to develop her talent.

1954

River of No Return: In spite of its class-A director, Otto Preminger, this picture is an uninspired Western, although when singing and in her scenes with the child actor Tommy Rettig, Marilyn delivered some of the best performances of her career.

There's No Business Like Show Business: Marilyn, playing a hatcheck girl who aspires to stardom, seems almost superfluous in this unimaginative musical. The film exhausted Marilyn. She worked hard at perfecting her musical routines, but she realized she was laboring over an inferior product.

1955

The Seven Year Itch: Here Marilyn reached the epitome of her appeal as woman-child and sex goddess. Tom Ewell's performance is exquisite: As a common man who wants to be told that he is "just elegant," he is the perfect foil for "The Girl."

1956

Bus Stop: Don Murray was perfectly adequate as the cowboy who sweeps Cherie off her feet, but Marilyn was right to want Rock Hudson, who would have endowed the cowboy's role with more of a sexual aura.

1957

The Prince and the Showgirl: Marilyn is at her most graceful and beatific in this film, but her performance is sabotaged by Olivier's uninspired direction and humorless approach to his role. The film needed an actor like Peter Ustinov to make it sparkle.

1959

Some Like It Hot: Without Marilyn, this film would not have worked. Her effervescent melancholy (a contradiction that only she could bring off) is what really drives the film, beginning with the shot of steam from the train locomotive that propels her and the film into a rollicking and comic exploration of sexual relationships disguised as a gangster movie. As Billy Wilder said, Marilyn was irreplaceable.

1960

Let's Make Love: This is perhaps the only one of her films in which Marilyn seems dull and uninspired.

1961

The Misfits: Although Marilyn acquits herself well in a dramatic role, the turgid screenplay and John Huston's sluggish direction did nothing to help her, as she fully realized. Her character, Roslyn, is yet another male fantasy, albeit a more down-to-earth one.

1962

Something's Got to Give: Judging by both the photographs and the out-
takes, Marilyn was at the peak of her talent here. She seems utterly at
ease, even as one grueling take followed another. Her scenes with Wally
Cox and Dean Martin are funny even in their uncut versions. Although
Marilyn had her doubts about the script, her work is nothing less than
professional and skillful.

Annotated Bibliography

BOOKS

Arnold, Eve. *Marilyn Monroe*. New York: Abrams, 2005. Print.
This collection consists of photographs taken by one of Marilyn's most perceptive photographers.

Baker, Roger. *Marilyn Monroe: Photographs Selected from the Files of United Press International/Bettmann*. New York: Crown, 1990. Print.
Black-and-white photographs are divided into chapters: "Chapter I: Norma Jeane," "Chapter II: Norma Jeane Dougherty," "Chapter III: Marilyn Monroe," "Chapter IV: Marilyn DiMaggio," "Chapter V: Marilyn Miller," "Chapter VI: Marilyn Monroe." This is a reasonably comprehensive collection, beginning with childhood photographs and early publicity shots, and including her first appearances in important films, film stills, her tour of Korea, two-shots with Marlon Brando, Joe DiMaggio, Arthur Miller, Jack Warner, Laurence Olivier, Billy Wilder, Tony Curtis, Yves Montand, Montgomery Clift, and others.

Banner, Lois W. *Marilyn: The Passion and the Paradox*. New York: Bloomsbury, 2012. Print.
Banner's is the most recent and most thorough biography, exploring the influence of Christian Science and the impact of various foster families on Norma Jeane. Banner also relies heavily on material from Anthony Summers's investigation of Monroe's last days. The biographer also analyzes various accounts of sexual abuse that occurred during Marilyn's

childhood. Banner suggests Marilyn had several sexual relationships with women. The photo insert includes important photographs taken by Milton Greene.

———. *MM—Personal: From the Private Archive of Marilyn Monroe.* New York: Abrams, 2010. Print.
    This treasure of primary sources includes Banner's informative introduction and a timeline. Among the many never before seen photographs included are: examples of Monroe's files and folders; her filing cabinets; receipts for purchases; letters to and from her; early shots of her on stage; newspaper clippings; classic photographs by Cecil Beaton; memos; telegrams, magazine covers; articles of her clothing; notebooks; jewelry; and works of art she purchased.

Bernard, Susan, and Bruno Bernard. *Bernard of Hollywood's Marilyn.* New York: St. Martin's, 1993. Print.
    This is a beautifully produced collection of Bernard's work, some of the best photography of the Hollywood Studio portrait period. Bernard's daughter, Susan, contributes an introduction explaining how her father worked and discussing his early recognition of Marilyn's photogenic qualities. The book is divided into six chapters: "Norma Jean," "The Birth of Marilyn," "The Goddess," "Persona," "Renaissance," and "The Legacy." Included in each chapter are excerpts, beginning in 1946, from Bernard's journal describing himself as a father and big brother figure for this "child-woman." This description is born out in the first chapter, which shows Marilyn in poses that evoke the wholesome outdoors girl, as well as a very young model in two-piece bathing suits looking not so much seductive as fetching. The second chapter features shots of Marilyn in satiny gowns and negligees, looking far sultrier than Norma Jeane ever did. The "Goddess" chapter dovetails with Bernard's journal entries documenting the progress of an actress deliberately perfecting her erotic appeal by searching for poses that amplify her playful sexuality. "Persona" is dominated by shots from *The Seven Year Itch*, including a two-shot with Joe DiMaggio and Walter Winchell watching the filming of the skirt-blowing scene. Later shots show Monroe at work on *Let's Make Love*, *The Misfits*, and *Something's Got to Give*.

Buchthal, Stanley F., and Bernard Comment. *Marilyn Monroe: Fragments.* London: HarperCollins, 2010. Print.
    This indispensable collection of Monroe's letters, notes, diaries, poems, drawings, recipes, and photographs includes: a snapshot of Norma Jeane

with James Dougherty in his coast guard uniform; a shot of Marilyn dancing with Truman Capote; pictures of Marilyn conversing with Carson Mc-Cullers, Isak Dinesen, Edith Sitwell, Carl Sandburg, and Lee Strasberg; and many photographs of her reading books by Heinrich Heine, James Joyce, Michael Chekhov, Walt Whitman, Arthur Miller, and a study of Goya. Two pages exhibit the covers of books in her personal library: *Madame Bovary*, *The Secret Agent*, *The Unnamable*, *Paris Blues*, *Winesburg, Ohio*, *Sister Carrie*, *A Farewell to Arms*, *The Sun Also Rises*, *Tortilla Flat*, *On the Road*, *The Fall*, *Invisible Man*, *Once There Was a War*. The book concludes with what is called Marilyn's favorite photograph, taken by Cecil Beaton at the Ambassador Hotel in New York in 1956: Holding a flower resting just below her right shoulder, a prone Marilyn gazes up at the camera.

Brown, Harry, and Patte B. Barham. *Marilyn: The Last Take*. New York: Dutton, 1992. Print.

Brown and Barham have produced a thorough study of Marilyn's last year and her work on *Something's Got to Give*. No photographs.

Buskin, Richard. *Blonde Heat: The Sizzling Screen Career of Marilyn Monroe*. New York: Billboard, 2001. Print.

Based on documents and interviews, this is the best-detailed account of Marilyn's screen career. Buskin begins with a chapter on "Marilyn the Actress," and with a quotation from Jack Lemmon that reflects the seriousness of Buskin's purpose: "Most of us maybe use eighty or eighty-five percent of our talents in a hot take, but I think Marilyn came close to using a hundred percent in the takes that were printed. She could use what she had more fully than anybody I have ever worked with." Buskin's next chapter, "Bit Roles and Broken Dreams: 1946–1950," features stills from the films Marilyn made during this period, but also includes very early shots of Monroe as a starlet sitting beside a pool with Johnny Hyde, while Natasha Lytess towers over her, followed by a list of Marilyn's rumored appearances as an extra. Plots of her films are summarized and followed by sections titled "Behind-the-Scenes Facts and Opinions," "The Critics' Views," and "Public Reaction"—a structure Buskin maintains throughout his book. For her early period, Buskin also provides revealing details about Marilyn's various screen tests, accompanied by a few stills of her performances. The next chapter, "The Fox Playmate 1951–1952," describes Monroe's cheesecake period and begins with a quotation from her: "I think cheesecake helps call attention to you. Then you can follow through and prove yourself." In the following chapter, "After You Get What You Want

You Don't Want It: 1953–1954," uses one of Marilyn's songs in *There's No Business Like Show Business* to chart her growing dissatisfaction with the substandard roles Hollywood offered her. Again, Buskin allows Marilyn's own words to tell the story: "I never have a chance to learn anything in Hollywood. They worked me too fast. They rushed me from one picture into another. It's no challenge to do the same thing over and over. I want to keep growing as a person and as an actress, and in Hollywood they never ask me my opinion. They just tell me what time to show up for work." This chapter includes costume shots for *Gentlemen Prefer Blondes* that were never used because the studio had received complaints about her revealing outfits, and ordered designer Billy Travilla to "cover her up!" The result, as Buskin also shows, was a much more elegant and understated dress. Marilyn's television appearances were so rare that Buskin devotes two pages to her on *The Jack Benny Show*, in which the comedian has fun with skits that show Marilyn expressing her adoration of him. Chapters on *How to Marry a Millionaire*, *There's No Business Like Show Business*, *River of No Return*, and *The Seven Year Itch* follow the same format. The rest of Marilyn's career is covered in a chapter titled "Running Wild, Mighty Bold: 1955–1962," with stills from *The Prince and the Showgirl*, *Some Like It Hot*, *Let's Make Love*, *The Misfits*, and *Something's Got to Give*. Buskin's view of this period and of her work life is summarized in a quotation from David Wayne, who starred with Marilyn in *We're Not Married* and *How to Marry a Millionaire*: "Later in her career she had the power to say, 'If I have to do 50 takes, I don't care, and nobody else should care either.' Because by then she knew that she was something, and she truly was something." Buskin includes two pages on Marilyn's *Person to Person* interview with Edward R. Murrow, concluding with her own view that she had not come off well.

Carroll, Jock. *Falling for Marilyn: The Lost "Niagara" Collection*. New York: Friedman/Fairfax, 1996. Print.

The volume includes an introduction (the article Carroll wrote for *Weekend Magazine*) while Marilyn was filming in Canada. He photographed her in bed reading the *Niagara* script; against the backdrop of the Falls; doing her famous walk, which became so controversial when the film was released; visiting a local silverware factory; shopping and walking barefooted; sitting cross-legged reading a book, her hair done up and without makeup; and another with bobby pins in her hair, a newspaper on her bed, and a book in her hand, turned to a chapter in *The Thinking Body* called "The Tongue." She is also pictured with her makeup man, Whitey Snyder, taking direction from Henry Hathaway while smoking in bed (practicing for *Niagara*).

Churchwell, Sarah. *The Many Lives of Marilyn Monroe*. London: Granta
  Books, 2004. Print.
  Churchwell's book is an indispensable assessment of the literature and
  art about Marilyn Monroe. No photographs.

Clayton, Marie. *Marilyn Monroe: Unseen Archives*. Bath, UK: Parragon,
  2003. Print.
  The subtitle of this wide-ranging collection is misleading. The photographs are not from some new collection, but instead culled from already
  published pictures. Some of the photographs, the introduction suggests,
  are "less well known"—an assessment that would only be true for someone
  who has not looked at other published collections of photographs. The
  book is divided into seven chapters, all taken from titles of Monroe's films.
  The book also includes a chronology, a brief biographical narrative in each
  chapter, and a bibliography. The first chapter, *"Ladies of the Chorus,"* includes stills from that film and publicity shots (Marilyn shown babysitting;
  on the phone; modeling a swimsuit; exercising; standing on her head),
  but also stills from *A Ticket to Tomahawk*, *The Asphalt Jungle*, *All About
  Eve*, and *As Young As You Feel*. The second chapter, *"Gentlemen Prefer
  Blondes,"* includes stills from the film, publicity photographs: a big close-
  up of Monroe and Russell putting their hands in cement at Grauman's
  Chinese Theatre; Monroe in a high-collared dress; Monroe with DiMaggio; swimsuit poses; an Idaho potato sack shot; two shots with director
  Henry Hathaway, Jack Benny, and Billy Travilla; pictures of Darryl Zanuck
  and Spyros Skouras; and stills from *Clash by Night*, *We're Not Married*,
  Monkey Business, *Niagara*, *How to Marry a Millionaire*, and *River of No
  Return*. Chapter Three, *"There's No Business Like Show Business,"* includes
  stills from the film; close-ups of Marilyn and Joe DiMaggio; pictures from
  her trip to Japan and Korea; a shot of her tearful announcement of the
  divorce from DiMaggio; pictures taken on the set with Billy Wilder and
  Tom Ewell in *The Seven Year Itch*; a shot of Marilyn at dinner with Milton Greene, Mel Torme, and Sammy Davis Jr.; a two-shot with Natasha
  Lytess; photographs of Marilyn with Milton Berle and Truman Capote;
  portraits of Lee Strasberg and Marilyn at the Actors Studio; and a shot
  of Marilyn riding an elephant in Madison Square Garden. Chapter Four,
  "The Prince and the Showgirl," contains stills from the film; publicity shots
  with Laurence Olivier and Vivien Leigh; photographs of Marilyn standing
  and seated close to Arthur Miller, playing with their dog Hugo, and seeming the contented and adoring wife; two-shots with Milton Greene, James
  Cagney, and President Sukarno; and stills from *Bus Stop*. Chapter Five,
  "Some Like It Hot," features stills from the film; photographs of Marilyn
  at charity events; and two-shots with Arthur Miller, on the set with Paula

Strasberg, and with the writers Isak Dinesen and Carson McCullers. Chapter Six, "*The Misfits*," includes stills from the film; photographs of Monroe's work with Montand in *Let's Make Love*; shots of her conferring with John Huston and Arthur Miller; the famous shot of her hugging a tree; somber vignettes with Miller that reflect their estrangement; and candids of her emerging from Columbia Presbyterian and relaxing with Joe DiMaggio. Chapter Seven, "*Something's Got to Give*," includes costume shots from the film; two-shots with José Bolaños, Rock Hudson, and Joe DiMaggio: Marilyn's nude swimming scene; photographs of her bedroom after her death; and pictures from her funeral, including a grieving Joe DiMaggio, Eunice Murray, and Ralph Greenson and his family.

Clark, Colin. *The Prince, The Showgirl, and Me*. New York: St. Martin's Press, 1996. Print.
    See the title below, which adds material to Clark's account of the making of the film.

_____. *My Week with Marilyn*. New York: Weinstein Books, 2011. Print.
    This memoir by a third assistant director, the son of the art historian Kenneth Clark, is a detailed account of his observations while he was working on the production of *The Prince and the Showgirl*. Clark has been criticized for making more of his relationship with Monroe than in all likelihood existed.

Cunningham, Ernest W. *The Ultimate Marilyn*. Los Angeles: Renaissance, 1998. Print.
    Chapters cover Marilyn's career as a sex symbol; the best things she said or were said about her; the men who claimed to have affairs with her; the women in her life; her costume designers; her films; films about her; her imitators; a biographical dictionary of the figures in her life; descriptions of her principal photographers; an account of her life as presented in the tabloids; Marilyn in art; discussions of Marilyn biographies; accounts of her death; and Monroe websites. The section of color photographs consists mostly of film stills.

Curtis, Tony, with Mark A. Vieira. *The Making of "Some Like It Hot"*. Hoboken, NJ: Wiley, 2009. Print.
    A detailed account of the making of the film, this book includes film stills and candid shots of Curtis, including makeup sessions; Wilder directing Curtis in the bathtub scene; and off-screen shots in costume.

DiMaggio, June, and Mary Jane Popp. *Marilyn, Joe & Me: June DiMaggio Tells It Like It Was*. Roseville, CA: Penmarin, 2006. Print.
This is a work of dubious biographical importance. Except for a few anecdotes that reveal Marilyn's enjoyment of the DiMaggio family, this book is mainly of interest because of the candid snapshots of Monroe enjoying holidays with the family, and for a sequence of shots taken on *The Misfits* set, in which she seems happier and healthier than in other photographs taken at the time. A few of Marilyn's brief, handwritten notes are also reproduced. She is shown: smoking atop a New York skyscraper; getting dressed; doing her hair and makeup; putting on Chanel No. 5; conferring with Milton Greene; signing photographs; speaking intimately with Milton Berle; reading; apparently napping; in the subway at Grand Central; seemingly lost in thought; wearing one of her favorite terry cloth robes; examining the costume for her elephant ride; putting on her stockings seated in a limousine; and, finally, atop the elephant.

Feingersh, Ed, and Bob LaBrasca. *Marilyn: March 1955*. New York: Delta, 1990. Print.
This volume consists of a fascinating documentary series of photographs following Marilyn for a week as she prepares for two appearances: opening night of *Cat on a Hot Tin Roof* at the Morosco Theatre, and riding an elephant in a charity event at Madison Square Garden.

Gilmore, John. *Inside Marilyn: A Memoir*. Los Angeles: Ferrine Books, 2007. Print.
Gilmore's is a perceptive account by an actor who knew Marilyn reasonably well and saw her work on movie sets. He includes many shots of early Marilyn, and a quite youthful portrait photograph of Gladys Baker, as well as other rare pictures of Gladys Baker and her mother Della, Grace McKee Goddard, Ana Lower, Johnny Hyde, Joe Schenck, Elia Kazan, and Ralph Roberts.

Guiles, Fred Lawrence. *Legend: The Life and Death of Marilyn Monroe*. New York: Stein and Day, 1984. Print.
This is a rewritten and updated version of *Norma Jean*.

———. *Norma Jean: The Life of Marilyn Monroe*. New York: McGraw-Hill, 1969. Print.
The first comprehensive biography of Marilyn Monroe, Guiles's work is the product of extensive interviews with Lee Strasberg, Rupert Allan, Arthur Miller, and others close to the actress. No photographs.

Haspiel, James. *Marilyn: The Ultimate Look at the Legend*. New York: Henry Holt, 1991. Haspiel's book is an intermittently revealing account of Marilyn written by a fan who was present to record some of her daily doings.

Hoyt, Edwin P. *Marilyn: The Tragic Venus*. New York: Duell, Sloan, and Pearce, 1965.
This early account is still valuable because it draws on Hoyt's interviews with Monroe's fellow actors and friends.

Kidder, Clark. *Marilyn Monroe: Cover to Cover*. Iola, WI: Krause Publications, 1999. Print.
The most extensive collection of cover photographs, Clark's volume is an indispensable resource for documenting Marilyn Monroe's presence in the media. Includes an index of featured magazines.

Leaming, Barbara. *Marilyn Monroe*. New York: Crown, 1998. Print and Kindle.
One of the best Marilyn Monroe biographies, Leaming's work is especially illuminating in its discussions of Monroe's business dealings, her work with agents like Charles K. Feldman, and her relationships with Elia Kazan and Arthur Miller. A photo insert includes pictures of Joe Schenck, Elia Kazan, Paula Strasberg, and George Cukor.

Luijters, Guus. *Marilyn Monroe: A Never-Ending Dream*. New York: St. Martin's, 1987. Print.
This book includes: film stills and commentary; publicity shots; two-shots with Marilyn's mother, Gladys, James Dougherty, Ben Lyon, John Huston, Jack Paar, Marlon Brando, Joe DiMaggio, Arthur Miller, Nunnally Johnson, Montgomery Clift, Henry Fonda, Clark Gable, Robert Mitchum, and Yves Montand; a photograph of Harry Cohn: a photograph of Johnny Hyde; and shots Marilyn's performances in Korea and other events. The book lists her recorded albums and songs, and a selective bibliography of books about Marilyn with pictures of their covers.

Mailer, Norman. *Marilyn: A Biography*. New York: Grosset & Dunlap, 1973. Print.
Mailer's is one of the more controversial Marilyn Monroe biographies. The book includes many fine photographs by her principal photographers: Lawrence Schiller, Sam Shaw, Milton Greene, Bert Stern, George Barris, and several others.

_____. *Of Women and Their Elegance*. New York: Simon and Schuster, 1980. Print.

Here Mailer collaborates with Milton Greene, whose photographs enhance Mailer's writing, which attempts to capture Marilyn's own voice in a fictional autobiography.

Marilyn Monroe and the Camera. Boston: Bullfinch Press, 1989. Print.

This volume, which ranks with David Wills's *Metamorphosis*, includes photographs by all of Monroe's important photographers. It begins with a stunning André de Dienes color photograph of Norma Jeane taken on the beach in 1945, and a David Conover shot of Norma Jeane combing her hair outdoors by the shore, then more de Dienes shots of her along California highways. Her early career is documented in photographs by Richard Miller, Bruno Bernard, and others, with film stills from *Love Happy* and the famous Phillipe Halsman shot of Monroe seated on the floor, gazing out of a group of seven other starlets. Also included are superb film stills from *The Asphalt Jungle* and *Don't Bother to Knock*, and many glamour shots by Frank Powolny, Bruno Bernard, and others. A Philippe Halsman 1952 photograph of Marilyn working out with hand weights includes Halsman's commentary: "On the floor were two barbells. 'Are you using them?' I asked. 'Yes,' she replied. 'I'm fighting gravity.'" Marilyn is shown eating an ice cream sundae in a 1953 de Dienes photograph. Full color stills from *Niagara*, *Gentlemen Prefer Blondes*, and *How to Marry a Millionaire* are featured, as are color images of the marriage to DiMaggio and the trip to Korea. Stills of *River of No Return* and *There's No Business Like Show Business* are followed by a photograph, taken by Weegee, of Marilyn arriving in New York to shoot scenes from *The Seven Year Itch*. Tight close-ups taken for *Bus Stop* and images of the Monroe-Miller-Greene-Olivier period are captured in several two-shots and crowd scenes. Marilyn's work in *Some Like It Hot*, *Let's Make Love*, and *The Misfits*—with more attention to her last completed film—segue to a single shot of her in *Something's Got to Give*, and then Bert Stern's "Last Sitting" photographs, including one Marilyn rejected, marking it with grease pencil. This volume also includes a short foreword by Jane Russell, George Belmont's interview with Monroe, a filmography, and a biography annotated with important dates.

Marshall, David. *The D. D. Group: An Online Investigation of the Death of Marilyn Monroe*. New York: iUniverse, 2005. Print and Kindle.

This work consists of a fascinating dialogue and point-by-point examination of the conflicting accounts of how, when, and why Marilyn Monroe died.

McCann, Graham. *Marilyn Monroe*. New Brunswick, NJ: Rutgers University Press, 1988. Print.

McCann's insightful scholarly study of Monroe as a phenomenon of society also makes shrewd observations about her performances and the management of her career. A small selection of photographs tends to favor her more elegant and intelligent work with Richard Avedon and Cecil Beaton and film stills from *Some Like It Hot*.

McDonough, Yona Zeldis. *All the Available Light: A Marilyn Monroe Reader*. New York: Simon and Schuster, 2011. Print and Kindle.

Essays by Joyce Carol Oates, Marge Piercy, and others cover many aspects of Monroe's persona as sex symbol, icon, and victim, as well as her cultural role.

Meyers, Jeffrey. *The Genius and the Goddess: Arthur Miller & Marilyn Monroe*. Chicago: University of Illinois Press, 2009. Print.

Meyers, who knew Arthur Miller, is stronger on Miller's point of view than on Marilyn's. The book contains photographs of Miller and his first wife, Mary Slattery, with Norman Rosten and Hedda Rosten, as well as shots of Johnny Hyde, Natasha Lytess, Milton and Amy Greene, the Strasbergs (Lee, Paula, and Susan), and Joe DiMaggio.

Miracle, Berniece Baker, and Mona Rae Miracle. *My Sister Marilyn: A Memoir of Marilyn Monroe*. Chapel Hill, NC: Algonquin of Chapel Hill, 1994. Print.

A memoir by Marilyn's half-sister, the Miracles' includes photographs of Berniece and Marilyn together; a photograph of their grandmother Della; a childhood photograph of Gladys; photographs of Norma Jeane at sixteen and seventeen; a shot of a family dinner featuring Norma Jeane, Gladys, Grace, and Ana Lower; a picture of Grace McKee Goddard; and a family tree.

Monroe, Marilyn, and George Barris. *Marilyn—Her Life in Her Own Words: Marilyn Monroe's Revealing Last Words and Photographs*. Secaucus, NJ: Carol Publishing Group, 1995. Print.

This volume includes a complete record of Barris's July 1962 photographic session, as well as Monroe's interview with him, in which she attempts to correct the errors printed about her life. Most of the shots show her relaxing at her Brentwood home and on a nearby beach. She describes in terms more graphic than in *My Story* the boarder who sexually molested

her when she was eight years old. Some of the shots show the same athleticism she displayed in her early modeling pictures.

_____. *My Story*. Illustrated edition. Foreword by Joshua Greene. Print.
Joshua Greene provides some explanation of the context in which his
father took certain important photographs. These photographs, however,
were not originally meant to illustrate Monroe's autobiography. Indeed,
they were all taken after Monroe's collaboration with Ben Hecht on her
autobiography had ceased.

Morgan, Michelle. *Marilyn Monroe: Private and Undisclosed*. New York:
    Carroll & Graf, 2007. Kindle.
Morgan's is one of the most reliable biographies and is full of new information based on extensive interviews and research into public records.
The book includes photographs of Los Angeles General Hospital where
Marilyn was born; a "stylish Gladys Pearl Baker"; Marilyn as a toddler on
the beach with playmates (even the shot of the Children's Cross that Marilyn helped to form at the Hollywood Bowl); the white piano Gladys bought
for Norma Jeane; Norma Jeane as a teenager; the Los Angeles Orphans
home; Sula Dewey, superintendent of the orphanage; Ana Lower; Emerson Junior High school; a remarkable section of "unseen photographs" that
document Norma Jeane in her mid-teens and during her first marriage;
the Florentine's nightclub, where Norma Jeane and James Dougherty
celebrated after their wedding; Norma Jeane on Catalina Island and during a Radioplane picnic; a shot of the Blue Book Modeling Agency in the
Ambassador Hotel; Bill Pursel (who dated Norma Jeane in the late 1940s);
Berniece Miracle, Norma Jeane's half-sister; Joe Schenck's home, where
Marilyn was a frequent visitor; the Hollywood Studio Club, where Marilyn
lived during her starlet days; on the *All About Eve* set with Anne Baxter;
conferring with Cary Grant on the set of *Monkey Business*; the photograph
with baseball player Gus Zernial that got Joe DiMaggio's attention; the
booth at the Villa Nova Restaurant, where Marilyn and Joe had their first
meal together; several shots of Marilyn during the filming of *Niagara*;
Marilyn's dressing room at Fox, which used to belong to Betty Grable;
site of the Wrong Door Raid during Marilyn's involvement with singing
coach Hal Schaefer; the East 57th Street home where Miller and Monroe
resided on the thirteenth floor; working with her dance instructor Jack
Cole on routines in *Let's Make Love*; her Doheny Drive apartment; and
the street leading to her last home on Fifth Helena Drive in Brentwood.

Murray, Eunice, and Rose Shade. *Marilyn: The Last Months*. New York: Pyramid, 1975. Print.
Although Murray's version has been challenged on a number of points, her own account still provides important details about Marilyn's final days.

Riese, Randall, and Neal Hitchens. *The Unabridged Marilyn: Her Life from A to Z*. New York: Congdon & Weed, 1987. Print.
This comprehensive and reliable book is one of the best sources of information on Monroe. Included are unusual photographs of Marilyn during her modeling career; elegant shots by Jack Cardiff (her cinematographer on *The Prince and the Showgirl*); pictures of Marilyn cooking with Arthur Miller's mother; a two-shot with Jayne Mansfield; Billy Travilla's sketches for the gowns in *Gentlemen Prefer Blondes*; and shots taken on a movie set with Sidney Skolsky and Billy Wilder.

Rollyson, Carl. *Marilyn Monroe: A Life of the Actress*. Revised and updated. Jackson: University Press of Mississippi, 2014.
This work remains the best account of Monroe's development as an actress.

_____. *Female Icons: Marilyn Monroe to Susan Sontag*. New York: iUniverse, 2005. Print and Kindle.
This collection includes essays about the process of researching Monroe's life and reflecting on her cultural importance.

Rosten, Norman. *Marilyn: An Untold Story*. New York: Signet, 1973. Print.
Rosten's is one of the best memoirs written about Marilyn.

Sakol, Jeannie, and Joseph Jasgur. *The Birth of Marilyn: The Lost Photographs of Norma Jean by Joseph Jasgur*. New York: St. Martin's, 1991. Print.
This work consists of a fascinating collection of early Norma Jeane photographs, taken March 6, 10, 18, and 23, 1946, as well as a section devoted to the photographs Jasgur took while Norma Jeane worked for the Blue Book modeling agency. The latter includes one fetching pose showing Norma Jeane with her frizzy brown hair tamed in a kind of tiara atop her head, even as she holds a cup of coffee and smiles like the girl next door. In another shot, she sits on a bale of hay, dressed in a sweater and skirt with a Dalmatian at her side. The accompanying text by Jeannie Sakol is quite informative about both Norma Jeane and the photographer's

early impressions of her. Jasgur wanted to photograph the whimsical side of Norma Jeane, and he got results. As Sakol notes, "Getting her to draw the heart in the sand and stick out her tongue had somehow triggered the zany aspect of her personality which would ultimately express itself in her high comedy performances in *The Seven Year Itch* and *Some Like It Hot*."

Schiller, Lawrence. *Marilyn & Me*. New York: Nan A. Talese, 2012. Print and Kindle.
Schiller's book is a brief but insightful account of his photo sessions with Monroe—especially the nude swimming scene in *Something's Got to Give*.

Schwartz, Ted. *Marilyn Revealed: The Ambitious Life of an American Icon*. Lanham, MD: Taylor Trade, 2009. Print.
Schwartz's book reflects a good research job and includes some new details about Marilyn's life. A photo insert contains the customary photographs.

Shaw, Sam. *The Joy of Marilyn: In the Camera Eye*. New York: Exeter Books, 1979. Print.
As Shaw says in his foreword, "This is not a Hollywood picture book. I don't think I've got one glamor shot." A close friend of Marilyn's, Shaw shows her in everyday settings: dressed in jeans with her back to the camera; out on the streets of New York City greeting fans; sitting next to a couple as she reads a newspaper and they seem to ignore her; snacking in Battery Park; standing in front of the Manhattan Bridge on East River Drive; rowing in Central Park; at Ebbets Field; multiple shots of her talking on the phone, dressed in white slacks and blouse, and lying across her bed, phone in hand; at the beach in a one-piece swimsuit looking languorous; playing in the surf; getting herself in shape; adjusting her dress, perhaps for a glamour girl shot; seated at her makeup table, touching her nose (the caption reads, "I have a bulbous nose"); with Richard Avedon as he prepares her for a photo session; dancing around a tree on her wedding day with Arthur Miller; at her Connecticut home with Arthur Miller and their dog, Hugo; in conversation with her wardrobe mistress; and getting dolled up for a scene in *The Seven Year Itch*. She seems by turns wistful, self-involved, and outgoing. Shaw includes a marvelous shot of Elia Kazan in a kind of improvised turban on the set of *Viva Zapata*, another of a remarkably relaxed Joe DiMaggio in a two-shot with Marilyn, and others with Sidney Skolsky and then with Natasha Lytess on the set of *The Seven Year Itch*. Shaw includes Marilyn's well-composed photograph of

the Rostens with their daughter Patricia, and a reproduction of Marilyn's hand-drawn, flamboyant self-portrait with the caption, "What the Hell, that's life!" The final sections of the book juxtapose shots of Norma Jeane and early Marilyn and also feature several film stills.

Shaw, Sam, and Norman Rosten. *Marilyn among Friends*. New York: H. Holt, 1988. Print.

Sam Shaw and his camera were present at some of the most important events of Marilyn's life, including crucial moments in her romance with Arthur Miller and their wedding. Marilyn is also pictured rowing a boat in Central Park and shown the night in New York City when Shaw shot the iconographic skirt-blowing stills (Shaw even includes a shot of the man who operated the wind machine under the street grating during the scene). He also caught candid photographs of her on New York City streets and at her makeup table (all of which are included in this book, along with Norman Rosten's sensitive commentary). Shaw includes shots of Marilyn working with Billy Wilder and Tom Ewell; enjoying an interview with columnist Earl Wilson; at a session with her favorite makeup man, Whitey Snyder; during a night out with actor David Wayne and photographer Milton Greene (her business partner); at home on the telephone; with Joe DiMaggio; dancing with Clifton Webb; picnicking with Norman and Hedda Rosten and their daughter Patricia; drinking at a table with her one-time agent and producer, Charles Feldman; and sitting and talking with Darryl Zanuck. One of the classic shots included here is Marilyn seated on a park bench reading a newspaper while a young couple, thoroughly absorbed in one another, ignore her. The book concludes with several photographs of Marilyn at the beach—sometimes posing with Arthur Miller and sometimes caught in spontaneous, antic attitudes. A final shot shows her in mid-flight, so to speak, her arms lifted upward and her left leg thrust backward, an angel in the air.

Spada, James. *Marilyn Monroe: Her Life in Pictures*. Kindle edition, 2013.

As the title suggests, this is a comprehensive collection, beginning with photographs of Marilyn as an infant and ending with some of the last shots taken of her.

Spoto, Donald. *Marilyn Monroe: The Biography*. New York: HarperCollins, 1993. Print.

Superbly researched, this biography corrects the record that in many instances has been distorted by previous biographers. Spoto portrays a Marilyn much more in control of her life than the woman presented in earlier biographies. He launches an all-out attack on Dr. Ralph Greenson, whom, Spoto believes, destroyed any opportunity Marilyn might have had to act independently. Excellent photographs of Gladys, Ida Bolender, and Norma Jeane as infant and schoolgirl, as well as a rare photograph of Grace McKee Goddard grace the volume, which also includes good photographs of Marilyn with Johnny Hyde; Natasha Lytess; Edward G. Robinson; of Marilyn recording a song for RCA Records (Spoto believes she could have had a successful singing career if she had wanted to pursue it); a great shot with Sidney Skolsky leaning against a bookcase as Marilyn, considerably taller, looks down at him; a very good three-shot of Lee, Paula, and Susan Strasberg; and a charming two-shot with Milton Greene. A rather unflattering picture of Ralph Greenson reinforces Spoto's negative view of him. Another shot, of Paula Strasberg entering a room looking like an aging servant bringing Marilyn (lying on a sofa) her meal, and shots of a triumphant Marilyn looking back at the camera during the shooting of *Something's Got to Give* illustrate Spoto's sense that the star took charge of her career virtually in the moment of her death.

Steinem, Gloria, and George Barris. *Marilyn*. New York: H. Holt, 1986. Print.
 This biography, written from a feminist point of view, relies primarily on secondary sources, but includes a good selection of George Barris's color photographs.

Stern, Bert. *Marilyn: The Last Sitting*. New York: Random House, 2007. Print.
 This volume consists of a sumptuous collection of semi-nude and fashion shots Stern took near the end of Monroe's life.

Strasberg, Susan. *Marilyn and Me*. New York: Time Warner, 1992. Print.
 This vivid memoir of Marilyn's friendship with Susan also includes reminiscences of Lee and Paul Strasberg.

Summers, Anthony. *Goddess: The Secret Lives of Marilyn Monroe*. New York: Macmillan, 1985. Print.
 As the subtitle suggests, Summers presents the testimony of many figures with stories to tell about Monroe's unreported activities, including many accounts of her relationship with the Kennedys. Summers conducted more than six hundred interviews and as a result uncovered much new information, some of which another biographer, Lois Banner, has

verified. Summers includes photographs of Gladys Baker; Marilyn without makeup; Ralph Greenson; and a controversial autopsy shot.

Taraborelli, J. Randy. *The Secret Life of Marilyn Monroe*. New York: Grand Central, 2009. Print.
Taraborelli includes some new anecdotes and documents, as well as several excellent photographs of Gladys, including one where she is holding the infant Norma Jeane, and pictures of the Bolenders and Stanley Gifford (Marilyn's purported father), and unusual shots of Marilyn socializing with Pat Kennedy Lawford, Peter Lawford, and Frank Sinatra.

Ventura, Michael. *Marilyn Monroe: From Beginning to End*. London: Blandford Press, 1997. Print.
This collection of Earl Leaf's photographs is divided into chapters: "The Woman and the Cameraman," "1950: The Last of the Secret Years," "1952: First Year of Stardom," "1953: The Super-Star," "1956: A Touch of Genius," "1958: The Downturn," "1962: Farewell, My Lovely," and "1997 Postscript." Monroe seems to have met the fan magazine photographer at a party in 1950. A very young Marilyn, a starlet, seems to enjoy posing with a Chihuahua; reading a script; doing handstands; and smiling invitingly with producer Darryl Zanuck in the background. Other pictures feature Monroe with Bogart and Bacall, and an unusual low-angle shot of Marilyn taken at the time she was filming *Something's Got to Give*. The text is innocuous, and the photographs have no captions.

Victor, Adam. *The Marilyn Encyclopedia*. Woodstock, NY: Overlook, 1999. Print.
This work is comparable to *The Unabridged Marilyn*, but it has better, full-color photographs, as well as several useful bibliographies of books Monroe read, films and books about her (including comic books), and fictional characters based on her. Excellent shots of her early modeling career and appearances in advertisements, original movie posters, fan magazine covers, and production shots are included, as well as two unusual photographs of Norma Jeane and Gladys; shots of Marilyn's Doheny Drive apartment; her houses in Amagansett, Roxbury, and Brentwood; a two-shot of Fred Karger and Jane Wyman, who Karger married after his involvement with Monroe; one of Tom Kelley with his famous nude calendar shot; a studio portrait of Elia Kazan; Josh Logan directing Marilyn on the set of *Bus Stop*; Joseph Mankiewicz with Marilyn on the set of *All About Eve*; Otto Preminger directing Marilyn on crutches in *River of No Return*; a portrait of Clifford Odets; Marilyn with her secretary May

Reis; with her co-star Tommy Rettig in *River of No Return*; with her voice coach Hal Schaefer; with President Sukarno of Indonesia; and appearing on *The Jack Benny Show*. This book's usefulness is enhanced by an index of names.

Vitacco-Robles, Gary. *Cursum Perficio: Marilyn Monroe's Brentwood Hacienda: The Story of Her Final Months*. San Jose, CA: Writers Club, 2000. Print.
Vitacco-Robles provides the most comprehensive record of Marilyn's last home, complete with floor plans, photographs of furnishings, rooms, and grounds, and narrative chapters about Marilyn's last months in the home and what they meant to her.

Weatherby, W. J. *Conversations with Marilyn*. New York: Paragon House, 1992. Print.
This book consists of revealing exchanges between a skilled reporter and Marilyn, who reflects on her life and career with unusual candor while remaining guarded about certain private matters.

Wills, David, and Stephen Schmidt. *Marilyn Monroe: Metamorphosis*. New York: It, 2011. Print.
This volume is the most beautiful, comprehensive, and aesthetically structured collection of Marilyn photographs published so far. The collection begins with a stunning portrait of a smiling Norma Jeane in pigtails, dressed in a white blouse with a red border that matches the red ribbons on her pigtails and her lipstick. Her hair is brown and frizzy, and her pre-Hollywood hairline is uneven—it is very much a mid-1940s portrait. The next photograph is of the young starlet in a two-piece swimsuit, sitting on a diving board above a pool. Her right leg is raised and bent at the knee, forming a triangle with her left thigh resting on the board as her calf dangles down toward the water. She is smiling and looking back at the camera in a very inviting pose. Every important Marilyn Monroe photograph is featured in this book. The shots in the opening section are not placed in chronological order, but rather so as to highlight her infinitely inventive skill as a camera subject. Thus a publicity shot of her in a red dress is cropped to show only her figure from the bust line up, with her rather dreamy yet shrewd expression framed by her left hand, which is brought up and bent at the elbow, so that her forearm frames her head resting against lush green velvet fabric. A few photographs later, shots of her taken during the filming of *The Misfits* and *Something's Got to Give*, show not only an older Marilyn, but also a woman whose eyes seem to

gaze past the camera, as though it is no longer the present moment that counts. Such juxtapositions seem calculated to arouse a consciousness of how Marilyn was simultaneously present in the moment and yet eternal. This effect seems to refer to the book's title, *Metamorphosis*. After this opening section, the book is divided into chapters: "Chrysalis: Norma Jeane 1942–1946," "Transfiguration: Starlet 1947–1951," "Sirius: Superstar 1952–1954," "Renaissance 1955–1961," "Icarus: Goddess 1962." In his introduction David Wills notes:

> [I]mages of Norma Jeane are today far better preserved than those of Marilyn. Her modeling career launched at the height of mid-1940s Kodachrome, Norma Jeane had the benefit of being captured by perhaps the richest, clearest, most brilliant, and chemically dependable color film stock in history. With the popularization in the early 1950s of cheaper, faster, and smaller-format negative and transparency films, this standard of quality disappeared. Through saturated at the time, Marilyn's impression on the emulsion has deteriorated, faded, and turned to magenta over the decades. Through digital restoration, we are now able to breathe new life into these images, but it is not the same. A certain depth and authenticity of color are lost. Yet Norma Jeane remains unchanged.

As befits the title of his book, Wills calls Marilyn "a work of art in progress . . . perfectly adapted to each passing decade." Wills also notes that Marilyn made "at least one major contribution to fashion and style: she loosened things up. In contrast to the structured forties, and despite the complexity of her appearance, there was a casualness about her that always suggested she just rolled out of bed, threw on a dress, and showed up. . . . [I]t was Monroe who helped catapult society into the dawn of the sexual revolution."

What follows in the first chapter of this extraordinary book are color shots of Norma Jeane, frolicking indoors and outdoor in perfect images of what she was like before her Hollywood transformation; in early magazine covers; athletic shots; and in a windswept pose (at the end of this chapter) that seems to reflect her joy in discovering what she had to offer the world. Chapter two presents a starlet sans makeup, then seated while she applies makeup to herself or is ministered to by others, and then shown in a series of athletic poses that illustrate how Marilyn was absorbing what Norma Jeane could do and making athleticism sexual provender for the camera. Her hard work as a performer is shown in a shot of her on the floor apparently putting on a dance slipper. Film stills and cheesecake shots are juxtaposed with photos of her reading a copy of *How to Develop Your Thinking Ability*. Chapter three shows how Marilyn's superstardom depended on a sexuality that (in a gown designed by Billy Travilla) became the gold standard. She is photographed as if she were gold-plated, with the lines of her dress seeming to be veins of precious metal. This phase of her career is again captured on a magazine cover that noticeably emphasizes what in his introduction David Wills calls her most distinctive feature: her mouth. Open or closed—or half-open or half-closed—her mouth is the synecdoche for her moods, her face, her figure, shot from every conceivable attractive angle. Of special importance in this chapter are shots from *The Seven Year Itch*, perhaps the only film that really shows her brilliance as an actress in both motion pictures and still photography. So much of the iconic Marilyn, as *Metamorphosis* demonstrates, resulted from the acting she did on screen, in the street, and in the photographer's studio. Chapter four pairs the title "Renaissance" with a shot of Marilyn leaning over the parapet of a Manhattan skyscraper, looking down at New York City. She was on top of the world at this point in her career, as she abandoned Hollywood, hoping for a new life in the urban world of stage actors. This is her Milton Greene period, and Wills does full justice to the sophisticated "new Marilyn" that emerged in Greene's dramatic and elegant setups. Sam Shaw, Richard Avedon, Cecil Beaton—all of Marilyn's best photographers—display her in inventive poses. *Some Like It Hot,* second only to *The Seven Year Itch* in its presentation of the iconic Marilyn, is amply represented—especially in the contact sheets that show Marilyn going through a gamut of emotions in just one of the Sugar Kane scenes. The final shot of this chapter shows Marilyn alone on the desert floor during the scene in *The Misfits* when she pulls away from her cowboy lovers and denounces them. The shot suggests just how *alone* she had come to feel in a movie that depended so much on idealizing her as the cynosure of males who see in her the renewal of their own lives, even as she is coming to the end of her own. Chapter Five emphasizes the dreamy, ethereal Marilyn Wills describes in his introduction and whom Lee Strasberg called a "supernatural beauty." She seems at one with the camera in the stills from *Something's Got to Give*, so that it is hard to imagine an existence for her outside the boundaries of the visual field that cameras yield.

Wolfe, Donald H. *The Last Days of Marilyn Monroe.* New York: William Morrow, 1998. Print.

Wolfe devotes too much time to a "secret conspiracy." Like Anthony Summers, he believes in Slatzer's credibility and cites a few people who vouch for Slatzer. But none of the principal people in Monroe's life ever met Slatzer or believe he had a significant relationship with Marilyn. A photo insert includes a good representation of Marilyn and the people in her life, including her mother, Stanley Gifford, James Dougherty, Natasha Lytess, Billy Wilder, Joe DiMaggio, Jerry Giesler, Johnny Hyde, Yves Montand, Simone Signoret, Ralph Greenson, José Bolaños, Whitey Snyder, and Peter Lawford. Also included are several shots of Pat Newcomb and of Marilyn's bedroom and home after her death.

Zolotow, Maurice. *Marilyn Monroe*. New York: Harcourt, Brace, 1960. Print.
This, the first reliable biography of Monroe, is based on several interviews with her. The book remains a key source for biographers and other students of Marilyn's career.

WEBSITES

The sites listed below are representative examples. There are many more devoted to Marilyn's life and work and to individual films and books about her.

Bio.com. A&E Networks Television. "Marilyn Monroe Biography."
This site includes videos of documentaries about Marilyn Monroe.

CursumPerficio.
This useful website includes a detailed chronology, files on Monroe's individual films and on the people in her life, a bibliography of books, links to other sources of information, and an extensive section of comments.

IMDb. "Marilyn Monroe."
This entry includes 616 photographs, forty-nine videos, 4,157 news articles, a biography, and message boards. The photo gallery documents many phases of Marilyn's life and includes many film stills. Videos include clips from her films and movie trailers.

Immortal Marilyn Front Page—Marilyn Monroe.
This up-to-date website has the latest news about books and other items concerning Monroe. The site also has a link to its Facebook page.

Official Marilyn Monroe Website.
In spite of its name, this is not a comprehensive source. It provides some news, a brief history of Marilyn, and photographs that can be purchased.

Rotten Tomatoes. "Marilyn Monroe."
The site consists of reviews of books and movies.

Wikipedia. "Marilyn Monroe."
The Monroe entry includes biography, extensive notes, and links to other sources.

Index

321

About the Author

Carl Rollyson is the author of *Marilyn Monroe: A Life of the Actress* (revised and updated, 2014), *American Isis: The Life and Art of Sylvia Plath, Amy Lowell Anew: A Biography,* and several other biographies and works of literary and film criticism. He is currently at work on *A Real Character: Walter Brennan and the World of Hollywood Players.*